Journey to Excellence

How Baldrige Health Care
Leaders Succeed

Also available from ASQ Quality Press:

On Becoming Exceptional: SSM Health Care's Journey to Baldrige and Beyond
Sister Mary Jean Ryan, FSM

Insights to Performance Excellence 2009-2010: An Inside Look at the 2009-2010 Baldrige Award Criteria
Mark L. Blazey

The Making of a World-Class Organization
E. David Spong and Debbie J. Collard

The Executive Guide to Understanding and Implementing the Baldrige Criteria: Improve Revenue and Create Organizational Excellence
Denis Leonard and Mac McGuire

Solutions to the Healthcare Quality Crisis: Cases and Examples of Lean Six Sigma in Healthcare
Soren Bisgaard, editor

Lean-Six Sigma for Healthcare, Second Edition: A Senior Leader Guide to Improving Cost and Throughput
Greg Butler, Chip Caldwell, and Nancy Poston

The Public Health Quality Improvement Handbook
Grace L. Duffy and John W. Moran, editors

Lean Six Sigma for the Healthcare Practice: A Pocket Guide
Roderick A. Munro

A Lean Guide to Transforming Healthcare: How to Implement Lean Principles in Hospitals, Medical Offices, Clinics, and Other Healthcare Organizations
Thomas G. Zidel

Improving Healthcare Using Toyota Lean Production Methods: 46 Steps for Improvement, Second Edition
Robert Chalice

Benchmarking for Hospitals: Achieving Best-in-Class Performance without Having to Reinvent the Wheel
Victor Sower, Jo Ann Duffy, and Gerald Kohers

To request a complimentary catalog of ASQ Quality Press publications, call 800-248-1946, or visit our Web site at http://www.asq.org/quality-press.

Journey to Excellence

How Baldrige Health Care Leaders Succeed

Kathleen J. Goonan, MD
Joseph A. Muzikowski
Patricia K. Stoltz

ASQ Quality Press
Milwaukee, Wisconsin

American Society for Quality, Quality Press, Milwaukee, WI 53203
© 2009 by ASQ
All rights reserved. Published 2009.
Printed in the United States of America.

15 14 13 12 11 10 09   5 4 3 2 1

Library of Congress Cataloging-in-Publication Data

Goonan, Kathleen Jennison.
Journey to excellence : how Baldrige Health Care leaders succeed / Kate Goonan,
Joseph A. Muzikowski, Patricia K. Stoltz.
    p. cm.
Includes bibliographical references and index.
ISBN 978-0-87389-735-8 (alk. paper)
1. Baldrige National Quality Program (National Institute of Standards and Technology)
2. Health services administration. I. American Society for Quality. II. Title.
[DNLM: 1. Baldrige National Quality Program (National Institute of Standards and
Technology) 2. Outcome and Process Assessment (Health Care)—methods—United States.
3. Benchmarking—United States. 4. Health Facilities—organization & administration—
United States. 5. Organizational Case Studies—United States. 6. Quality Indicators,
Health Care—standards—United States. 7. Total Quality Management—United States.
W 84 AA1 G659j 2009]
RA971.G625 2009
362.1068—dc22

2009011722

Publisher: William A. Tony
Acquisitions Editor: Matt T. Meinholz
Project Editor: Paul O'Mara
Production Administrator: Randall Benson

ASQ Mission: The American Society for Quality advances individual, organizational, and
community excellence worldwide through learning, quality improvement, and
knowledge exchange.

Attention Bookstores, Wholesalers, Schools, and Corporations: ASQ Quality Press books,
videotapes, audiotapes, and software are available at quantity discounts with bulk
purchases for business, educational, or instructional use. For information, please contact
ASQ Quality Press at 800-248-1946, or write to ASQ Quality Press, P.O. Box 3005,
Milwaukee, WI 53201-3005.

To place orders or to request a free copy of the ASQ Quality Press Publications Catalog,
including ASQ membership information, call 800-248-1946. Visit our Web site at
www.asq.org or http://www.asq.org/quality-press.

♾ Printed on acid-free paper

Quality Press
600 N. Plankinton Avenue
Milwaukee, Wisconsin 53203
Call toll free 800-248-1946
Fax 414-272-1734
www.asq.org
http://www.asq.org/quality-press
http://standardsgroup.asq.org
E-mail: authors@asq.org

Contents

List of Figures

Foreword

There are no secret answers. No magic bullets. But there are rational approaches that achieve results. This book is about those approaches and the results they achieve. This book is about the "brutal truth" health care organizations need to accept. It is about seeking the truth of your current reality for your organization, making sense of that reality, and changing the organization to achieve the results that lead to a sustainable reality, high performance, and engaged partners on your staff, among your patients, and in your community.

This book is presented in a compelling manner, with key points at the end of every chapter and many examples from real organizations that are succeeding through use of the Baldrige Criteria and a systematic approach to managing, improving, and changing their organization for the better. The Baldrige process provides discipline that many organizations never achieve. The authors provide a studied approach for achieving this discipline: the LASER elements (Leadership, Assessment, Sensemaking, Execution, and Results). They provide their insights from a unique vantage point. They are all experienced Baldrige examiners and judges, who have had the opportunity to assess the performance of many organizations. They combine that insight with a research study of Baldrige Award recipients, quoting from the recipients' discussions with them and sharing the recipients' processes for enterprise management. The result is "aha" moments that you will be able to apply directly to your organization. Then they synthesize what they have learned into useful tips, such as the five critical behaviors of successful leaders in Chapter 4 and important questions health care leaders should ask in Chapter 8.

In recent years, half of Baldrige Award applicants have been health care provider organizations. Thousands more are using the Baldrige Health Care Criteria. That is surprising when one compares the number of health care institutions with the much larger number of businesses and education institutions in the U.S., which make up the bulk of the other half. Why is this so? I believe it is because of a singular overlap between what the Baldrige Criteria provide and the challenges health care is facing: to improve quality, to reduce cost, and to do it in a way that is strategically sustainable. If you can identify with this challenge, Baldrige might be right for your organization, and this book will give you easy insights to begin your journey.

Harry S. Hertz
Director
Baldrige National Quality Program

Preface

PURPOSE

Leading change in the best of times is difficult. In uncertain times, it is daunting. This book is for health care leaders at all levels seeking to guide successful transformational change even in the most challenging circumstances. We appreciate that this audience is broad and diverse, from senior executives to administrators and managers to clinicians, in complex organizations that vary substantially in size and scope of service. Our goal is to provide you with the strategy and knowledge to advance your personal effectiveness as an agent of change and help you lead your organization to greater achievements in performance.

This book is *not* a Baldrige educational manual, nor is it a "how to" book about the Baldrige process, although it includes lots of practical information about the successful use of Baldrige. Many resources are available to help you learn the Baldrige Criteria and how they are applied, starting with those provided by the Baldrige National Quality Program on its Web site, http://www.baldrige.nist.gov.

This book is about the strategy for leading successful change in a complex environment and what the nine health care organizations that have received the Baldrige Award since 2002 can teach us in this regard. All nine used the Baldrige framework and the Health Care Criteria for Performance Excellence as their diagnostic self-evaluation tool and guide for improvement. At the same time, each organization customized their use of Baldrige to fit their organizational culture, values, and goals. We learned many surprising lessons about the role Baldrige played—and did not play—in their accomplishments. This book focuses on the journeys of these nine organizations and seeks to convey what is common in their approaches that can help other health care leaders drive transformational change.

METHODS AND FINDINGS

The idea for this book first took shape in about 2002. Health care was under fire for quality and performance problems. Jim Collins had shown in *Good to Great* that certain organizational habits and disciplines could predict success. The Baldrige process, effectively used for more than a decade by manufacturing and service companies, had opened to health care and the first recipient, SSM Health Care, had been named. And we had begun working with organizations seeking to create their own journey from "good to great" using the Baldrige Criteria.

Our experiences as Baldrige Award judges and examiners had allowed us to analyze the practices of some of America's highest performing organizations. We knew *what* those practices were. What we wanted to understand better was *how* organizations used Baldrige to transform and create truly high-performance cultures. We recognized the potential value for health care leaders of an in-depth and thoughtful analysis of how these organizations went about the job of making transformational change. Our curiosity and our sense of the importance of our question grew as the pressure on health care for better performance intensified, increasing numbers of health care organizations became Baldrige users, and new Baldrige Award recipients were named in the health care sector. Late in 2006, we launched our plan for this book.

We studied the application summaries of Baldrige recipients from health care and other sectors and material they presented at Quest for Excellence, the annual showcase of Baldrige recipient practices, and in other forums. We conducted in-depth personal interviews with twenty senior leaders from the nine health care recipients. Finally, we went back to the application summaries of our study organizations, their Quest for Excellence presentations, and our interviews to examine similarities and differences in their approaches to transformational change.

Two key findings emerged from our analysis. First, the recipient organizations we studied followed a common path once they started using Baldrige. Kate Goonan recognized this common path as a journey marked by five clearly discernible stages: Reaction (stage 0), Projects (stage 1), Traction (stage 2), Integration (stage 3), and Sustaining (stage 4). Second, we recognized that a set of critical activities, continually practiced and integrated one with another, seemed to support progress on the journey. These are the key components of what we came to call the LASER model: Leadership, Assessment, Sensemaking, Execution, and Results.

STRUCTURE

Chapter 1 lays out the context in which health care leaders work today and describes our overall findings. Here we introduce the "journey" and the stages of transformation that emerged from our research. Chapter 2 provides an overview of Baldrige and how it is used in the context of a larger change process. Our aim is to provide "just enough" basic information to understand the process and the journey taken by the nine health care award recipients. Readers with an in-depth knowledge of Baldrige may choose to skim or skip this chapter. Readers who are new to the subject, on the other hand, may want to download and review the Criteria before continuing with the remainder of the book. Chapter 3 offers a more detailed description of the journey, including the five stages and their sequence. This chapter provides the foundation for the LASER model practices. Chapters 4 through 8 describe each of the LASER elements in detail. Chapter 9 offers our conclusions. We designed these chapters so that the reader can benefit from reading each independently. If you choose to read the Leadership chapter and nothing else, you can skip to the Results chapter and Conclusion on a subsequent read. You might come back to the Assessment chapter at a time when you are seriously considering starting an assessment for your organization.

Each chapter features figures and side bars to illustrate recipient best practices and concludes with key points to summarize the chapter. At the end of the book, we address briefly a short list of the questions about Baldrige most often asked of leaders in health care recipient organizations and of us as consultants. Throughout this book, we quote extensively from our interviews to bring these health care leaders and their experiences to life as we illustrate their journeys. We also provide abundant examples of their practices and their results, primarily from publicly available material that you can explore yourself in more detail.

ACKNOWLEDGMENTS

Many valued colleagues contributed their talent and their time to support us in writing this book. First and foremost, we extend our deepest gratitude and admiration to leaders at the nine health care recipient organizations who made themselves available to us. At the end of the Preface, we list each organization and the individuals who contributed their expertise to this book.

We are indebted to others who made significant direct contributions to this book. Marsha Kessler, deputy director of the Massachusetts General Hospital Center for Performance Excellence, provided significant strategic and analytic support to the overall project. She created the database of research findings, worked as an essential partner with Kate Goonan on development of the LASER model by synthesizing the research findings and Kate's experience into a useful framework. She worked with the team of authors defined the details behind the elements of the model. Other colleagues made significant contributions: Marti Beltz, Sherry Bright, Steffanie Bristol, Len Denault, Jessica Marder, Sherry Martin, and Katherine Reller. In particular, we thank Sherry, Sherry, Marti, and Len, who offered helpful suggestions on our early drafts. We are grateful also to the dozens of leaders in organizations we have been privileged to support over the last six years. Partnering with them to shape their organizational change strategies has taught us so much and influenced our thinking in this work.

This book would not have been possible without the support of David Blumenthal, MD, director of the Institute for Health Policy, Massachusetts General Hospital/Partners, on leave to serve as the country's National Coordinator of Health Information Technology, Department of Health and Human Services. David is a visionary health care leader who recognized the potential power of the Baldrige process to change health care performance and provided us a spawning ground to test that hypothesis. Through his sponsorship, Massachusetts General Hospital/Partners supported the creation of the Center for Performance Excellence, home to our work as a team.

We also want to express our gratitude to Harry Hertz, director of the Baldrige National Quality Program, for his leadership of the program and for the insights and opportunities for learning he has shared with us as colleagues over many years. Each of us in our careers has been supported and influenced by other leaders and mentors. It would be difficult to name them all here and communicate their singular contributions to our knowledge. But we will always be grateful.

Finally, we want to thank our families. They have learned to tolerate our near obsession with this project and provided endless patience and support to us throughout.

Kate Goonan
Joe Muzikowski
Trish Stoltz

HEALTH CARE AWARD RECIPIENT ORGANIZATIONS AND LEADERS INTERVIEWED

2008 – Poudre Valley Health System

Poudre Valley Health System is a locally owned, private, not-for-profit health care organization serving residents of northern Colorado, western Nebraska, and southern Wyoming. Founded in 1925, it provides a full spectrum of health care services through two hospitals (Poudre Valley Hospital in Fort Collins, Colorado, and the Medical Center of the Rockies in Loveland, Colorado) and a network of clinics and care facilities.

Rulon Stacey
President and CEO
Poudre Valley Health System

Priscilla Nuwash
Director, Process Improvement
Poudre Valley Health System

Sonja Wulff
Performance Excellence Manager
Poudre Valley Health System

2007 – Mercy Health System

In 1989, Mercy Hospital was a single stand-alone community hospital primarily serving Janesville, Wisconsin. Today, Mercy Health System is a fully integrated health care system with three hospitals and a network of sixty-four facilities, including thirty-nine multi-specialty outpatient centers located in six counties throughout southern Wisconsin and northern Illinois. Mercy Health System provides a complete spectrum of integrated health care services to more than one million patients annually.

Javon R. Bea
President and CEO
Mercy Health System

2007 – Sharp HealthCare

Sharp HealthCare is San Diego County's largest integrated health care delivery system, serving greater than 27 percent of the county's more than three million residents—some 785,000 people—each year. A not-for-profit organization, Sharp has an annual net revenue of greater than $1.9 billion, employs a workforce with more than 14,000 staff members and 2,600 affiliated physicians, operates four acute care hospitals and nineteen outpatient medical clinics, and manages its own health insurance plan.

Michael W. Murphy
President and CEO
Sharp HealthCare

Nancy Pratt
Senior Vice President, Clinical Effectiveness
Sharp HealthCare

2006 – North Mississippi Medical Center

Established in 1937, North Mississippi Medical Center has grown from Tupelo's solitary "hospital on the hill" to the flagship hospital and referral center for North Mississippi Health Services, a not-for-profit health care delivery system serving twenty-four rural counties in northeast Mississippi and northwest Alabama. With more than six hundred beds, staffed by 3,875 employees and 277 physicians, North Mississippi is the largest non-government hospital in the state and the largest rural hospital in the country.

John Heer
President and CEO
North Mississippi Health Services

Ken Davis, MD
Former Chief Medical Officer
North Mississippi Medical Center

Jan Englert
Former Director, Clinical Outcomes
North Mississippi Medical Center

Chuck Stokes
Former President
North Mississippi Medical Center

2005 – Bronson Methodist Hospital

Founded in 1900, Bronson Methodist Hospital today is a state-of-the-art facility with all private rooms, the flagship organization in the Bronson Healthcare Group. Designed as a peaceful, healing environment, the hospital features an indoor garden atrium complete with lush trees, plants, and bubbling water. Located on a 28-acre urban campus, Bronson Methodist Hospital provides medical care for the nine-county region in southwest Michigan surrounding Kalamazoo, Michigan.

Frank J. Sardone
President and CEO
Bronson Healthcare Group

Michele Serbenski
Vice President, Performance Excellence
Bronson Healthcare Group

2004 – Robert Wood Johnson University Hospital at Hamilton

Located on a 68-acre campus, Robert Wood Johnson University Hospital at Hamilton is a private, not-for-profit, acute care community hospital serving more than 350,000 residents in Hamilton Township, New Jersey. The hospital is part of the Robert Wood Johnson Health System and Network and is affiliated with the University of Medicine and Dentistry of New Jersey – Robert Wood Johnson Medical School.

Ellen Guarnieri
President and CEO
Robert Wood Johnson University Hospital at Hamilton

Deborah Baehser
Senior Vice President, Clinical Services, and Chief Nursing Officer
Robert Wood Johnson University Hospital at Hamilton

Diane Grillo
Senior Vice President, Chief Learning and Communications Officer
Robert Wood Johnson University Hospital at Hamilton

2003 – Baptist Hospital, Inc.

The First Baptist Church of Pensacola, Florida, established Baptist Hospital in 1951 as a community-owned health care facility founded on Christian values. That single hospital evolved into Baptist Health Care, today the largest, most comprehensive health care system in the Florida Panhandle. Baptist Hospital, Inc., a subsidiary of Baptist Health Care, includes Baptist Hospital, a 492-bed tertiary care and referral hospital; Gulf Breeze, a 60-bed medical and surgical hospital; and Baptist Medical Park, an ambulatory care complex.

Al Stubblefield
President and CEO
Baptist Health Care Corporation

David Sjoberg
Vice President, Strategic Services
Baptist Hospital, Inc.

2003 – Saint Luke's Hospital of Kansas City

Founded in 1882, Saint Luke's Hospital is the largest hospital in the Kansas City, Missouri, metropolitan area. Affiliated with the Diocese of West Missouri of the Protestant Episcopal Church, it is a not-for-profit comprehensive teaching and referral health care organization that provides 24-hour coverage in every health care discipline. Saint Luke's is driven by its vision, "The Best Place to Get Care, The Best Place to Give Care," and its core values of Quality/Excellence, Customer Focus, Resource Management, and Teamwork. Specialized care capabilities for very ill people are Saint Luke's hallmark.

Eugene E. Fibuch, MD
Vice President and Medical Director for Quality
Saint Luke's Health System

G. Richard Hastings
President and CEO
Saint Luke's Health System

Sherry Marshall
Vice President, Quality
Saint Luke's Health System

2002 – SSM Health Care

Sponsored today by the Franciscan Sisters of Mary, SSM Health Care is a private, not-for-profit health care system based in St. Louis, Missouri. The system owns, manages, and is affiliated with 21 acute care hospitals and three nursing homes in four states: Illinois, Missouri, Oklahoma, and Wisconsin. Nearly 5,000 physician partners and 23,000 employees work together to provide a wide range of health care services through inpatient, outpatient, emergency departments, and ambulatory surgery settings. SSM Health Care offers additional services that include physician practices, residential and skilled nursing, home care and hospice, and information services.

Sister Mary Jean Ryan, FSM
President and CEO
SSM Health Care

Paula Friedman
Corporate Vice President, Strategy and Systems Improvement
SSM Health Care

1

Introduction

*"Knowing is not enough; we must apply.
Willing is not enough; we must do."*

– Goethe[1]

Over the last decade, the U.S. health care system has endured mounting public scrutiny and declining public trust, prompted by well-researched and publicized evidence of far-reaching problems in safety, patient experience, and performance. After a half-century as a symbol of U.S. strength and extraordinary achievements in technologically advanced diagnostics and treatments, health care delivery is under fire from every direction for fundamental shortcomings in every facet of operational excellence.

Few people are happy with the current delivery system—not the people using it, the people working in it, or the people paying for it. For every story of medical triumph and human compassion, there are many more accounts of errors, ineffectiveness, and insensitivity. Good care happens almost in spite of organizational systems, too often requiring tremendous effort by patients, their families, and their health care professionals to overcome operational barriers.

The Centers for Medicare and Medicaid Services (CMS) is fully committed to transforming payment incentives into tools that reward quality and efficiency and exercising its legal authority to punish laggards.[2] CMS has put more hospitals on "Immediate Jeopardy" status for quality and safety problems in the last four years than in the preceding four decades, threatening to pull federal funding until issues are fully addressed.[3] Naturally, private payers follow the lead of CMS in such situations. In 2009, The Joint Commission instituted its own version of "Preliminary Denial of Accreditation" based on judgments about the immediacy of risk to patients.[4]

Providers and delivery systems ultimately control care and its quality and efficiency. To succeed in these challenging times, the focus must be on building the *capability* of provider organizations to deliver safe, reliable, and effective care.

Leaders of health care delivery organizations recognize and live with the consequences of this harsh environment every day. The forces of change and strategic challenges facing health care organizations—economic recession with rising unemployment, shrinking reimbursements, rapidly emerging safety and quality standards, expanding transparency on performance metrics, pay-for-performance, workforce shortages and poor staff morale, and consumer demands—create enormous turmoil for front-line health care providers and stress for their leaders. Over the last decade, most organizations have tried multiple strategies to address these challenges including quality improvement in its various forms and methods. Nevertheless, leaders typically find cultural transformation and sustainable performance excellence beyond reach for their organizations.

HEALTH CARE'S GROWING INTEREST IN BALDRIGE

In this unprecedented environment for health care, a startling trend has emerged highlighting a potential path forward for many health care organizations. The Malcolm Baldrige National Quality Award, the most competitive performance excellence award in the United States, has been dominated by health care applicants since 2002. As Figure 1.1 shows, since the Baldrige Award process opened to health care organizations in 1999, 40 percent of all applicants have come from this sector.[5] In 2007, 42 health care organizations applied at the national level, while 130 applied for state-level Baldrige-based performance excellence awards.[6] In 2008, there were 43 health care applicants for Baldrige. It is widely believed that award applicants are the tip of an iceberg of Baldrige users, organizations using the Criteria to integrate their developing business, operational, and quality activities around a culture striving for excellence.

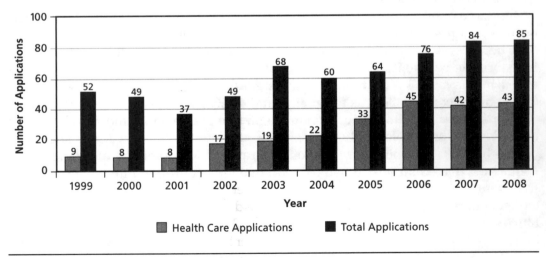

Figure 1.1 Baldrige applications by year.

Why would so many organizations, in the face of unprecedented cost and quality challenges, choose to compete for the Baldrige Award? At a time when the number of Baldrige applicants from manufacturing and service industries has declined to a mere handful annually, health care organizations are making the significant investment required to apply. The fifty-page application describes precisely how their organization is led and managed, including some 100 graphs and charts of results demonstrating performance in quality and safety, customer experience, financial and market performance, workforce and improvement capability, and ethics/regulatory compliance. Unlike most award applications, this task cannot be delegated to junior staff. Writing a Baldrige application requires significant input by senior leadership. What could explain this investment and what return does the effort produce?

We interviewed CEOs and senior leaders from all nine Baldrige recipients to-date from the health care sector.[7] Our goal was to understand why they made this investment and what they got out of it. We also wanted to know how they approached their "Baldrige journey" and what other health care leaders should do to reap similar benefits. A common belief is that Baldrige requires significant commitment of time and resources, yet so many health care organizations are using the approach. We set out to understand the return on that investment.

The answers were remarkable. Assessing their organizations' performance against the Baldrige Criteria proved to offer benefits far beyond the hoped-for recognition of the Baldrige Award. Although three of the nine health care recipients entered into the Baldrige process with aspirations of a quick award, they soon learned that this is not a typical award program. All nine recipients uniformly and unequivocally report persisting over years for the genuine and lasting benefits of the process itself. Both the task of developing the application and receiving the detailed scores and feedback proved enormously valuable to these organizations. They used the assessment and feedback process to steer a path toward higher performance in every aspect of business and performance excellence.

Rich Hastings, president and CEO of Saint Luke's Health System, put it simply: "We needed a business model, a total process model to evaluate how well we do what we do. Baldrige was the only organizational tool we could find to do that, to help us align everything we were doing. Applying for the award made us a stronger organization."

"Health care can be so fragmented…the Baldrige Criteria provide an integrated framework," explained Javon Bea, president and CEO, Mercy Health System.

All the Baldrige recipients from health care came to similar conclusions about the return on investment. Sister Mary Jean Ryan, president and CEO, SSM Health Care, summed it up: "Baldrige is the single most powerful tool for change available. There is no other way to get better faster."

These remarkable responses made us even more curious about what these organizations did to benefit from using the Baldrige process. The National Institute for Standards and Technology supports the Baldrige Criteria for Performance Excellence and the award program (see Chapter 2, Baldrige). The Baldrige Program oversees biannual public updating to ensure that the Criteria for Performance

Excellence reflect what Director Harry Hertz often calls "the leading edge of validated management practices." Assuming Hertz is correct, the robust design of the Criteria still does not explain exactly how using Baldrige helped these organizations accomplish significant, enterprise-wide improvement across multiple dimensions of performance.

To understand the journey for these nine organizations and their return on investment, we explored their stories in detail. We studied their fifty-page award applications, presentations at national and regional meetings, other publications by or about them, and most important, we interviewed their CEOs and other senior leaders at length. Our interview questions can be summarized in three basic themes:

- How did you successfully use the Baldrige framework to drive improvement?

- What would you recommend other organizations do to gain the value you have from a Baldrige journey?

- What can we learn from you that would help other organizations manage their improvement journeys to maximize the value they gain?

We analyzed these data for common trends and themes that could be generalized for other organizations, and two overarching findings emerged. First, there is a progression of stages that characterize a successful journey over time (Figure 1.3). With remarkable consistency, the nine recipient organizations evolved through a series of stages and common patterns of leadership action to become high performers. Despite significant differences between them, their experiences were remarkably similar. The path, which we call "the journey," appears to be consistent across health care organizations as well as other industries, based upon our knowledge of Baldrige recipients across all sectors. Second, a common set of leadership actions emerged. We found five basic areas where there were similar executive decisions and actions that enabled these organizations to progress successfully over time (Figures 1.4 and 1.5). The journey as well as the leadership practices are introduced here and detailed in later chapters. Before we describe these findings and practices, here is a short description of the Baldrige Criteria and process to orient you to what these organizations did and how they benefited.

BALDRIGE BASICS

We want to share a few basics here as we introduce what our research taught us about successful use of Baldrige as a strategic enterprise framework. Chapter 2, Baldrige, describes the Criteria and framework in straightforward, non-technical language, providing the context to decide how and whether a Baldrige-based approach can prove useful to your situation.

"Baldrige" generally refers to the Baldrige Criteria for Performance Excellence, a public domain compilation of leading-edge management practices for building a high-performance enterprise in any sector of the U.S. economy. The Criteria are non-prescriptive, provocative questions that challenge leaders to clarify their approaches to creating value and accomplishing objectives in seven categories:

1. Leadership

2. Strategic Planning

3. Customer Focus

4. Measurement, Analysis, and Knowledge Management

5. Workforce Focus

6. Process Management

7. Results

The Criteria require evidence of how your organization is led and managed, and how all of this activity links together in a system that produces results. Results are defined broadly, encompassing the performance domains addressed by the Institute of Medicine Six Aims and also diverse business and operational results (market and finance, patient engagement, workforce engagement, improvement capability, community service, and governance).[8] A small sampling of the Criteria is displayed in Figure 1.2. The Baldrige Criteria and scoring method are widely considered to be the gold standard of objective, comprehensive performance assessment tools. The Malcolm Baldrige National Quality Award is the highest honor that a business or organization can achieve in one of six sectors of the U.S. economy. The award is based upon an objective evaluation of an organization's entire operation, from quality to the bottom line, measured against the Criteria. Numerous countries use similar criteria and award programs to evaluate and honor companies and organizations for excellence.[9]

- Leadership: *How do your senior leaders create and promote a culture of patient safety? How do leaders foster accountability for results?*

- Strategic Planning: *How do you develop and deploy action plans throughout the organization to achieve your key strategic objectives? How do you ensure that the key outcomes of your action plans can be sustained?*

- Customer Focus: *How do you follow up with patients and stakeholders on the quality of health care services, patient and stakeholder support, and transactions to receive prompt and actionable feedback? How does your complaint management system enable aggregation and analysis of complaints for use in improvement throughout your organization and by your partners, as appropriate?*

From the Baldrige National Quality Program, *2009-2010 Health Care Criteria for Performance Excellence,* available at www.baldrige.nist.gov/HealthCare_Criteria.htm.

Figure 1.2 Sample Baldrige Criteria questions.

RESEARCH FINDINGS OF A JOURNEY

Our research revealed a consistent pattern of development, a journey over time for individual organizations using Baldrige. Each progressed through five stages on the way to high performance as measured by the Baldrige Criteria. Based on our years as Baldrige experts evaluating many different organizations, we believe the stages are universal and found in any sector or industry.

Stage 0 – Reaction

Reaction refers to the stage when organizations opt to wait for mandates and regulations, and implement change when required to maintain the status quo. While they may experience occasional random or even planned acts of improvement in some areas, there is no overarching impetus to drive the organization to higher levels of performance beyond complying with externally imposed requirements as challenges arise.

Stage 1 – Projects

The *Projects* stage characterizes an organization in which leaders acknowledge the performance problems and commit to finding an effective approach to improvement. Initial steps tend to include learning and implementing quality improvement tools and methods. Often this project-focused phase brings new capabilities to execute initiatives and implement processes learned from others. Many organizations become competent with quality improvement methods and tools and achieve islands of success, but the overall culture does not change. Improvement is still reactive to problems or deficiencies. Proactive approaches to organization-wide performance excellence do not exist. The connection between strategic goals, operational plans, daily operations, and improvement projects is haphazard or non-existent. Ultimately Stage 1 generates only modest improvements, causing leaders to seek more systematic approaches to transformational change.

Stage 2 – Traction

Traction occurs when senior leaders begin to gain traction in their organizational strategies. Organizations that adopt Baldrige as their framework for transformation assess their enterprise-wide operations and results against the Criteria (see Figure 1.2 for sample questions) and begin systematic benchmarking of best leadership and management practices during the Traction stage. For Baldrige-using leaders, this phase represents gaining a toehold on overseeing their enterprise as a system of processes that cause measurable results to happen across multiple performance domains. The Traction phase marks the transition from the singular focus on change through projects, however well executed, to systematic design, evaluation, and improvement of leadership processes. Projects continue to be a key element of the landscape, but they become more focused and aligned with overall strategy. Cycles of Baldrige assessment and feedback lead to building leadership capability to spread improvements and hardwire change.

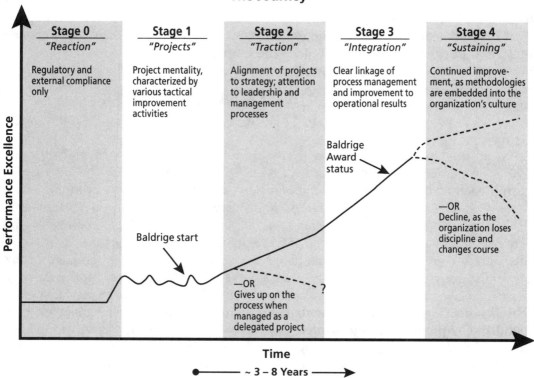

Figure 1.3 The journey and stages of progression.

Stage 3 – Integration

Integration represents a later phase when organizations become more skillful and integrated at executive functioning. Approaches and processes of leadership, such as values deployment and culture building, begin to link and align with strategic planning and action planning, scorecards and dashboards, job descriptions and performance review methods, and other operational processes. Projects are embedded into operational process management. Nonaligned improvement initiatives are dropped or postponed as focused effort replaces frenetic and often duplicative activity. The nine health care organizations we studied were well along in the Integration stage when they were named Baldrige Award recipients. Many recipients report that they experienced their greatest improvements and gains in alignment and integration in the year just before or right after receiving the award.

Stage 4 – Sustaining

Sustaining is a challenge for any high-performance organization. The health care environment is anything but static. New demands emerge, and challenges continue to mount. Even for high performers, maintaining past performance is not an option for future competitiveness. Organizations go in one of two directions at this stage: either they continue to perform well or decline as they lose focus and the drive to excel.

The particulars about these stages and how our study organizations progressed through them are detailed in Chapter 3, The Journey.

LASER – FUNDAMENTAL ELEMENTS GUIDE THE JOURNEY

As we studied the health care Baldrige recipients and their developmental journeys, five basic elements emerged that drove their forward momentum. The approaches within each of the five elements explain how these organizations gradually, over several annual cycles of evaluation and improvement, built systematic and disciplined capability to plan for and meet their unique strategic challenges and achieve notably better results. None of these organizations became perfect, but all of them grew significantly more capable and focused. Their leaders and workforce generally grew more engaged. As they evolved, they improved their measured performance against the Baldrige Criteria in each of the seven categories, including their results. We introduce these elements here and then describe them in more detail in Chapters 4 through 8, with examples from our study organizations. We derived LASER, the acronym for these five essential elements—Leadership, Assessment, Sensemaking, Execution, and Results—from the analysis of all our data sources, including the interviews.

The fact that our study organizations followed such similar paths and stages was unexpected. Equally striking was the similarity in how they did it, how they achieved their early traction and increasing integration and alignment over time. LASER is a set of behaviors and actions that focused these organizations and accelerated their journeys, the five strategic building blocks that form a foundation for transformation.

Early on in the journey, these elements function in sequence, as an organization shifts from project mentality to gaining traction under transformational change. Clear patterns are visible in Leadership that drive the shifts necessary to build systematic approaches to enterprise operations that are new and different for organizations. Assessment plays a critical role, in providing the objective feedback essential to motivate innovation and change. Sensemaking is a collaborative process by senior leaders to understand current enterprise performance and identify how leadership and management processes must change to achieve different and better results with less effort and resources. Execution is the critical element of setting focus and accomplishing the work of change. The Results provide the evidence, the measured outcomes of a successful strategy to achieve higher performance.

Leadership

Every approach to organizational change, from the micro system to the macro system, acknowledges the important role of *leadership*. In building a Baldrige-based approach, we found the three essential steps:

- Recognize that fundamental change is needed to realize the enterprise vision

- Welcome objective evaluation and "brutal facts" feedback[10]

- Commit to building a culture of organizational learning and improvement

Effective and successful organizations establish a discipline of evaluating and improving their leadership and management approaches. By welcoming evaluation and feedback, these leaders modeled a commitment to learning and growth that is essential to competitive success. Improvement projects, though an essential ingredient, were not sufficient to hardwire lasting change, change that could be sustained beyond committed individual champions and spread successfully across work units. Feedback framed by the Baldrige Criteria provides the critical element of "brutal truth" that can identify both strengths and vulnerabilities in current cultural and leadership practices that move a successful project into a repeatable, systematic, and transferable process. Finally, leadership practices that characterized our study organizations shared a common commitment to learning and improvement at all levels of the organization. The Baldrige evaluations served as a structured discipline for enterprise-wide performance review, an objective measure of progress in building culture and focusing results.

Assessment

Assessment reflects the decision to systematically evaluate leadership and management practices, cutting across traditional organizational charts and structures, viewing the organization from the perspective of the customer. This decision must come from the top of an organization, whether the scope is a 20-bed intensive care unit, a 200-bed hospital, or a 20,000-employee integrated delivery system. Assessment feedback serves as a critical input to strategic planning, ensuring that goals and targets include building business competencies into operations. Our study organizations focused on three necessary actions:

- Describe the organization's culture, approaches, and processes against the Baldrige Criteria

- Conduct periodic enterprise-wide evaluations

- Receive scoring and feedback on leadership and management practices and capacity to achieve organizational vision for the future

This practice of periodic enterprise evaluation is akin to the practice of regular individual performance reviews, but applied to the entire organization. It can be accomplished through a myriad of methods ranging from simple self-assessments to national award program applications with their detailed feedback reports. Specific information on how organizations accomplish assessments is provided in Chapter 2, Baldrige, and Chapter 5, Assessment.

Sensemaking

Sensemaking is a concept first introduced by Karl E. Weick to describe the critical role of leaders in interpreting and explaining the facts of a challenging environment and framing what is required for successful operations of a complex system such as health care delivery.[11] The oversight of transformational change requires engaged senior leaders who build a system of management processes and culture that drive results. The fundamental activities of sensemaking include the following, which can only be accomplished by senior leaders:

- View the organization as a system of leadership and management processes that generate results

- Interpret assessment feedback in light of current organizational capabilities

- Define and focus priorities for changing leadership and management practices to achieve better results with less effort and resource

Sensemaking is a critical step in building traction under a transformational change strategy. In our study organizations, particularly in the early stages of the journey, there was often resistance to this step by some on the senior team. Systems thinking is not a natural fit for some leaders.

Execution

In the LASER model, *Execution* refers to the focused action necessary to achieve results. It is the critical work of changing *how* your organization runs in order to produce higher performance. Leaders in recipient organizations developed their capacity to execute on a set of actions that translate the learning from their assessments and sensemaking into better results. Through cycles of evaluation and improvement, they built processes and practices that allowed them to address challenges in their market and environment proactively. They developed in their organizations the capability to execute the strategy. The critical actions we found among the recipient organizations include the following:

- Make changes from day one by formalizing their informal processes

- Set priorities to focus on critical actions as well as discontinuing tangential activity

- Establish accountability and develop action plans for priorities to improve leadership and management of key work processes

- Integrate addressing Baldrige feedback into strategic and operational planning to ensure steady improvement in overall operations

Execution is an area of significant weakness for health care organizations generally. The Baldrige recipients used their journeys to grow steadily in their effectiveness at execution of strategy and improvement. As they progressed to later stages in their journey, they demonstrated increasing ability to identify performance gaps and address them efficiently with measurable results.

Results

In the end, a successful Baldrige journey is all about the *results*, comparison to the organization, and appropriate benchmarks over time that demonstrate undeniable and significant improvement in areas of importance. Each of these organizations demonstrated numerous quality, service, workforce, market, and financial areas of noteworthy achievement. None of them proved to be perfect, but they all demonstrated excellence and capability to meet challenges successfully. Their results demonstrated the following characteristics:

- Strong performance on a comprehensive set of measures in areas important to patients, stakeholders, and markets

- Beneficial trends over time in areas of importance to the accomplishment of the organization's mission

- Key results evaluated against relevant comparisons and/or benchmarks showing areas of good to excellent relative performance

- Alignment with key organizational strategies and goals

Health care organizations tend to be full of data and measures but weak on focus, weaker still on action linked to analysis of performance. These organizations demonstrated continual improvement in their efficient and effective use of data to improve enterprise results.

Within each of the LASER elements, we found similar practices and approaches among our study organizations. Stepping back from our findings and looking at the commonalities across organizations, we could see clearly that these elements formed a foundation for successful use of the Baldrige framework. In Chapters 4 through 8, we use examples from our study organizations to describe how each of the five strategic LASER elements evolved over the course of their journeys. The essentials worked in synergy over time, fostering culture change and enterprise-wide improvement. The LASER practices matured as the enterprise progressed through the stages of the journey, eventually becoming embedded in the leadership of each organization, while each retained its own values, culture, and style.

LASER Practices Changed Through the Journey

During the first year, successful organizations moved through the LASER elements in sequence (Figure 1.4). They initiated Leadership practices to set the change process in motion and committed to periodic objective evaluation of their culture and operational systems. Then they conducted Assessments, customized to their circumstances and needs. Leadership used their feedback for Sensemaking, to gain insight about how their enterprise runs and why it gets the results it gets. They addressed Execution by developing action plans to focus initiatives and align projects. Finally, they took a comprehensive objective look at their baseline Results across all key dimensions of performance.

Over time and through multiple cycles of assessment and feedback, the LASER elements became more interconnected and continuous (Figure 1.5). Senior leaders embodied organizational commitment to periodic assessment; learning and change became a routine part of their work. As leadership and management processes become more visible and subject to periodic redesign, senior leaders spend less of their time running the organization or fighting fires and more of their time thinking about how to hardwire change and innovate. Though a formal comprehensive assessment might be performed once every year or two, evaluation of specific activities such as strategic planning, complaint management, or incident reporting, becomes routine. Staff and leaders come to see their work as processes; over time, they build in process steps to measure, assess, and improve these processes efficiently when needed.

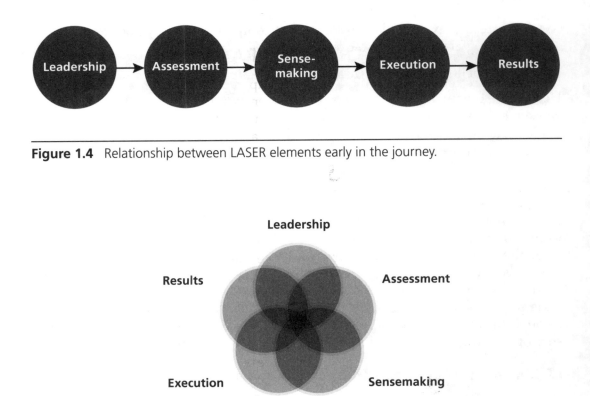

Figure 1.4 Relationship between LASER elements early in the journey.

Figure 1.5 Relationship between LASER elements later in the journey: connected and continuous.

We found that organizations early in the journey waited to get their feedback before embarking on productive change work. Over time, they were able to anticipate their feedback on their own, before the official report arrived. This shift to continuous evaluation, learning, and process improvement allowed them to accelerate their journey. By this point in the journey, the formal feedback was a critical input into strategic planning, allowing the enterprise to address culture change and leadership processes explicitly. Organizational goals evolved to include building competencies and high-performing leadership processes in addition to achieving traditional performance objectives.

The Impact of LASER Over Time

Over time, each of the award recipients grew more capable of solving problems and achieving goals. They developed the capacity to adopt new ideas and spread best practices faster than before. None became perfect but all grew significantly more competent. Competition and the ever-changing health care landscape continue to challenge them, but their capacity to lead, plan, and execute helps them to be far more successful than they were "pre-journey." Although their leadership and management processes are hardwired, they generally remain committed to periodic evaluation of all key processes. With less effort and greater speed, they are able to achieve better results.

PROCESS LITERACY

As we analyzed the award recipients and compared them to other less successful organizations, another fundamental concept emerged. During our research team conversations, we developed a shorthand phrase to characterize more mature organizations that had grown competent and agile at improving both leadership and daily work processes, that had moved beyond random, often externally driven projects. They had acquired, through cycles of Baldrige assessments and feedback, the capacity to identify and manage their key processes. They had grown "process literate."

They had gained the capacity to see, as W. Edwards Deming often said, that all work is a process. Gradually, they came to identify their key processes, the owners of these processes, and the short list of actionable measures of performance managers can use to determine process effectiveness. Whatever their chosen improvement methodology, it was used periodically to redesign key processes as these organizations grew more capable and proactive. They applied their improvement methodology to leadership and management processes, such as communications and strategic planning, as well as to daily work processes, such as drug dispensing, diagnostic testing, and staff hiring. Although it did not develop in a few months and in most cases it took a few years, by the time successful organizations entered the Integration phase, they were well along in becoming process literate. Throughout this book, you will find descriptions of how the Baldrige recipients evolved into process literate organizations. In Chapter 6, Sensemaking, we detail more of the specific applications of this fundamental business competency.

BENEFITS OF THE JOURNEY

What characterizes Baldrige recipient companies and organizations, in health care and in other industries, when they reach later stages of their journey? They have a refined performance improvement system that uses methods, tools, and resources effectively and efficiently to improve key processes and address the organization's unique aspirations and challenges. They have developed leadership and operational capability to address the following challenges:

- Build culture that engages the entire workforce in the achievement of their unique mission, vision, and goals

- Understand and manage their enterprise as a system of processes that generate value for all customers and stakeholders

- Benchmark and systematically improve key processes, both those of leadership and daily work processes

- Achieve results that meet organizational and market requirements and measure up favorably against other comparable organizations

What the Baldrige process provided the health care recipient leaders was a framework—a framework to align strategy, processes, and improvement; measure organizational progress; and systemically identify new opportunities for change. Through cycles of assessment, feedback, action, and re-assessment, all nine organizations made substantial improvements in results across multiple dimensions. According to Frank Sardone, president and CEO, Bronson Healthcare Group, Bronson "achieved results faster than we predicted. We're the preferred hospital in the county, with 40 percent growth in admissions since 2000, and recognized for six years in a row as a great place to work and great place to bring your patients. No question about the benefits."

Asked how they would counsel other leaders in terms of readiness to begin, the health care recipient leaders spoke with one voice. Baptist Hospital's David Sjoberg, vice president of strategic services, said an organization "can start any time, from any place."

"The most common misconception," said Sister Mary Jean, "is that you should wait until you are 'ready.' No one is ever ready. You have to start somewhere and you can only get better by getting your report."

Baldrige recipients are not perfect, but they are competent across a wide range of governance, leadership, and management capabilities. They are also not alike; each is competent to accomplish its own unique aspirations and solutions. Baldrige provides a much-needed enterprise framework, a proven organizational roadmap, for a path to higher performance. This book is about how and why organizations successfully improve comprehensive operational performance using Baldrige. The approach is widely applicable, regardless of an organization's size, breadth of services, or current performance level. Creating a Baldrige-based developmental strategy supports successful transformational change across the spectrum of health care organizations.

2

Baldrige

"I see the Baldrige process as a powerful set of mechanisms for disciplined people engaged in disciplined thought and taking disciplined action to create great organizations that produce exceptional results."

– Jim Collins[1]

I s Baldrige just an award program or a roadmap to improve organizational performance? Our research found that Baldrige serves as a strategic business framework, providing leaders a means to align and focus their entire team on improving overall results. The Baldrige process provides diagnostic assessments to evaluate and monitor your organization's capabilities to execute against every type of challenge. Assessment scores and feedback serve to integrate leadership activities around a comprehensive framework, providing actionable answers to three fundamental questions:

1. How well is your organization performing?

2. Are your leadership systems capable of meeting your strategic challenges?

3. What are your strengths and opportunities to improve?

BALDRIGE – A SYSTEMS FRAMEWORK

The Baldrige Criteria provide a systems framework applicable to enterprises of any scope and size. The framework is comprehensive, inclusive of all operations and all desired results. The Criteria are non-prescriptive. They do not dictate any particular approach or method; rather, the Criteria are used by highly trained examiners to evaluate how you use your chosen approaches to achieve results. For example, some organizations use Lean, others use Six Sigma, and still others use Plan-Do-Check-Act as their approaches to performance improvement. Many organizations select a

Baldrige Award Program

The award program is named in honor of Malcolm Baldrige, Secretary of Commerce (1981-87) and a strong proponent of quality as a way to strengthen the United States' competitiveness worldwide. Congress enacted legislation establishing the award to raise awareness about the importance of quality and performance excellence, naming it in honor of Baldrige and his legacy after he died tragically in 1987. Originally established to honor businesses, the Baldrige Award is now open to virtually any U.S. organization regardless of size, sector, or purpose. Awards may be given annually to manufacturing, service, small business, education, health care, and nonprofit organizations. The education and health care sectors were added for eligibility in 1999, and the nonprofit sector was added in 2007. The award is given to organizations that demonstrate performance using a rigorous, unbiased scoring and judging system based on the Criteria for Performance Excellence. The Criteria are comprehensive, assessing organizational excellence in every fundamental domain of strategy and operations. Although the Criteria concepts are consistent across sector, size, and type of organization, the Criteria language is customized to the unique terminology of education and health care in specific Criteria booklets as well.[2] Since the award was established in 1988, there have been seventy-nine awards given to a wide diversity of businesses and organizations, including nine health care awards to five hospitals and four health care systems.

combination of these methods or create their own approach, adapting their choices to their unique culture and circumstances. The Criteria examine whether an organization has an approach to performance improvement, how effectively methods are used, and the evidence that improvement is systematic and successful.

Baldrige assesses the effectiveness of your chosen approaches to deliver your desired results and determines whether your methods fit your situation and are used by the appropriate work units. It evaluates your organization's capability to overcome your unique challenges and to accomplish your particular mission, vision, and goals. Assessments do not compare individual organizations to one another. Rather, the Criteria are used to evaluate your organization against a gold standard of excellence and provide specific feedback about the gaps between your current state and your desired future state. Baldrige provides an objective measure of enterprise culture, competence, and capability to deliver desired results.

The framework, shown in Figure 2.1, provides a high-level overview of the Criteria for Performance Excellence and illustrates how the Criteria provide a systems perspective. Each box represents a fundamental aspect of business operations, categories that every organization must address. When each category of activities operates synergistically and effectively, the organization as a system can deliver desired results, Category 7.

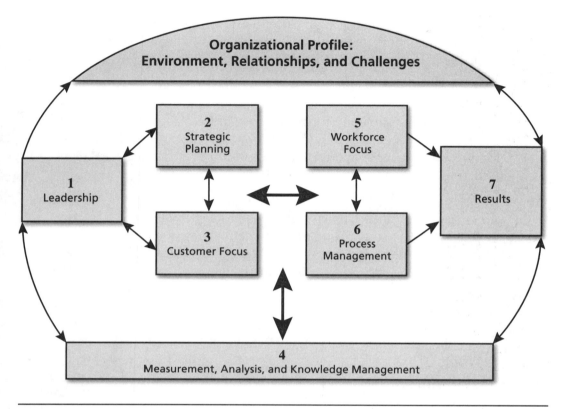

Figure 2.1 Criteria framework—a systems perspective.[3]

From top to bottom, the framework has three basic elements: the organizational profile of your unique situation and approaches to excellence, the system operations and the results produced by those systems, and the foundational infrastructure for measurement, analysis, and knowledge management.

- The *Organizational Profile* (top of the figure) describes fundamental information about your organization's unique environment, key working relationships, and strategic challenges and advantages. The Organizational Profile summarizes your performance improvement system and provides the key information about your unique circumstances. Examiners use this information to evaluate your leadership and management approaches. They assess the effectiveness of your approaches in producing desired and needed results, in light of your environment, circumstances, and aspirations.

- Enterprise operations (middle of the figure) comprise two linked triads.

  - The *Leadership Triad* consists of the Criteria on (1) Leadership, (2) Strategic Planning, and (3) Customer Focus. These three critical elements provide the direction and set expectations for the enterprise. The responses to these Criteria questions provide a description of your organization's approaches in these areas. The evaluation process tests whether your approaches are systematic and effective.

– The *Results Triad* includes the Criteria on (5) Workforce Focus, (6) Process Management, and (7) Results. These three elements focus on how your workforce is supported and key processes managed to generate your overall performance results.

- *Measurement, Analysis, and Knowledge Management*, Category 4, underpins the operational system and forms the base of the Baldrige framework. In essence, it provides the roadmap for the journey, through your use of information to assess performance of your key processes and direct improvement and innovation.

The arrows connecting the boxes indicate the importance of building an integrated leadership system that links elements such as strategic planning (Category 2) to workforce processes (Category 5) and improvement of key work processes (Category 6). Measurement, Analysis, and Knowledge Management are critical functions that support all operations. Taken all together, the framework and Criteria provide an overall gestalt on how the enterprise functions as a system and the evaluation provides an assessment of the integration and alignment of each element as a system.

John Heer, president and CEO, North Mississippi Health Services, spoke very clearly about the importance of learning to view your organization as a system and how the Baldrige process helped him in this regard. "After four years, I realized we really needed to focus on alignment of our approaches [in each of the categories]. We learned the Baldrige score was not about knocking the socks off one or two categories. You have to perform in all categories to win." Leaders oversee their enterprise as a system of processes that together produce strong results across multiple dimensions of performance.

The Criteria continue to evolve ensuring they address the highly dynamic environment for all types of organizations and businesses, including health care. First developed by business performance experts in the 1980s, the Criteria have kept pace with the leading edge of management practices as well as evolving

---

Generic Strategic Framework

While the language of the Health Care Criteria is customized to our sector, the basic framework and structure is generic and applies to your organization or business regardless of whether you manufacture computer components, provide housing and food to homeless people, or educate college students. This feature supplies one of the greatest benefits of Baldrige diagnostic assessments, enabling benchmarking across industries to find innovative approaches. For example, many role model practices for strategy development and strategic plan deployment come from industries outside of health care. The generic Baldrige framework makes cross-industry learning more accessible.

Cause and Effect
Just as there is a causal link between any process and its outcomes, organizations as systems cause or create their enterprise outcomes. The notion of cause and effect between processes and the results they generate is fundamental to the Baldrige framework and evaluation methodology. For example, there is a cause and effect relationship between the processes to engage the workforce and the results on surveys and other measures of workforce engagement. As leaders refine their approaches to workforce engagement, the measured levels of engagement increase. Similarly, the processes of infection control correlate with the measurable results regarding hospital-acquired infections. The same reasoning applies across all critical work systems and processes.

standards for health care quality. A public process managed by the U.S. Department of Commerce updates the Criteria every two years to collect insights from every business sector, refining the Criteria to keep pace with new knowledge and best practices.

WHERE TO USE BALDRIGE

Baldrige can be applied in virtually any organization or circumstance. The journey found in our research describes a similar progression regardless of size or scope. Some started in crisis. Others were well along in achieving performance excellence when they adopted Baldrige to help them accelerate the journey. Mercy Health System president and CEO Javon Bea often describes how his organization was in the midst of a major financial crisis when he came into his leadership position and soon thereafter started using Baldrige. Sharp HealthCare president and CEO Mike Murphy told us they were well along in the Sharp Experience transformation when they turned to Baldrige as a tool to evaluate their progress, integrate all the pieces, and identify the necessary steps to go to the next level. Most award recipients were skilled at projects when they picked up on Baldrige, but even this was not uniform. The bottom line is that each transformation story is unique.

"Organization" refers to any enterprise or subunit operating in the health care sector, providing services to patients.[4] According to Michele Serbenski, vice president of performance excellence, Bronson Healthcare Group, "The Criteria can be used for any type of organization of any size." We have seen Baldrige used to design new hospitals, to steer through a crisis, and to move an organization from pretty good to demonstrably better and unquestionably great. Some of the award recipients we studied are individual hospitals, while others are health systems with medical groups, nursing homes, and other health care related business units. We know of health plans and nursing homes that have used Baldrige as a platform for change.

The Criteria can also inform and frame efforts at the micro-system level, such as intensive care units or a transplant service. Our study organizations used the Criteria in a variety of ways, to design new services and processes. "Once we started really understanding the Criteria, we used them to establish processes and structures, for example, for determining and listening to all our customer groups," explained Diane Grillo, senior vice president and chief learning and communications officer, Robert Wood Johnson University Hospital at Hamilton. For most organizations, Baldrige and the Criteria operate in the background as an executive tool, not a term in regular use broadly throughout the workforce. The mission, vision, values, and performance measures are routine topics of conversation. "Baldrige" is a technical term describing the strategic framework for enterprise evaluation and transformation. The CEO and senior leadership may grow familiar with the Criteria and use the Categories to discuss their organizational competencies, but few organizations train employees in Baldrige.

While Baldrige functions in the background, it is an ever-present reminder to senior leaders of the objective current performance of the enterprise. Executives monitor the overall and category scores and feedback, engaging as active learners in the assessment and strategic activities to continually improve organizational capabilities.

AWARDS ARE ONLY PART OF THE STORY

The Criteria are used widely across industries, countries, and professions as the gold standard of organizational evaluation and architecture for high performance.[5] According to a 2003 Booz Allen Hamilton study, "The Baldrige Award enjoys very broad, positive recognition among leaders in each of the Baldrige Award-eligible sectors.... More than 70 percent of leaders surveyed among Fortune 1000 companies said they are likely to use the Criteria for Performance Excellence."[6] Several million copies have been distributed since the first edition in 1988, and reproduction and electronic access multiply that number many times over. Thousands of organizations conduct periodic self-assessments using the scoring method to monitor progress of cultural change initiatives. The diagnostic and monitoring functions of the Criteria and assessment process may in fact be their greatest impact. A Baldrige assessment provides explicit clarity about strengths and gaps. Assessments ensure systematic benchmarking within and across industries. Ellen Guarnieri succeeded Christy Stephenson as president and CEO of Robert Wood Johnson University Hospital at Hamilton, after the organization received the award in 2004. Asked why health care leaders are interested in Baldrige, Guarnieri replied, "We face increasing need to maintain public trust, to move to transparency. The IOM Chasm Report created a sense of urgency. Health care leaders feel increasing responsibility to comply with and excel at meeting payer and community requirements for disclosure. Benchmarking moved from 'nice to do' to 'must do.'" Ken Davis, MD, former chief medical officer at North Mississippi, echoed this and noted that the

Baldrige process fosters serious benchmarking in and out of health care for role model practices to emulate. "It forced us to look at benchmarks outside health care, on national scale. How do you know who's the best in the world? How do you do compared to them? What did you find? Benchmarking for us was both encouraging and enlightening." When an assessment notes a specific opportunity to improve in (for example) service recovery and customer complaint processes, the former Baldrige recipients' application summaries are a readily available public domain source of best practices.[7]

CRITERIA FOR PERFORMANCE EXCELLENCE – OVERVIEW

The Criteria consist of eighteen topic items divided among seven categories of the framework. Answering the Criteria themselves generates incredibly valuable dialogue and learning. By design, they provoke strategic, crucial conversations.

We asked Sherry Marshall, vice president of quality, Saint Luke's Health System, why they were attracted to the Criteria. She responded, "They are so logical. The Categories address processes that every organization needs to perform extremely well to get the outcomes they want. If you perform these well, it drives results you want to achieve. So it made good common business sense. Frankly, it reinforced what we all knew from business school. The Criteria provide the tool to have the conversations we needed to have to be successful."

For Al Stubblefield, president and CEO, Baptist Health Care Corporation, and other Baptist Hospital leaders, a light went on after spending three hours in a workshop on the Criteria: "This could be a wonderful platform for taking what we had accomplished and going to the next level. We decided to meld what we had already done to build a great organization with the Baldrige framework. It helped us identify our gaps and get perspective on our strengths."

The Organizational Profile

The assessment begins with answering the questions in the *Organizational Profile* (Figure 2.1). These answers serve as the lens through which your enterprise is evaluated. The Profile outlines fundamental information about your organization used by examiners to base their evaluation of your performance management systems and analyze the effectiveness of your leadership approaches. The Profile summarizes your:

- Organizational and competitive environment

- Purpose, mission, vision and culture

- Key strategic challenges and advantages

- Performance improvement system

The Profile is an abstract of the forces against which your organization operates. It serves as the starting point to evaluate the effectiveness of your leadership and management approaches. In an assessment process, examiners use the information in the Profile to evaluate your organization's capability to produce intended results. You are judged against your own competence to deliver on your organizational vision.

The Process Criteria

Although the Criteria and framework are designed to focus on key outcomes and performance results, looking only at results does little to diagnose *how* your organization operates to generate these results. There are six categories of fundamental processes that contribute to current performance and the process criteria questions ask you to describe your approaches in each category. Each category is broken into two parts called "items." During the evaluation process, examiners evaluate and score the application at the item level.

1. *Leadership* examines how senior executives guide and sustain the organization, setting organizational vision, values, and expectations. Topics addressed include how senior leaders communicate with your workforce, measure and review organizational performance, create an environment that fosters high performance and ensures ethical, legal, and community responsibilities are met. Item 1.1 analyzes how senior leaders lead while Item 1.2 addresses governance and social responsibilities of the organization.

2. *Strategic planning* looks at how the organization develops and deploys its strategic and action plans, how it ensures adequate resources to execute those plans, and how accomplishments are measured and sustained. Item 2.1 describes how you develop your strategy, and Item 2.2 looks at how you deploy your strategy.

3. *Customer focus* examines how the organization determines requirements and expectations of patients, stakeholders, and markets; how it builds relationships with patients and stakeholders; and how the organization identifies key factors that lead to patient and stakeholder engagement. Item 3.1 evaluates how you engage patients and stakeholders to serve their needs and build relationships. Item 3.2 addresses how you obtain and use information from your patients and stakeholders.

4. *Measurement, analysis, and knowledge management* focuses on how an organization manages and uses its data, information, and knowledge assets to review and improve its performance. This category is depicted on the bottom of the framework to indicate it represents the "brain center" for alignment of your data and information in support of competitive position and strategic growth. Item 4.1 looks into how you measure, analyze, and

then improve organizational performance. Item 4.2 analyzes how you manage your information, organizational knowledge, and information technology.

5. *Workforce focus* examines how the organization engages, manages, and develops its workforce in alignment with the mission and strategic goals. This category addresses key workforce practices, those directed toward creating and maintaining a high performance workplace with an engaged workforce. Item 5.1 assesses how you engage your workforce to achieve organizational and personal success. Item 5.2 examines how you build an effective and supportive workforce environment.

6. *Process management* looks at how the organization determines its core competencies and work systems across administrative and clinical areas. It examines key work systems and processes that support the organization's mission and how it designs, manages, and improves these key work processes. Item 6.1 analyzes how you design your work systems. Item 6.2 looks at how you design, manage, and improve your key organizational work processes.

The process Criteria are non-prescriptive. They do not presume any one approach is better than others or right for all organizations. The questions investigate whether you have systematic methods that enable your organization to improve when and where performance is lagging, and whether you use these methods effectively. They examine whether improvement projects align with and support your strategy by targeting key work processes. As organizations move along in their journey, they refine their approaches to process management. As a result, improvement becomes ingrained in routine work, focusing on and improving key processes that are critical to enterprise success and sustainability.

The Process Evaluation Factors

Assessments use four evaluation factors—Approach, Deployment, Learning, and Integration (ADLI)—to determine how capable an organization is in any of the six process categories. You receive a percentage of the total point score allowable for each category or items within categories, depending on how completely each of the evaluation factors is addressed. Examiners are trained to analyze the description or application to determine how to score a particular approach or item. The evaluation factors for the process categories, Categories 1–6, are listed in Figure 2.2.

Examination and scoring based upon these evaluation factors leads to a percentage of total points available. The scoring methodology and examiner training is designed to achieve standardization in ratings across examinations and examiners.

Approach	**Definition:** "Approach" refers to • The methods used to accomplish the process • The appropriateness of the methods • The effectiveness of the methods as implemented • The degree to which the methods are repeatable and based on reliable data and information (that is, systematic)
	Questions to ask when analyzing approach: • What method or collection of methods is presented? • Is the method systematic (repeatable steps; use of information and data; built-in opportunity for learning)? • Is there evidence that the approach is effective in achieving the intended purpose?
Deployment	**Definition:** "Deployment" refers to the *extent* to which • Your approach is applied consistently • Your approach is used by all appropriate work units
	Questions to ask in analyzing deployment: • Do all appropriate organizational units or work groups follow the method or process? • Is the approach or process consistently followed? • What evidence confirms how completely the process is deployed?
Learning	**Definition:** "Learning" refers to • Refining your approach through cycles of evaluation and improvement • Encouraging breakthrough change to your approach through innovation • Sharing refinements and innovations with other relevant work units and processes in your organization Organizational learning is achieved through research and development, evaluation and improvement cycles, employee and customer ideas and input, best practice sharing, and benchmarking. To be effective, learning should be embedded in the way an organization operates.
	Questions to ask in analyzing learning: • Has the approach or process been evaluated and improved? • Is there evidence of breakthrough changes to this approach through innovation? • Is there evidence that learning from this approach or process is shared with other organizational units/other work processes (organizational learning)?
Integration	**Definition:** "Integration" refers to the extent to which • Your approach is aligned with your organizational needs identified in the Profile and other process categories • Your measures, information, and improvement systems are complementary across processes and work units • Your approaches, processes, results, analyses, learning, and actions are harmonized across processes and work units to support organization-wide goals Effective integration goes beyond alignment and is achieved when the individual components of a performance management system operate as a fully inter-connected unit.
	Questions to ask in analyzing integration: • How well is the approach or process aligned with the organizational needs identified in the Profile and other Criteria? • How well is the approach integrated with these needs? • Are the measures, information, and improvement systems complementary across processes and work units?

Figure 2.2 Process evaluation factors.

The Results Criteria

The seventh category of the Criteria is designed to put the diagnostic focus on whether an organization's approaches generate intended results. The analytic model evaluates the causal link between your enterprise leadership and management and the measurable outcomes produced by your approaches. The scoring methodology assigns 450 out of the 1,000 potential points to the results category, demonstrating the focus on organizational results. The results category is broken down into six items, or groups of results.

> 7. *Results* examine the organization's objective performance and improvement in all of its key areas: health care outcomes, customer-focused outcomes; financial and market outcomes, workforce outcomes, process effectiveness outcomes, and leadership outcomes.

There is a high degree of congruence between these six results areas and the six aims identified in the Institute of Medicine's *Chasm* report as the priority performance dimensions to address the gaps in health care generally:[8]

1. Safe – avoiding injuries to patients from the care that is intended to help them

2. Effective – providing services based on scientific knowledge to all those who could benefit, while refraining from providing services to those not likely to benefit

3. Patient-centered – providing care that is respectful of and responsive to individual patient preferences, needs, and values, and ensuring that patient values guide all clinical decisions

4. Timely – reducing wait times and sometimes harmful delays for both those who receive and those who give care

5. Efficient – avoiding waste, including unused equipment and supplies, ignored ideas, and unnecessary expenditures of energy

6. Equitable – providing care that does not vary in quality because of personal characteristics such as gender, ethnicity, geographic location, and socioeconomic status

Since the *Chasm* report was published in 2001, many health care organizations have built performance measures around the six aims, and they find the multidimensional focus of the Baldrige results category a good fit with their existing framework (Figure 2.3).

Baldrige Results ▶ IOM Aims ▼ Care is:	7.1 Health Care Outcomes	7.2 Patient- and other Customer-focused Outcomes	7.3 Financial and Market Outcomes	7.4 Workforce-focused Outcomes	7.5 Process Effectiveness Outcomes	7.6 Leadership Outcomes
1. Safe	•			•	•	•
2. Effective	•			•	•	•
3. Patient-centered		•				
4. Timely					•	
5. Efficient			•	•	•	
6. Equitable	•					•

Figure 2.3 Relationship between the Baldrige Results Criteria and the IOM Six Aims.[9]

The Results Evaluation Factors

Four evaluation factors—Levels, Trends, Comparisons, Integration (LeTCI)—are used to assess an organization's performance. The evaluation factors for the results category, Category 7, are listed in Figure 2.4.

Taken together, the evaluation of your processes and results generates a comprehensive analysis of the capabilities of an enterprise. It provides the detail to understand the current state of organizational strengths as well as the opportunities to improve and achieve desired results.

THE ASSESSMENT PROCESS

Throughout this book, we describe the "aha" moments of our study organizations, stories of times during their journey when important learning happened through trying to answer a Criteria question or reading their assessment feedback. Many stories illustrate why these leaders consider their journey a cornerstone of their success, far beyond the award.

One such story comes from SSM Health Care, which president and CEO Sister Mary Jean Ryan describes in her presentations and her book, *On Becoming Exceptional*.[10] In 1999, the first year the Baldrige Award opened to health care, SSM submitted their first application. As Sister Mary Jean tells the story, their journey had already helped them to see that they were not functioning as a system and not positioned to achieve their goals. They had an uninspiring corporate mission statement, eighty-five words long, and each SSM facility had created its own

Levels	**Definition:** "Levels" refers to
	• Your current level of performance
	Numerical information that places an organization's performance on a meaningful measurement scale. Performance levels permit evaluation relative to past performance, projections, goals, and appropriate data comparisons. Levels of performance require a meaningful scale and must be related to what is in the Profile, the process Categories (Categories 1-6), or the results category (Category 7).
	Questions to ask when analyzing levels:
	• Do the results provided address the Criteria requirements?
	• Is the performance level excellent, average, or poor?
	• For graphed data, are the axes and units meaningful?
Trends	**Definition:** "Trends" refers to
	• The rate of your performance improvement or the sustainability of good performance (that is, the slope of performance data)
	• The breadth (that is, the extent of use your performance results)
	Numerical information that shows the direction and rate (slope of the trend line) of performance improvements. A minimum of three data points is needed to begin to ascertain a trend, with more data points needed for a statistically valid trend. Trends show the direction of change. The number of data points is dependent on the cycle time of the process being measured.
	Questions to ask in analyzing trends:
	• Are results tracked over time? Are results sustained? Is there consistency of results—favorable, unfavorable, or no change? If there is no change, is it OK because the organization's results show sustained high performance?
	• Does the organization understand the trends?
	• Does the organization demonstrate understanding of the trends and explain the cause of favorable or unfavorable trends or specific data points?
Comparisons	**Definition:** "Comparisons" refers to
	• Your performance relative to your competitors and others providing similar services
	• Your performance relative to benchmarks or industry leaders
	• Your performance relative to the best-in-class in any sector
	Numerical information that establishes the value of results by their relationship to similar or equivalent measures. Comparisons can be made to the results of competitors, industry averages, and best-in-class organizations. The maturity of the organization may help determine which comparisons are most relevant.
	Questions to ask in analyzing comparisons:
	• Are comparisons provided for a few, some, or many graphs?
	• Are comparisons provided for the most important results?
	• Are the comparisons with local, industry leader, or best-in-class organizations?
	• Are the comparisons provided relevant for the maturity of the applicant?
	• Are the comparisons consistent across related measures?
Integration	**Definition:** "Integration" refers to the *extent* to which
	• Your results address important customer, product and service, market process, and action plan performance requirements identified in your Profile and your process categories (Categories 1-6)
	• Your results include valid indicators of future performance
	• Your results are aligned work processes and work units to support organization-wide goals
	Questions to ask in analyzing integration:
	• What results are most important to the organization (that is, key measures, key segments, key processes, action plans)?
	• Do results link to responses to the process categories (Categories 1–6)?

Figure 2.4 Results evaluation factors.

mission statement. Beginning in 1998, they engaged some 3,000 employees over two years to create a single thirteen-word mission statement, appropriate for all their more than twenty facilities. This process had already created tremendous energy and focus for employees, and by the time of their 1999 site visit, they "couldn't stop talking about it" to the examiners who came onsite.

SSM Health Care Mission Statement

Through our exceptional health care services, we reveal the healing presence of God.

Soon the feedback report arrived. They had what Sister Mary Jean calls their "biggest 'aha' moment" in what would be four years of Baldrige assessments. The examiners acknowledged that the new mission statement was simple, memorable, and engaging, but it raised two questions for them: "What do you mean by 'exceptional'?" and "If you want to be exceptional, why are you content to compare yourselves to the average?"[11] The evaluation identified a glaring weakness for the SSM leadership. They realized their mission statement was wonderful only if it changed how people work on a daily basis. It was really a success only if they could demonstrate evidence that what they meant by "exceptional health care services" was defined, deployed, and measured. The feedback pointed them in a new direction on their journey. It gave them insight and a new focus: to ensure that "exceptional" was explicit and that every employee knew exactly what they needed to do to make their contribution to fulfilling the mission.

The assessment underlying a Baldrige examination is both rigorous and elegant in design. It assesses how well an individual enterprise is led and managed to meet its own unique mission, overcome its specific challenges, and make continuous improvement toward its goals. Later on in the journey, for some organizations, comes the award recognition, granted when role model levels of performance are achieved in most areas after cycles of improvement and learning. Several organizations liken this journey to climbing a mountain and as they reach higher and higher levels, their measures of performance improve as well as their Baldrige assessment scores.

The core activities of a Baldrige approach are conducting objective enterprise-wide assessment and implementing improvements to address the assessment score and feedback. We devote an entire chapter on this subject, Chapter 5, Assessment. Baldrige users engage in periodic evaluation of their current approaches and processes, identifying the strengths and opportunities for improvement of their organizational approaches. Using the feedback, they prioritize and execute changes to current approaches. Evaluation and learning become integral to the culture, a regular and valued aspect of the organization's way of life.

Assessments can be internal (self assessments) or external (submission of an application to a state or the national award program for independent scoring and detailed feedback). Both internal and external assessments begin with a description of the organization's operations organized around the Criteria questions, referred to as an assessment document or an application. With internal assessments, organizations use internal staff, trained examiners, or consultants to score the assessment document. Award programs use teams of trained examiners in a confidential process to score and provide feedback to applicants.

Assessments lead to two kinds of learning. First, self-learning comes from the insights gained while answering the Criteria questions and writing the application. Second, the feedback report provides detailed objective analysis of the organization's strengths and opportunities for improvement. An assessment process provides a rich source for organizational learning from both of these perspectives. "The Baldrige process is the best consulting you can buy," explained North Mississippi's Ken Davis, MD. "It's relatively inexpensive, compared to other options. Preparing the application involves answering useful and provocative questions. But the feedback comes back to show very specific gaps. We used the gaps to improve how we work, what we were doing."

Many state programs offer several award levels, ranging from basic ten-page applications to full detailed fifty-page applications similar to the Baldrige Award program. This allows organizations to make early steps and develop over time to full-scale applications.

Our interviewees strongly discourage waiting to start assessments until you believe your organization is ready to be a potential award recipient. This defeats the fundamental purpose of evaluation and precludes the potential learning from struggling with the Criteria questions as well as gaining from objective feedback. It also inhibits progress. Stepping up to receive what Jim Collins calls the "brutal facts" can be humbling but very valuable, as many of our interviewees described. "No one ever feels ready; just jump in and get started with the feedback. Waiting will just delay the learning and growth," explained North Mississippi's John Heer.[12]

Typically, a first-time assessment identifies questions that have yet to be answered by senior leaders. For example, it is common to find that senior leaders have not identified key customer segments and their requirements in any meaningful way. Similarly, it is typical to find that the critical strategic challenges and advantages and core competencies have never been articulated or used effectively in strategic planning. Reaching agreement among the senior leadership team on the answers to these and other Profile questions can be a critical conversation. Communicating these answers to the governance board, other leaders, and staff can serve many important purposes for an organization.

THE SCORE

The evaluation methodology includes a numeric scoring system. Each category is scored separately, with a total potential of 1,000 points, as listed in Figure 2.5. It is important to note some key facts about the scoring methodology. First, 450 out of the 1,000 potential points are assigned to results. This design feature is intended to ensure that high scores correlate with high comparative performance levels and trends. A second important feature is that organizations commonly score in the 200-point to 300-point range in their early assessments, even high profile ones and those that go on to eventually achieve the award. This is because the Criteria evaluate every aspect of competence and even high-profile organizations have vulner-abilities. Recipients typically score in the 550-point to 700-point range. Third, the score is not the sole deciding factor used to identify award recipients. When the Panel of Judges selects organizations, the numeric score is critical but not the determining element in that decision. Judges seek to identify role model companies and organizations. Even award recipients receive a fifty-page feedback report detailing their strengths and opportunities to improve. Finally, the scoring process is designed to foster standardization across examiners, providing scores that are as consistent and reliable as possible. This is critical to the use of feedback to monitor organizational transformation.

The perspective and logic built into the scoring system attracted Sharp HealthCare to the Baldrige process. "It is a Criteria-driven award, not win-or-lose type award. It's about the process of getting better and not an award or prize. That's why it appealed to us. We used the scoring and feedback to improve our systems," explained Nancy Pratt, senior vice president of clinical effectiveness.

Category	Point Score Potential
Leadership	120
Strategic Planning	85
Customer Focus	85
Measurement, Analysis, and Knowledge Management	90
Workforce Focus	85
Process Management	85
Results	450
Total Points	1,000

Figure 2.5 Point values.

In this context, opportunities to improve do not imply doing more projects; rather, they indicate areas where more effective approaches and processes will yield higher performance and sustainable success for the organization.

THE AWARD PROCESS

Organizations that elect to do an assessment by participating in their state or the Baldrige Award program find that their application is subjected to at least two, and possibly three, rounds of review (Figure 2.6). Throughout the process, there is a standard procedure and protocol used to ensure consistency, confidentiality, and fairness in the process for all applicants.

During the first phase, independent and consensus review, about six examiners review the application and analyze it against the scoring methodology described previously. Every item within each category is scored. Typically each examiner spends 40 to 60 hours analyzing your assessment document. They are prohibited from seeking out other sources of information and will have been screened for any personal bias or connections. After the independent reviews are complete, all applications go through a consensus evaluation when their team of examiners share and cross reference their findings with one another. They reach a shared consensus score along with feedback about strengths and opportunities for improvement (OFIs – pronounced "O-fees") for each item.

After the consensus review is complete, the Panel of Judges selects high-scoring applicants to receive site visits. This step is blinded for the judges, based entirely on the scores. After selecting the site visit applicants, the names and details of the selected organizations are revealed to the judges, who must declare any real or perceived conflicts of interest. Judges in conflict with an applicant are excluded from any subsequent review or discussion about that organization. Judges in some cases may also be excluded from discussion for an entire sector to ensure the objectivity of the decision-making process.

If an applicant is selected to receive a site visit, the examiner team identifies a series of issues based on the consensus report to verify the content of the application and clarify issues that were not fully comprehensible from the application. Site visit teams will interview a significant percentage of the organization's employees, at all levels, and will review relevant documents and data. Site visits have a defined process and protocol, just like the other steps in the award process, to ensure consistency and fairness to the applicants. This includes the on-site presence of a "monitor" from the program, whose role is to ensure the process is followed.

After a site visit is completed, the examiner team prepares a final site visit scorebook. The Panel of Judges reviews this extensive report and makes final recommendations on which applicants should receive the award. All site-visited organizations receive a feedback report based on the findings of the site visit. By the time the review is over, some applicants will have received more than 1,000 hours of evaluation in all.

Applicants that are not selected to receive the award may continue to apply each year. Several of the health care recipients went through multiple application cycles, including site visits, at the state or Baldrige level, or both, before receiving the award. Once an applicant becomes an award recipient, it is precluded from applying again for five years. In a way, receiving the award has a downside: the lack of ongoing, objective feedback to drive improvement. To address this, many recipients subsequently apply at the state level or do self-assessments so they can maintain momentum and ongoing learning.

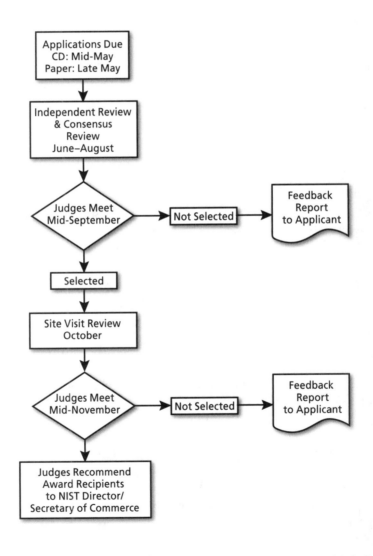

Figure 2.6 The Baldrige Award cycle.[13]

THE FEEDBACK REPORT

Applicants receive a feedback report detailing the organization's strengths and opportunities for improvement in each area addressed by the Criteria. Applicants go through at least two rounds of evaluation. The consensus review builds upon and integrates the independent scores of the entire team of examiners. During consensus, the examiners spend several hours together analyzing the assessment document and refining their feedback to ensure it is accurate, meaningful, and actionable. The assessment document is their only source of information in scoring the application.

A feedback report begins with a scoring band descriptor, which provides a broad overview of the applicant's overall performance.[14] This is followed by a series of "key themes" that serve as the executive summary of the report. The themes detail major, cross-cutting issues for the organization, both strengths and opportunities for improvement. The key themes section of the feedback report is one significant difference between a Baldrige assessment and other types of consulting—it focuses on cause-and-effect relationships, both across processes and between processes and results.

Next in the report is a series of item-level comments, typically about six comments per item, meaning that an applicant can expect to receive more than 100 specific comments in its feedback report. The comments include strengths, to confirm and reinforce the important things that applicants do well, as well as OFIs. Comments are not prescriptive—they point out only "what" is good or not good; they don't address specifically "how" an applicant should go about fixing things. OFI comments include language to help the applicant understand the significance of the comment (that is, why it's important to address this gap). Even award recipients find that they have a long list of OFIs to address.

Together, the strengths and OFI comments form the basis for objective scoring. While an applicant does not receive a specific overall score as part of the feedback, the scoring band descriptor places the overall organization in a general level of performance. In addition, the item-level summaries include a scoring range for the item (for example, 50%–65%) that helps the applicant understand its relative strengths and weaknesses for each of the eighteen items in the Criteria.

BALDRIGE NATIONAL QUALITY PROGRAM

The National Institute of Standards and Technology (NIST) administers the Baldrige National Quality Program. NIST is a non-regulatory agency of the U.S. Department of Commerce. It is charged with developing and promoting measurements, standards, and technology to enhance productivity, facilitate trade, and improve the quality of life. NIST is supported in managing the Baldrige Program through a strong public/private-sector partnership, the foremost component of which is the award's Board of Examiners. More than six hundred experts from manufacturing and service organizations, educational institutions, health care, government agencies, and non-profit organizations volunteer thousands of hours each year to learn the Criteria and its systematic scoring methodology, review applications, conduct site visits, select award recipients, and develop feedback reports for all applicants.

SIMILAR AWARD PROGRAMS

There are nearly fifty state, regional, and local Baldrige-based quality award programs in the United States. Since 1991, these programs have received more than seven thousand award applications, produced the same number of feedback reports, and trained thousands of examiners.[15] More than seventy countries world-wide, from Japan to Sweden, have programs similar to Baldrige.[16]

The Robert W. Carey Performance Excellence Award is an annual award sponsored by the Secretary of Veterans Affairs. This award recognizes organizations within the department that have implemented management approaches that result in sustained high levels of performance and service to the veterans. This award is named in memory of Robert W. Carey, a publicly recognized VA quality leader and a champion for excellence in the federal government. He was the director of the Philadelphia Regional Office and Insurance Center from 1985 until 1990. The Carey award criteria are aligned with the Baldrige Criteria.

The use of Baldrige by the U.S. Department of Defense is perhaps broadest of any of these alternative uses of the Criteria. Since 1994, the Army, Navy, and Air Force have had internal Baldrige programs that encourage full applications, with scoring, site visits, and feedback for internal units. The all-state National Guard units participate in the Army program annually. "I believe this is one of the reasons why the National Guard is considered to have the most ready units they have ever had," explained Donelle Denery, chief of strategic management and process office, Enterprise Management, U.S. Army Armaments Research, Development and Engineering Center, 2007 recipient of the Baldrige Award in the nonprofit sector.

Baldrige is a generic public domain tool, built by volunteers as a living set of Criteria that change every two years to keep pace with current leading-edge management practices. While the Criteria themselves can be intimidating and there is a role for technical expertise in their interpretation, successful use of the Baldrige process is remarkably simple. It involves stepping back periodically to evaluate how your organization is run and the results you achieve as an enterprise. It requires willingness to compare to high performers and to learn better ways of leading and managing. In the next chapter, we turn to the journey that Baldrige recipients traveled and how they transformed over time.

KEY POINTS IN THIS CHAPTER

- The Baldrige Criteria serve as a strategic business framework, providing leaders a means to align and focus their entire team on improving overall enterprise-wide results. The Criteria are comprehensive, bringing everyone to the table and holding all functions accountable for their results.

- Baldrige assessments provide diagnostic evaluations to assess and monitor your organization's capabilities to execute against every type of challenge.

- Baldrige applies to any type and size of organization, at any level of performance. The smallest award recipient had fewer than fifty employees while the largest had staff world wide in the tens of thousands.

- The Criteria and assessment process is completely customized to your unique circumstance, culture, and aspirations. You are evaluated against your potential to achieve your vision. Two entirely different organizations may score equally well against the Criteria.

- State and other similar programs offer avenues to get started on the journey.

3

The Journey

*"In the final analysis, change sticks when it becomes
'the way we do things around here,' when it seeps
into the bloodstream of the corporate body. Until new
behaviors are rooted in social norms and shared values,
they are subject to degradation as soon as
the pressure for change is removed."*

– John P. Kotter, *Leading Change* [1]

With remarkable uniformity, Baldrige Award recipients portray their experience as a journey. They describe fundamental cultural transformation progressing through a series of stages. While each story is unique, we found a universal roadmap that others can follow. Award recipients began at various levels of performance, ranging from struggling to "pretty good." Once committed to fundamental change, each progressed through cycles of assessment and feedback, coupled with focused action to develop and refine their leadership systems. They grew more competent, ready to meet competitive and strategic challenges, and make the most of their strategic advantages. Results improved dramatically across diverse measures of performance. None was perfect in the end, but each transformational journey led to strong capable leadership and operational practices. Accounts of both personal and organizational growth fill their interviews and publicly available documents.

Recipient CEOs are quick to point out that their journey never ends. When faced with the question, "What's next?" inevitably they acknowledge getting fifty pages of feedback and a long list of opportunities for improvement (OFIs) just like every other applicant. Like astute senior executives in any competitive business, they recognize sustainability is always a challenge. Either you continue to improve or you decline. Baldrige provides the framework for continued improvement for organizations that choose to do so.

Most of these recipients had begun to improve before they adopted Baldrige as their management framework. Each had developed improvement project capability. Some had completed customer service programs and initiated broad-based cultural change strategies. Javon Bea, president and CEO, Mercy Health System, described years of culture change and leadership building that predated the introduction of Baldrige, paving the way for their major financial turnaround and system growth in the late nineties: "We had built an effective senior leadership team. So there were no issues with engagement. There was an extensive culture change initiative already in place for years before we implemented Baldrige." But they all had reached a plateau in their results. They recognized the need for a comprehensive business model to accelerate and integrate their efforts to achieve competitive performance in all areas. These CEOs all describe their Baldrige assessments and the actions the feedback provoked as critical to their overall organizational success.

While none of the recipients characterize Baldrige as a "silver bullet," most described seeking a systems model to help them unify around one common framework. They identified Baldrige as a means to achieve high aspirations. Rulon Stacey, president and CEO of 2008 recipient Poudre Valley Health System, had come from SSM Health Care, where he had been introduced to Baldrige. When he arrived, Poudre Valley was looking for a comprehensive model for enterprise-wide improvement. They wanted something that would set their sights really high and give them a focus on improvement for years, to help them build a total system for excellence for the long run. "We wanted a goal that could *not* be easily achieved," he explained. "We wanted to get better every year and we needed a target to shoot for. The speed of the journey was less important than the process." His organization explored Total Quality Management, ISO, and others, and they settled on Baldrige as the best approach.

Our research team wanted to understand multiple elements of the journey, what leaders did and how they did it. We set out to grasp the depth and breadth of change that each organization accomplished using Baldrige. While each story is unique, there are instructive universal strategies, tactics, and lessons learned. We analyzed our data to understand the following:

- The roadmap they followed

- Similarities and differences that characterize the progression

- Activities of leaders at each stage and how they changed

- Leverage points and critical success factors that could benefit others

Many organizations are not interested in pursuing Baldrige for the award. Far more business leaders use the Criteria as a strategic business framework than apply for awards.[2] The number of companies is unknowable, but these leaders use the Criteria to assess and monitor organizational capabilities. We focus on Baldrige

Award recipients because their journey proved successful. Their status as role models was determined through the most objective process in existence, a process free of personal bias, financial or other influence. Their Award application summaries are comprehensive and public, and they were eager to share how they operate as high-performance organizations.

FIVE STAGES OF THE JOURNEY

Our research showed organizations progress through five developmental stages:

- Reaction – reacting to problems and complying with external requirements

- Projects – conducting projects, when teams and individuals learn to solve problems through improvement tools and methods

- Traction – gaining traction under their efforts to transform their culture

- Integration – building proactive and integrated approaches to leadership

- Sustaining – maintaining levels of high performance through renewing and innovating competent leadership approaches (or not)

Throughout a successful Baldrige journey, change initiatives grow more integrated with strategic goals, more powerful against their unique organizational and environmental challenges, and more readily spread throughout their enterprise. Silos across professional and functional boundaries weaken and alignment grows. Work becomes increasingly focused on processes that cut across departments and disciplines. Improvement becomes a routine competency of leaders. Measured results grow stronger compared to industry standards, broader and deeper in scope, and more connected to overcoming key strategic challenges.

The common journey for these organizations is figuratively illustrated in Figure 3.1. Each organization added Baldrige to their strategy at a unique point in their development but all adopted the framework and discipline of system-level assessment. Typically this occurred as they reached the limits of change inherent in spreading projects and adding initiatives. Figure 3.2 describes the characteristics of each stage in the journey. The terms and descriptions reflect our interpretation of the evidence and were not created by the recipients themselves. The remainder of this chapter describes the characteristics of each stage in greater detail, highlighting the activities and impact of the Baldrige process on these leaders and their organizations.

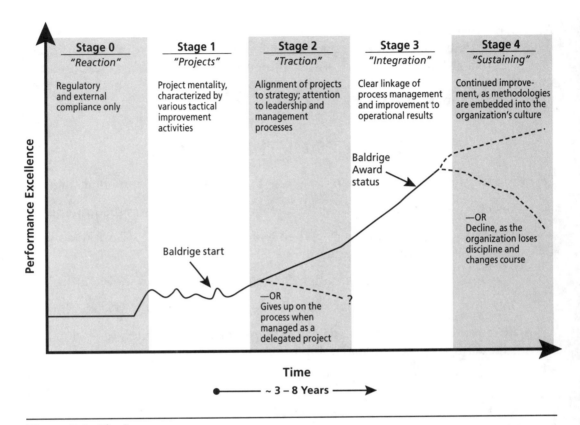

Figure 3.1 The journey.

STAGE 0 – REACTION

Reaction (stage 0) typifies leaders and organizations that chose a strategy of compliance to define and meet their obligations for clinical, financial, and operational results. They wait for mandated changes and implement them when required to maintain minimum industry standards. While they may experience occasional "random acts of improvement" through the efforts of motivated individuals, they lack an overarching impetus driving the organization to higher levels of performance.

We number this stage zero because it is reactive. Unfortunately, this is a common state among health care organizations. At this stage, organizations are merely compliance driven and priorities are set by outside entities. Leaders are constantly responding to external drivers without an internal compass. In *Redefining Health Care,* authors Porter and Teisberg describe "the strategies, organizational structures, and operating practices of many health care providers are misaligned with value, as revealed in the staggering array of evidence on poor performance and practice variation..."[3] "What is missing is an overall strategic framework."[4] Absent sufficient competitive drivers to improve operational performance, many health care delivery organizations carry on for a remarkably long

Stage	Descriptor	Characteristics of Organizational Approach
0	Reaction	Reacting to mandates and problems as they arise, no systematic approach to process improvement. Limited approaches to developing people as leaders and managers of processes.
1	Projects	General orientation toward improvement using project-based tools and methods, achieving some good results stemming from individual projects. Basic, traditional approach to developing people as leaders and managers of processes.
2	Traction	Early transition to a systems view. Beginning systematic evaluation and improvement of key processes (both daily work and leadership/management). Deployment of process improvements may still be variable. Measures begin to align with strategy. Improvements and/or good performance being achieved from many key processes. Early efforts to develop people as leaders and managers of processes.
3	Integration	Effective, systematic approaches and processes designed and in use in each Baldrige Category. As integration progresses, processes/approaches are refined and characterized by the use of key measures, good deployment, evidence of innovation, and very good results in most areas. Key leadership and daily work processes benefit from fact-based evaluation and improvement, and are being aligned and integrated with organizational goals. Approaches to development of people including systematic development of core organizational competencies becoming systematic. Results address key customer, market, and process requirements, and demonstrate many areas of strength including industry leadership in some key areas.
4	Sustaining	Refined processes/approaches characterized by the use of key measures, good deployment, evidence of innovation, and very good results in most areas. Organizational integration and spread of better practices are routine. People approaches refined and integrated with operations management. Results address many customer/stakeholder, market, process, and action plan requirements. The organization is an industry leader in some results areas. Successfully sustaining the momentum of a performance excellence journey is characterized by keeping up the rigor developed in earlier stages even when it appears that performance is "good enough;" otherwise performance declines.

Figure 3.2 Stages of progression along the journey.

time in the Reaction stage. Growing external drivers do give rise to meaningful improvement (such as The Joint Commission National Patient Safety Goals, Centers for Medicare and Medicaid Services publicly reported comparative performance data, and private sector campaigns). These drivers have made basic improvement project capability a standard feature of Stage 0 organizations. It is now a requirement to prevent "never events," at the very least.[5] Arguably these and other external drivers are raising the floor of health care performance and having significant impacts on patient care safety and quality. But Stage 0 organizations remain compliance focused, waiting for the next external mandate to improve, not capable of broad-scale measurable excellence or innovation. These organizations lack systematic approaches to strategy and culture, relying on individuals to solve problems and manage crises as they arise. If they measure results, they limit measurement and information to what is required for regulators and payors.

Leaders of all the recipient organizations are ambitious, typically early adopters of quality improvement, customer service approaches, or leadership philosophies and practices that distinguish their organizations. We did not learn much about their time in Stage 0 as our evidence about them largely begins after they were well into the next stage, exploring various strategies and tactics to accelerate their journey to achieve performance excellence.

STAGE 1 – PROJECTS

Projects (stage 1) refers to when organizations gear up with improvement methods and tools and indeed achieve measurable improvement in key areas. They adopt a "general improvement orientation that is forward looking."[6] Their acts of improvement are no longer entirely reactive. They often implement improvement methodologies to enhance the effectiveness of their projects, such as Plan-Do-Check-Act (PDCA), Plan-Do-Study-Act (PDSA), Define-Measure-Analyze-Improve-Control (DMAIC), their own homegrown version, and various statistical and process redesign tools. They conduct projects beyond requirements, tackling vexing operational, service, and quality problems that warrant attention. Examples include projects to improve patient safety and clinical quality, patient access, customer service, patient satisfaction, and a host of other important topics. Projects address problems and make a difference. They may be initiated by individuals aware of the quality chasm and motivated to overcome the gap, or they may come from a concerned Board member, external mandate, or voluntary campaign on a specific topic.

Proficiency at executing improvement projects is an essential organizational competency. The limitations of this approach, however, arise when the organizations seek transformational change, when leaders set out to achieve more fundamental and broad-reaching cultural change. Efforts to spread and multiply projects may have a temporary system-level impact, but proliferating projects will not lead to enterprise-wide results. As Tom Nolan, accomplished improvement expert and senior advisor to the Institute for Healthcare Improvement, wrote, "This plethora of ignition sources predictably results in a long list of worthwhile projects and measures, each of which makes sense on its own. However, the collection of projects is less likely to make sense as a coordinated whole aligned with the strategic direction of the organization.... No single initiative or set of unaligned projects will likely be enough to produce system-level results. Even aligned projects alone will not be sufficient."[7]

Baldrige recipients' descriptions of their experience in the Projects stage provide instructive lessons for others. Saint Luke's invested in statistical process control training in the late 1990s. "After several months, we realized people knew how to create statistical displays, but they didn't know why they were making them or when to use them," said Rich Hastings, President and CEO, Saint Luke's Health System. Mike Murphy, Sharp HealthCare president and CEO, described their experience at this stage as most unsatisfying: "We went to Boston for training and did a lot of projects in the nineties. But it wasn't leading us to transformational change." SSM Health Care, a pioneer in health care quality improvement, had a similar experience. "Our own CQI (continuous quality improvement) results were flat and we needed some way to accelerate our progress," Sister Mary Jean Ryan, SSM Health Care president and CEO, reflected. SSM adapted a curriculum used at Florida Power and Light and taught it widely, with some successful improvements. However, Sister Mary Jean went on, "We had people working on many different things and it took forever. There was no urgency, it was all voluntary. When we looked at Baldrige recipients in other industries, their projects were aligned with strategic goals and had timetables. Improvement was not optional. We could see these other sector recipients were simply better performing."

All our study organizations valued their improvement projects and resulting achievements; they celebrated the individual leaders and teams completing them. They maintained and even expanded their project skills training throughout their Baldrige journeys. Some recipients started with PDCA in the early years and stayed with that project model. Others launched PDCA but later added Lean or Six Sigma tools and refer to their own "tool box," including North Mississippi, Sharp, SSM, and Saint Luke's. These project skills proved invaluable over time and they continued to cultivate improvement skills and methods.

But "project spread" proved inadequate as a cultural change strategy for operational and quality performance excellence. Spreading projects failed to generate changes of the breadth and depth required to move the entire organization forward. "We needed a system to align all our staff and projects with the strategic plan. We could put together a bottom line but that didn't mean the culture was managed," said Saint Luke's Rich Hastings. Others found similar limitations. Sister Mary Jean explained, "We realized that we wanted to change the culture, not just conduct projects. It proved much harder than we thought but also much more important. The Baldrige Criteria asked how we developed and deployed our mission statement. We had to step back and build a common mission statement, then design a systematic approach to deploy our mission."

Even professionals responsible for quality and patient safety found they needed something to connect their work with the interests of their colleagues across the delivery system and from key administrative areas such as finance, marketing, human resources, and information technologies. Ken Davis, MD, former chief medical officer at North Mississippi, spoke passionately about their need for a system framework to evaluate and improve operations and integrate their work with that of other administrators. They needed this broad engagement to gain the full participation of practitioners and managers in each of the Care-Based Cost Management model projects they used to implement evidence based medicine.[8] At Bronson Methodist Hospital, the performance excellence journey began some years prior to their introduction to Baldrige. A board member encouraged Frank Sardone, president and CEO, Bronson Healthcare Group, to consider using Baldrige. "At this point we were not thinking of it as award potential but as a framework for achieving excellence. A few key people including Michele Serbenski [Bronson's vice president of performance excellence] picked up on it. They become familiar with the Criteria and how they applied to us," Sardone explained.

Typically early exploration and learning about the Baldrige framework, Criteria, and evaluation processes take place during the Project phase. Initial attempts to use Baldrige may be delegated and managed like a project. This approach typically flounders because without engaged and committed senior leadership, the initiative fails to gain traction toward fundamental cultural change.

STAGE 2 – TRACTION

Traction (stage 2) signifies the transition from sporadic improvements and projects scattered throughout subunits of the organization to early stages of alignment between values, mission, strategic goals, operations, and improvement projects. We call this phase Traction to reflect how senior leaders described their experience of gaining a toehold on cultural transformation. They explained a shift from managing fragmented operational and improvement activities to early glimmers of proactive oversight of key processes and intentionally generating desired results. As they transitioned to systematic processes for leadership and management, they described gaining "traction" under their transformation. Leaders at this stage must take full ownership of the transformational journey. Executives begin to see a real change in the effectiveness of their internal operations. It is during the Traction phase that executives begin consolidating and leveraging their investments in transformational change, allocating resources to identify and design key leadership and management processes. They start to gain momentum. As Rich Hastings explained, "I had vision of [Saint Luke's as] a system with alignment in all parts of the organization and the strategic plan."

The following typically happen during the Traction phase:

- Completion of a Baldrige-based assessment, with initial cycles of learning and feedback

- Feedback from award programs or self-assessments that generates insight and direction

- Action taken to address the feedback and accelerate learning, improvement, alignment and results

Figure 3.3 provides a visual model of the Baldrige process and how organizations successfully leverage assessments to strengthen operations. Chapter 5, Assessment, covers the assessment process with specifics and details, including suggested resources.

Stage 2 – Traction

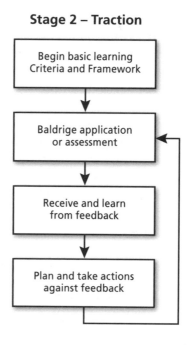

Figure 3.3   Steps to building traction.

Early Exploration of Baldrige

Several of the recipient organizations had undertaken a change process prior to the addition of Baldrige. The 2007 recipient, Sharp HealthCare, had launched The Sharp Experience, their cultural transformation initiative, in 2001. Mike Murphy explained: "We were on our own journey; we had ambitious goals for excellence under our Sharp HealthCare Six Pillars of Excellence (Quality, Service, People, Finance, Growth, Community). We had been on the journey for two years, rolling out tools, leadership education, behavioral standards, and Lean Sigma to build a culture of excellence. At a community event, someone introduced us to the idea of the Baldrige Criteria and CAPE, the California Award for Performance Excellence. Nancy [Pratt] made the link between the Sharp Experience and CAPE's Baldrige-based approach." Nancy Pratt, senior vice president of clinical effectiveness, Sharp HealthCare, explained their next steps: "So we considered if we should use the Criteria and the Award program as a way to measure milestones in implementing The Sharp Experience. We took it to the senior leadership in 2003 and asked them what to do. The reply was, 'Absolutely. How can we not?'"

During the Traction stage and throughout their journey, Baldrige and related activities are *not* the primary focus. Most recipients did *not* declare Baldrige as their organizational approach to excellence (although some identified Baldrige prominently in their change journey). If consultants and external experts were used, their role is downplayed in comparison to the role of internal leaders whenever possible.

Senior leaders explored using Baldrige to accelerate their change strategy, move beyond fragmented projects, measure their overall progress, and create traction under their own cultural change and excellence initiatives.

In 1999, Robert Wood Johnston University Hospital at Hamilton was working with service consultants and other experts on quality, but they wanted a performance excellence framework that would be a model for the whole organization. They adopted the Baldrige model and began annual assessments in 2000, receiving the Award in 2004. "We were experiencing some average results in service, quality, and market share and wanted to transform the organization," explained Deborah Baehser, senior vice president of clinical services and chief nursing officer. Then president and CEO Christy Stephenson introduced the idea of using Baldrige. While other senior leaders had heard of it, no one understood the Criteria or how to use them. "We educated ourselves about the Criteria and what they actually mean as our first step. Those early conversations really helped build senior leadership engagement," Baehser said. Bronson's Frank Sardone noted that the Criteria can be intimidating in the beginning. "People read them and throw their hands up. They seemed esoteric at first. We found looking at previous recipients' applications was really helpful. It took me a few rounds of feedback to 'get' it," he recalled.

Early Baldrige Assessments Build Traction

The early exploration of the Criteria led to completion of a Baldrige-based evaluation, through either a self-assessment or a state or national award application. We use the terms "assessment" and "application" interchangeably, because award recipients often do. David Spong, former CEO of two diverse Boeing companies in two different business sectors that both received the Baldrige Award, told us he called award applications "the assessment document" because it was the complete description of his organization, the basis for evaluation and scoring by trained Baldrige examiners.[9] He used this term to emphasize the goal was evaluation and learning, not just an award.

An assessment begins by documenting how the enterprise operates. A detailed description of how the organization operates is created by answering the Criteria questions. "Preparing the application involves asking very useful questions," explained North Mississippi's Ken Davis, MD. "We learned a lot about ourselves as a system and our culture from the task of answering the Criteria. Even when we couldn't answer a question, that taught us something."

Writing a Baldrige application is a challenge, but leaders describe a huge return on investment for accomplishing the task. "Go ahead and write an application, just tell your story, you will learn enormously from the process. It draws staff together and it reveals the gaps in your leadership. Writing the application is an invaluable experience," advised Sherry Marshall, vice president of quality, Saint Luke's Health System.

But writing and submitting an application for Baldrige is a challenging decision. When we asked Sister Mary Jean how she introduced the idea at SSM, she described telling people she had decided to go forward with an application. The reaction was negative. "We don't need another award." After reflection, Sister Mary Jean changed her message. Her new message proved to be the right one for her values and her organization. "We are going to use this application to help us improve patient care," she told her team. With this new approach, her team (including physicians) rallied around the goal. SSM Health Care went on to be the first health care recipient of the Baldrige Award in 2002, proving their capacity to create alignment from senior leader to front line.

At Sharp, leaders spent a day at first exploring where they were against the Criteria. "We did a one-day self-assessment workshop to determine how well positioned we were to respond to Criteria," explained Nancy Pratt. "From there we identified a group of leaders to write an application. Most Category teams were led by a senior leader."

Learning from Feedback

The next step in building traction comes with receiving and learning from Baldrige feedback. Recipients describe this step as enlightening and provocative but sometimes also painful. All the recipients welcomed the feedback but acknowledged it can be humbling. As Jim Collins described in *Good to Great*, confronting the brutal facts is critically important: "You must maintain unwavering faith that you can and will prevail in the end, regardless of the difficulties and, *at the same time*, have the discipline to confront the most brutal facts of your current reality, whatever they might be… Good-to-great companies continually refined the *path* to greatness with the brutal facts of reality."[10]

Sister Mary Jean had this to say: "It's not for the faint hearted. [Imagine] having experts come in from the outside, totally objectively, and say to you, 'this is what you say about yourself, but we can't find any evidence of it in your documents, which we studied for hundreds of hours.'" Although the examiners acknowledged that SSM had a great mission statement—"Through our exceptional health care services, we reveal the healing presence of God"—they asked two questions: "What do you mean by 'exceptional'?" and, "If you want to be exceptional, why are you content to compare yourselves to average?" This site visit occurred in 1999, before there were many comparative data sets available for health care organizations, and it was typical, at the time, for organizations to compare themselves to averages. Those questions made an enormous impact on the senior leaders of SSM Health Care. They realized even a great mission statement must be operationally defined and supported by strategy-focused measures. This feedback spawned serious introspection and redefined their focus for strategic planning the next year. The end result was a new direction, including system-wide goals and measures.

Award recipients describe the feedback as invaluable. "The state and Baldrige feedback helped reinforce the positive things we were doing. The feedback report provides a good external view of your performance. It has very specific details that you can use to direct improvements," noted Mercy's Javon Bea. Leaders at North Mississippi view the feedback as "the best consulting you can get and it's relatively inexpensive. The feedback comes back showing your gaps. We used the gaps to improve what we're doing. Improving the application was secondary to acting on the relevant and timely points of the feedback about how we work as leaders," Ken Davis, MD, explained. John Heer, president and CEO, North Mississippi Health Services, gave further details. "Senior leaders need to interpret the feedback and translate it into something that's actionable. People beyond the senior leadership team don't talk about Baldrige."

While Baldrige feedback is a great source of "brutal facts," new Baldrige users need to temper their instincts to tackle all of it at once. Even high-performing and high-reputation organizations are likely to score lower than they might expect on their early assessments. It is typical for a first assessment to put nearly every organization in band 2 out of a possible eight scoring bands.

Planning action to address feedback is a task senior leaders direct. This involves considering which strengths to build upon and which opportunities for improvement to address, and aligning and integrating any new activity into existing priorities. Many organizations find early feedback leads them to take initiatives *off the plate* rather than add new ones because the feedback highlights how some activities are *not* aligned and should be stopped or postponed. Freeing up resources to focus on high-leverage initiatives can be an early benefit of a Baldrige assessment.

It is important to address both strengths and OFIs in planning action in response to feedback. Based on a recent global survey of companies, McKinsey and Company reported that companies successful at creating organizational transformation "are far likelier to communicate the need for change in a positive way, encouraging employees to build on success rather than focusing exclusively on fixing problems."[11]

Taking Action on Feedback

The final steps in a single Baldrige cycle are planning and executing to address the feedback findings. Again, Jim Collins's research published in *Good to Great* had similar findings: "One of the dominant themes from our research is that breakthrough results come about by a series of good decisions, diligently executed and accumulated one on top of another."[12] Baldrige recipients report analyzing the feedback and crafting aligned, high-leverage actions. Just like the story about SSM Health Care and their 1999 site visit above, all of these organizations took their feedback and used it to (1) benchmark role model practices and approaches from organizations, inside and outside of health care and (2) redesign key leadership and management processes. Processes could be as significant and far reaching as enterprise-wide strategic planning and plan deployment or as focused and specific as complaint management and service recovery. The recipient application summaries posted on the Baldrige Web site are full of examples of the recipients' processes and approaches. (See also Chapter 6, Sensemaking, for a listing of critical leadership and management processes.)

Benchmarking is the practice of comparing your approaches and processes to others with potentially better process and results, with a goal of learning and improving. Baldrige recipient organizations are not only masters at benchmarking and adopting new practices from others, they are quick to do so and adapt these better practices to their own culture. They typically take ideas from others and modify them to make them "their own." They generally adapt them to their own culture and give them their own home-grown name. This is encouraged and common, as recipient practices are widely available for imitation and in the public domain.

Many organizations attempt to benchmark others in the search for innovative ideas and approaches but it often amounts to "industrial tourism," making visits and attending meetings without a systematic approach regarding which approaches to adopt. Using Baldrige feedback to frame benchmarking, recipient organizations describe systematically studying role model practices. Saint Luke's informal senior leadership triad (their CEO, chief medical officer, and vice president of quality), assigned each other specific questions to research. After completing these assignments, they would meet and talk about what they had learned about high-performing companies. Rich Hastings read some Harvard case studies on Boeing and went to meet with the CEO of the Boeing plant in Saint Louis. The Boeing officials showed Hastings the Baldrige model and how he could use it to develop a systems approach for the hospital. "We wanted a way to align the values of hospitals. Before pushing it out to others, we felt like we needed to understand the process and what our gaps were," Hastings explained.

State Versus National Awards

In the early stages of their journeys, all nine recipients applied to their state programs for feedback and recognition. The quality of these experiences varied and it appears that the state programs have been improving over time, particularly in terms of the value of the feedback. Later—sometimes much later—after receiving the national award, some announce plans to continue the discipline of annual assessments and a few declare commitment to reapply for the award after the mandatory five-year waiting period. Within hours of getting the call from the Secretary of Commerce about their 2005 Award, Frank Sardone announced to the Bronson Methodist Hospital executive team that he plans to reapply in 2011. This is not about collecting trophies; it's about maintaining a discipline that supports their goals of high performance.

Saint Luke's had a particularly positive experience with their state program. "Had we not had our state program, we would not have progressed as fast," explained Sherry Marshall. "Having a good state program can be invaluable. We relied on the state program for training in Baldrige. Saint Luke's had state quality award staff come in and do training for directors and rank-and-file employees. They did not mandate leaders to become examiners, but several decided to make that choice." North Mississippi started with their state program and then progressed to using the national Award program for their feedback. SSM has required its individual hospitals to use their state award programs for feedback and recognition as a business discipline.

> "Baldrige is a Criteria-driven Award, not a win-or-lose type of award. You get multiple scores you can compare to high performers in any industry. It's about the process of getting better and not an award or prize." Mike Murphy, president and CEO, Sharp HealthCare.

Challenges to Gaining Traction

Many organizations test Baldrige and complete one or two applications or assessments only to back away. Obviously, the Award recipients did not make this choice. At present, there is no objective evidence about how often this happens or why, but some recipient CEOs speculated that this is not uncommon.

Some organizations fail to gain traction with a Baldrige journey because the senior leaders treat Baldrige like a project. "When it's delegated to an individual or department as a project rather than managed as the work of the organization, you can see a clear difference. Getting real traction eludes organizations that keep it a project," explained Bronson leaders Frank Sardone and Michele Serbenski. Another barrier emerges for organizations that think of Baldrige as simply an award program. When staff and employees who are mired in the challenges of daily work assume leadership is making an investment of time and resources in another trophy, a cultural "award toxicity" appears that can undermine the learning process. Baldrige loses its power as a lever for change when staff see it as just another award senior leaders are trying to win.

Arguably, health care professionals have by nature a propensity for perfectionism. A strength in most respects, this trait can be an obstacle to engaging with a Baldrige journey. While precision and thoroughness are valued in any field and particularly in health care, the Criteria and the feedback can be intimidating. "We talk to lots of people who are interested [in Baldrige] but afraid to take the first step. Our recommendation: just get started," suggested Sardone and Serbenski. A final observation about the barriers to getting started and successfully gaining traction with a Baldrige journey came from Al Stubblefield, president and CEO, Baptist Health Care Corporation. "I suspect some leaders put a toe in the water and decide not to pursue it. It's very easy to get caught up in crises and abandon the journey. It's hard for organizations to do Baldrige when they have many short-term demands. For us, early sessions with a Baldrige expert were useful to build interest among senior leaders."

STAGE 3 – INTEGRATION

Integration (stage 3) follows Traction and usually occurs after a few cycles of assessment feedback and improvement. During this stage, senior leaders grow increasingly "process literate" in their sphere of responsibility and as they come to understand the Criteria deeply in one or more Baldrige Categories. Each of the categories represents a set of key leadership and management processes and over time, the senior leaders in those areas come to appreciate that these processes can be defined and improved, made more efficient and effective. The results achieved by those processes can be measured. Later in the journey, leaders recognize the connections between categories and the importance of working together as a system. Priscilla Nuwash, director of process improvement, Poudre Valley Health System, described it this way. "We looked to our Baldrige process to help everyone work together. We needed all the parts working together. Early on we used a bicycle to give people a visual [of integration], to illustrate that excellence requires the efforts of many working together."

For example, the senior leader responsible for planning often assumes account-ability for Category 2 of the Criteria (Strategic Planning). This person oversees the description of the organization's strategic planning and deployment processes as part of the early assessments or applications. After a few cycles of feedback and improvement, this leader will be much more knowledgeable about high-performance organizations and companies and their approaches to strategic planning. Many aspects of the organization's planning processes will have been redesigned and improved. Efficiency, effectiveness, and alignment of plan develop-ment and deployment will be noticeable by staff and the governing bodies. Strategy planning will coordinate with capital and budget planning. Information technology and human resource planning will align with strategy and capital and all planning will grow increasingly proactive and results oriented.

As the organization progresses, this leader will come to recognize the importance of integrating strategy development with customer listening processes (Category 3), measurement processes (Category 4), workforce capacity planning (Category 5), and daily work process management (Category 6). But these are more advanced steps, not likely to be relevant or accessible to an organization during their first assessment. After an organization gains traction on their transforma-tional journey and makes progress *within* individual Baldrige categories, leaders begin to see connections *between* categories that integrate key leadership and man-agement processes across the enterprise as a system. Integration functions as a learning system with clear evidence of leadership and management processes that produce measurable improvement in performance results lead to higher and higher scores against the Criteria. This cause-and-effect relationship between leadership and enterprise results is the hallmark of high-performing organizations and companies.

John Heer is the only health care CEO to lead two different organizations to become Baldrige recipients—North Mississippi in 2006 and Baptist Hospital in 2003. He reflected on the Baldrige process and how organizations progress to the Integration stage: "It takes three to five years to build a truly capable organization. After four years of learning and focusing on Baldrige Categories 1 through 6, we realized that we needed to focus on alignment and integration across the categories. The Baldrige scoring system is not about having pockets of excellence or scoring high in one or two categories. You have to perform well in all categories to be a recipient, a designated U.S. role model for others to follow." Evaluation and improvement of leadership and management processes, in addition to daily work processes, are routine when an organization reaches the Integration stage. Leaders have grown "process literate." We asked David Sjoberg, Baptist's vice president of strategic services, if there had been a focus on process management before Baldrige: "No, that was something we learned through Baldrige. We had some good processes but we didn't realize it….[until they went through a few cycles of organizational assessment and improvement]." One example Sjoberg described was when Baptist benchmarked Ritz Carlton Hotels and analyzed their approach to employee communications. Baptist adapted the Daily Line-up process used at Ritz-Carlton Hotels to develop a process in which all Baptist leaders and employees gathered at each shift to hear the *Baptist Daily*, a weekly 15-minute message delivered throughout the organization. Because they defined a systematic process, they could easily spread and hardwire this practice throughout their work units. This practice, common in health care today and advocated by many consultants as "daily huddles," was one of a number of role model practices Baptist promoted when they were a Baldrige recipient in 2003. Through their journey, they were provoked to align and integrate this communication process with other knowledge management processes of their organization as a system.

Saint Luke's journey evolved through trial and error over the years; in hindsight, competence with process tools such as Lean Sigma was a big factor in their success. "Everything keeps changing for the better. We recently did a detailed study—step-by-step action on the number of steps to register at one of our clinics. We improved it from the perspective of patients and clinicians. We are getting ready to embark on the fourth level of process design, deep into the organization. Looking back, once we started mapping and improving our processes, we started making changes for the better," said Hastings.

Leaders expanded the use of Baldrige from the hospital to the system. As described in the Saint Luke's Health System Missouri State Quality Award application, senior leaders set direction and performance expectations through the Strategic Planning Process, which produces Strategic Focus Areas (People, Clinical & Administrative Quality, Customer, Growth & Development, Finance) that are critical to the system's future success and the success of its entities. These five strategic focus areas align with the system's balanced scorecard and cascade down through the organization's work processes.[13]

Paula Friedman, SSM's corporate vice president of strategy and systems improvement, described how learning from their feedback reports grew as the years went by. "For us, the learning came from answering the hard questions. We didn't get that until we had been through it a number of times. But it's not about making everyone a Criteria expert either," she explained. She described the early years when they assigned individuals to focus on one Baldrige category. After a few cycles, they learned their own categories and were ready to look at the connections across all categories (including results). "Answering the questions drives you to really look at the connections between processes like strategic planning and human resource processes for example, and what measureable results prove that your leadership and management approaches are actually working," Friedman noted.

Bronson leaders told us about how their early years involved a small group intensely focused on the Criteria and studying the application when they first started in 2000. "By about 2003, the process blossomed," explained Michele Serbenski. They assigned senior leaders to Baldrige categories and integrated the Criteria requirements into their performance standards for employees and made progress updates a part of weekly meetings. "2004 marked the shift from managing Baldrige like a project to converting it to senior leader responsibility to help them do their work," she said.

At Mercy Health System, all senior executives reviewed the OFIs and developed action plans to address them. Progress was reviewed weekly in senior manager meetings, conversations that led to many new insights and critical decisions about how to improve operations as well as strategy deployment overall. One critical insight came during the Integration stage of their journey. Once Mercy leaders had improved and hardwired processes and approaches *within* Baldrige Categories, they were able to address a lack of integration across and between Categories. With the skills and process literacy developed through their early Traction years, they were able to improve integration throughout their business units and begin to function as an integrated system. "We revised our targets for our main scorecard measures at 98th percentile as part of this phase. Early on, we might have been reluctant to do this but after years of integrating and improving our processes, this was an easy decision," explained Mercy's Javon Bea.

During the Integration phase all of the recipients had adopted some approaches to maximize their improvement from the Baldrige feedback. For example, each had incorporated their feedback report as critical input to their strategic planning (see Chapter 7, Execution, for more details). "Starting in 2003, we embedded the feedback into our strategic planning process," described Michele Serbenski. Bronson's journey began in 2000 and culminated in 2005 when they received the Baldrige Award. Leaders from Saint Luke's, North Mississippi, and Baptist reported similar developments during the Integration stage of their journeys. Sister Mary Jean said, "Integration occurs through requiring action on the feedback, feeding it forward into the strategic planning process. We do this every February using the feedback received the previous fall." She described a number of examples where SSM's feedback led to specific performance goals for the following year. One year the feedback talked about inconsistencies in communication and complaint management. The following year, it was time to develop consistent approaches to both of these processes that were well aligned and integrated. "Another year our feedback pointed out that we had said in our application that people are our most important asset, noting that we didn't cover them in our strategic plan," said Ryan. SSM changed that the following year by building a human resources plan as an integrated part of their overall strategic plan. Rich Hastings described addressing key OFIs each year as part of strategic planning at

Saint Luke's: "The first year we linked employee performance and performance metrics, as part of an overall initiative to adopt the Boeing balanced scorecard approach." These examples are just a few of the dozens of improvements that built upon and accelerated the gains made earlier in the journey.

As leaders become more knowledgeable through their Integration stage, they grow comfortable with the concepts of approach, deployment, learning, and integration. This basic framework for evaluating any key process, whether infection prevention in the ICU, complaint management, or strategic planning, addresses four simple questions:

- What is your approach?

- How is it deployed to all who need to use it?

- How is this approach linked to related processes?

- How are related processes integrated throughout the organization?

The journey evolves over time as everyone learns what the Criteria ask for. Some people think of it as getting an "on-the-job" masters degree in business excellence. Ken Davis, MD, recalled that at North Mississippi the process took some time: "It took a while to learn the lingo and understand how to use the non-prescriptive Criteria, which are unlike accreditation standards. Once we got started getting feedback, the real learning began. We were not as good as we thought we were. It was hard and we reached a time after two or three applications when we reconsidered the value of the process. As we got more sophisticated we could anticipate our feedback, almost write it ourselves." Sherry Marshall made similar observations about Saint Luke's: "We had to drown leaders in their Categories first, then teach about linkages, then back to Categories... understanding the concept of alignment and integration took a couple years, for example linking to process design and setting up performance measurement. Understanding this linkage took a while."

All the journey stories we heard from recipients echoed the notion of patience as they made their way through cycles of assessment and feedback. Interviewees described both hard work and tremendous learning as they continued to refine their organizations' operations. In our estimation, all of these organizations were well into the Integration stage, perhaps even into Sustaining, when they received the Baldrige Award. By this time, however, using Baldrige as their framework was embedded in the leadership culture as a business discipline. Some leaders voiced concern that they lost some of that discipline after receiving Baldrige Award and several noted that their strongest year for improvement was the last year *before* the recognition. As Al Stubblefield reflected about Baptist's experience, "The site visits really built engagement, they were very positive, unlike other site visits we have. Our people got really excited about telling our story," Stubblefield explained. "But the real value was the consistent alignment and deployment of high quality business practices across the organization, they pay great dividends." We estimate that all of these organizations were well into the Integration stage when they were recognized as recipients of the Baldrige Award. But as SSM's Paula Friedman put it, "This process helped us keep the mission at the forefront and in focus. It kept us, and keeps us, honest. The award was secondary."

Poudre Valley experienced a major "tipping point" after their third site visit in 2007 when they did not receive the award. Priscilla Nuwash explained, "We were so disappointed, but we had an important awakening as a result. We realized it really is not about the award. We realized we might never get the award. But the process was helping us get better and if it helped us care for our patients, helped us to achieve our vision, then it was worth doing. Ironically, after that point, we gained a lot of momentum." Poudre Valley senior leaders said the year from 2007 to 2008 was a time of significant improvement, and the 2008 site visit was tremendously educational.

STAGE 4 – SUSTAINING

Senior leaders of Baldrige recipient organizations worry about sustainability like any executive in any business. They all agree that maintaining momentum is not easy for any organization, particularly as health care becomes more competitive and transparent along multiple dimensions of quality and efficiency. The difference is that these organizations built a system of leadership processes that enables them to address market forces more effectively. Never immune to challenges, they are positioned to identify new business challenges issues and change course proactively to maintain their successes with minimal risk to sustainability.

The annual award cycle is critical to sustaining momentum during the years before the Award. It becomes the driving timetable to address gaps and fully deploy strengths. John Heer welcomed the focus on a sustained effort. "The Baldrige process causes you and your team to stay focused and on course," Heer explained. "It gives you a clear target."

Sherry Marshall described it this way: "The award cycle holds your feet to the fire. Since Saint Luke's Hospital was successful [in 2003], we've been working at the system level. We wrote an application for the system in 2006 to move to the next level of performance for all eleven hospitals. We applied for the Missouri Quality Award in 2005 and won it in 2006. The feedback and timeline was very valuable to us."

Bronson has found the bright lights and scrutiny of being a recipient has helped to maintain their momentum for change. "Many organizations slow down after receiving the Award. The opposite happened for Bronson. The external validation brought people on-board. It helped us build momentum," described Frank Sardone.

In the early years of using Baldrige, some organizations chose to skip an application cycle but in hindsight, recipients uniformly remarked that good intentions succumbed to distractions during those years. Sister Mary Jean strongly encouraged or required SSM hospitals to submit applications at the state level, to ensure they were focused on improving organizational performance. When people asked to take a year off, she would explain that no one gets to take a year off from improvement. She felt that Baldrige couldn't be set on the side. Unlike a project that could be put aside for a year, improvement using Baldrige must be continuous. Over time, according to SSM leaders, the process of preparing applications became easier and executing on the feedback more routine.

Senior leadership commitment was a factor in success from the beginning through sustaining the gains from their Baldrige journeys. Seven of the nine recipients told us they plan to continue to conduct periodic Baldrige-based assessments or continue applying for the Award, as systems or subunits of their systems. The other two plan to continue using the Criteria to evaluate their operations, particularly as changes to the Criteria reflect advances in management thinking across industries.

CHANGES ON THE JOURNEY

Personal Changes in Leaders

Several senior leaders cited significant changes to their personal leadership style. Mercy's Javon Bea noted this is fundamental to successful use of Baldrige and worth serious consideration before embarking on a Baldrige journey. He theorized that it could hurt an organization to undertake Baldrige for just a year or two: "The CEO has to make a commitment to change. It's very personal, not just an award that we are talking about here."

Chuck Stokes, former president of North Mississippi Medical Center, reflected on how generations and culture changed during his watch there: "Young people have very different expectations today. When baby boomers first became executives and moved into the C-suite, they had other people build relationships for them [with their employees and medical staff]. It didn't work. I looked at companies like Toyota and saw that successful CEOs build relationships themselves. You have to be directly involved in every aspect of the improvement journey." Rich Hastings reflected on his leadership at Saint Luke's and recalled how he learned to have more fun with his people. They started a ritual of a boot camp and he dressed up in a general costume to playfully illustrate the importance of discipline and commitment to the cause. "If I had it to do over, I would have started with the fun stuff earlier. I didn't make it fun enough in the beginning," he said.

Poudre Valley's Rulon Stacey talked about his personal learning after his organization had a third site visit without receiving the award: "I needed to evaluate how my own comments and actions were leading people to measure success by the award. I needed to change my message. It was, and is, about achieving our vision for our patients. I truly believe this process has saved lives."

Certainly any successful senior executive learns and changes his or her personal style over time. This is one mark of a strong leader. What distinguishes these CEOs is how they measure their own personal success against the maturity of their organization and the degree to which they hardwired a leadership system that sustains beyond their personal involvement. Through their use of Baldrige, they established capabilities with the potential to carry on after the current executive team steps down.

Development of Process Literacy

Process literacy refers to the competency of high-performing leadership teams to run the enterprise through a system of leadership and management processes. During a Baldrige journey, senior leaders become increasingly process literate, meaning they come to understand that their organization is a system, both core work processes and administrative and leadership support processes that must be designed, managed, measured, and improved to achieve organizational goals and deliver value to stakeholders (see Chapter 6, Sensemaking, Figure 6.4). They come to understand that they accomplish their responsibilities through approaches and processes that can be designed, evaluated, and improved.

For most, this is a more advanced learning that comes once an organization is well along into Traction or Integration stage. For health care professionals in general, thinking in processes may be more challenging than for people working in other industries. Quality tools and methods teach how to improve discrete work processes and to understand that processes depend on multiple people and disciplines. Senior leaders grow to understand that they must also improve all key leadership processes and integrate those processes to become high performance systems. This is a skill set that evolves over time, in many cases over years.

WHY SOME JOURNEYS FAIL

While the number is unknown, clearly some organizations try Baldrige and quit. We asked the recipient organizations why they think organizations might reject Baldrige after exploring it. Here are some reasons they offered to explain why some organizations fail to get needed traction to go to the next level and sustain their Baldrige journey:

- Baldrige remains a project, an additional task for busy people.

- Activities are not sustained. Because the process is overwhelming, there is lack of discipline, or it bogs down in perfectionism.

- The focus is on the award instead of a leadership discipline.

- There is resistance to feedback.

- The process is not fast enough, not a silver bullet, results in lack of sustained commitment.

Sherry Marshall told us, "People at Saint Luke's would have tuned us out if we had been award-seeking. But if you can show results at the point of care, make that connection, you tap into motivation of health care workers. Leaders must have trust of employees and medical staff, of course. They were open to Baldrige because we made that connection early on. For example, by getting more efficient we can give more charity care."

Poudre Valley's Rulon Stacey summed up the journey in the following way: "[Becoming an excellent organization] is about being a workhorse, not a racehorse. It's about the direction, not the speed. We want to plow the field all day long, every day, for our patients."

KEY POINTS IN THIS CHAPTER

- Baldrige Award recipients uniformly portray their experience as a journey. They describe fundamental cultural transformation progressing through a series of five stages:
  - *Reaction* (stage 0): reacting to problems and complying with external requirements
  - *Projects* (stage 1): conducting projects, when teams and individuals learn to solve problems through improvement tools and methods
  - *Traction* (stage 2): gaining traction under their efforts to transform their culture
  - *Integration* (stage 3): building proactive and integrated approaches to leadership
  - *Sustaining* (stage 4): maintaining levels of high performance through renewing and innovating competent leadership approaches (or not)

- During a Baldrige journey, senior leaders become increasingly process literate. They come to understand their organization as a system of core work processes as well as administrative and leadership support processes that must be designed, managed, measured, and improved to achieve organizational goals and deliver value to stakeholders.

- Organizations can stop progressing at any stage and not complete the journey. Common causes include the following: treating Baldrige as a project to be delegated or an award rather than a transformational journey; actions and commitment are not sustained; feedback is ignored. All these potential roadblocks and ways to successfully manage them are addressed in the coming chapters.

4

Leadership

"Leaders are obligated to provide and maintain momentum.... Momentum comes from a clear vision of what the corporation ought to be, from a well-thought-out strategy to achieve that vision, and from carefully conceived and communicated directions that enable everyone to participate and be publicly accountable in achieving those plans."

– Max De Pree, *Leadership Is an Art*[1]

Our research showed a critical connection between leadership and the success of a performance excellence journey. This connection was so fundamental that it quickly became the first element of our LASER model. As we continued to research this aspect of the model, we discovered a remarkable consistency in the behaviors demonstrated by these leaders.

CRITICAL LEADERSHIP BEHAVIORS FOR A SUCCESSFUL JOURNEY

Leaders of a successful performance excellence journey consistently demonstrate five critical behaviors:

- Make a personal commitment to organizational transformation to achieve performance excellence

- Align people in support of the destination and the journey to get there

- Build a culture of organizational learning and improvement

- Continually motivate, inspire, and engage the workforce
- Build a results orientation and processes for personal and organizational accountability for results

In a landmark paper first published in 1990, John P. Kotter, a leadership and change management expert now retired from the Harvard Business School, identified three defining behaviors of leaders that he believed differentiated leaders' work from that of managers: make a personal commitment, align people, and continually motivate.[2] In successful leaders of performance excellence, we observed similar behaviors. In addition, however, we found that these leaders consistently focused on building an organizational culture of learning and improvement, one with a results orientation and accountability for high performance.

#1: MAKE A PERSONAL COMMITMENT TO LEAD ORGANIZATIONAL TRANSFORMATION

Successful leaders make a personal commitment to a process of organizational transformation to achieve success and sustainability. The commitment is long-term. Frank Sardone, president and CEO, Bronson Healthcare Group, explained that the hospital set a ten-year goal to be a Baldrige recipient as "one measure of long-term organizational success." Javon Bea, Mercy president and CEO, concurred, saying that he tells other CEOs, "You have to stick with it. In fact, it might hurt the organization if you were just to do this for a year or two and then give up.... It's not a two- or three-year process just to win an award." The CEO's commitment, Bea said, must be personal. He said he asks himself nightly, "What did I do for Baldrige today?" Bea's simple ritual kept a personal focus on organizational transformation.

Commit to a Transformational Journey, Not a Prize

Nancy Pratt, senior vice president of clinical effectiveness, Sharp HealthCare, pointed out that Baldrige is about the process of getting better, using a Criteria-driven award, not a win-or-lose type award. Yet, when organizations undertake a performance-excellence journey using Baldrige, an inappropriate focus on the award—on winning the prize—is a common pitfall at first. Sometimes top leaders themselves promote an award focus. Javon Bea admitted thinking Mercy could easily receive Baldrige and having to change his "message to the organization about why they were applying." Sometimes the organization has a culture that highly values external recognition, in which award-seeking is the norm. In such an organization, the workforce may assume that Baldrige is like many other competitions and the objective is winning the prize.

Excessive focus on the award can create a cultural backlash if the workforce sees the Baldrige process as seeking external recognition and does not appreciate the importance of periodic organizational assessments to realizing the organization's vision and goals. Establishing this understanding is a critical challenge for and responsibility of leadership.

A counterproductive award focus inevitably backfires. First, the award is not easily won. Rulon Stacey, president and CEO, Poudre Valley Health System, observed that it was "really hard the first years when we didn't win—and it was devastating for the organization." Second, and perhaps more important, award-seeking is not a driver of engagement and motivation for most health-care professionals. Failure to win "the prize" in one or two cycles leads to discouragement and diminishing interest in the practical benefits of the award program, understanding and taking action on objective feedback. Sherry Marshall, vice president of quality, Saint Luke's Health System, explained, "People at Saint Luke's would have tuned us out if we had been award-seeking, but if you can show results at the point of care, make that connection, then you tap into the motivation of health care workers. Our employees and medical staff followed because we made the connection early on. For example, we explained that by getting more efficient, we can give more charity care." Key to sustaining the effort, said Marshall, "are senior leaders who set direction based on their belief in the utility of Baldrige to improve patient care."

Position Baldrige as the Means to Achieve the Vision and Goals

Successful leaders use ongoing and carefully designed communication and their personal leadership actions to communicate and reinforce the organization's direction—its mission, vision, and values and, in particular, its patient-focused goals. Although awards and award-seeking do not engage or motivate health-care professionals, demonstrably better care does. Successful leaders ensure first that the workforce understands the vision and the goals, then position Baldrige as a method to help the organization track its progress and become capable of realizing the vision and goals. They may cite specific organizational gaps as barriers to higher performance and describe how the Baldrige process will help the organization address them.

To put Baldrige in context for his organization, Rich Hastings, president and CEO, Saint Luke's Health System, explained that the assessment process is a method to measure goal attainment, "to evaluate how well we do what we do…to measure how well the system is working." And because the feedback captures strengths as well as opportunities for improvement, the feedback gives leaders the opportunity to build energy and engagement by celebrating strengths and recognizing progress.

To avoid ambiguity and encourage an appropriate focus, they avoid public speculation about when the organization will "win" (or why it did not). When the feedback report arrives, they focus their attention primarily on the significance of the feedback, not the scores. When referring to Baldrige role-model organizations, they call them "recipients," not "winners." In some cases, leaders surface assumptions and reframe thinking: It's not a journey to win an award; rather, it's a journey to achieve the degree of excellence that would merit the award.

Leaders differ on the extent to which the term Baldrige should be used in organization-wide communication and added to the institutional lexicon. John Heer, who has led two health care award recipients organizations, explained his approach at North Mississippi this way: "We never said we are going to 'do Baldrige.' We used Baldrige as the platform…using the Baldrige initiative was pretty much writing the application. Senior leaders need to interpret the feedback into something that's actionable. People beyond the senior leadership team don't talk in [terms of] Baldrige." This approach may be particularly suitable if the organization has formed negative impressions of external review agencies, Heer advised. It may also work well in organizations that over the years have made a habit of regularly adopting, and then discarding, tools and approaches in the name of performance improvement, where the workforce is apt to be skeptical of the value and staying power of any new approach.

Regardless of the degree to which these successful leaders use the "B" word, they clearly put the focus on the organization's vision and goals. They seek to communicate the vision and goals to all levels of the organization in order to align everyone in support of the transformation. At Sharp HealthCare, an organization-wide performance excellence initiative called The Sharp Experience had been under way for a year when Mike Murphy, Sharp's president and CEO, and Nancy Pratt recognized how the Baldrige Criteria aligned with Sharp's six-pillar results framework and its focus on key stakeholders—for Sharp, its patients, physicians, and employees. They saw how the comprehensive framework and the discipline of periodic assessment promoted organizational learning in support of Sharp's values of Innovation and Excellence, and could accelerate the transformation of Sharp HealthCare into the "best place to work, best place to practice medicine, best place to receive care, and ultimately the best health-care system in the universe." Thus when Murphy and Pratt determined that Sharp would undertake a Baldrige process starting with the system-wide assessment at the state level in 2004, they did not see themselves introducing a new organizational initiative. Instead, like other successful leaders, their objective was not to foster engagement with Baldrige. Their objective was to foster engagement with the organization's vision and goals, and the urgency of achieving them, and offer Baldrige as a way to support and accelerate the journey.

Put the Award in Perspective for *Your* Organization

As organizations make progress on their performance excellence journey, however, some find that constructive award-seeking contributes additional energy. Saint Luke's Rich Hastings said, "If you want to get people motivated for quality, winning an award like that is a great lever. So it's not a problem starting with going for the process and [then shifting] to going for the award." Sherry Marshall, senior vice president of quality, Saint Luke's Health System, recalls the year before Saint Luke's received the award as "a big growth year…. Not winning gave us fire in the belly to address an OFI we knew we had. It was humbling not to win, but motivating." Even early on, for some organizations, aspiring to win the award can be energizing. At Baptist, according to Al Stubblefield, president and CEO, Baptist Health Care Corporation, pursuit of the award was "morale boosting for employees and motivating, so award seeking is not all bad." Initial low scores gave leaders the determination to understand Baldrige and succeed. Sports offer a helpful analogy. When you are becoming a great organization, receiving objective recognition that the workforce respects can be a motivator. Putting a spot on the wall after a few cycles of feedback and improvement can be viewed favorably by staff.

For other organizations, actively confronting and abandoning an award focus provides the necessary catalyst for progress at transformation. At Poudre Valley Health System, Rulon Stacey, president and CEO, and Priscilla Nuwash, director of process improvement, agreed that winning the award dominated their approach early on. "After our third site visit," Nuwash said, "we were so disappointed, but we had an awakening that it was not about the award. That was a huge tipping point. We had to realize we might not get the award. It was about our patients and about achieving our vision." Stacey admitted, "Even though we talked a lot about not it being about the award, in my comments I would steer the organization, just by some of the things I said, back to success being measured by the award." When Stacey and his team eliminated the term Baldrige, changed it to performance excellence, wrote a one-pager for staff explaining performance excellence, and Stacey reached out to the organization at multiple forums, "then momentum hit."

Ultimately, every successful leader must make a personal commitment to a process of organizational transformation. They must connect the transformation process to achieving the organization's vision and goals. Each must determine how to position Baldrige and the award, initially and over time, in a way that supports the organization's overall vision and goals and addresses the unique features of that organization's culture and environment. Again, the world of sports offers a good analogy, one that CEOs can employ in talking about their transformational journey: Does Tiger Woods seek to become the world's greatest golfer or win the most major tournaments? The answer is yes and yes. Priscilla Nuwash put it this way, "We had to realize it's not about the award, but we're so happy to have the award."

#2: ALIGN PEOPLE AT MULTIPLE LEVELS

Successful leaders align people at multiple levels in support of the destination and the journey to get there. These leaders use four principal methods to create this alignment: personal involvement and visibility, coalitions, strategic line of sight, and ongoing communication.

Demonstrate Active, Personal Leadership

Personal, active involvement in the assessment process is characteristic of all successful leaders. In every case, leaders engage personally in developing the assessment document and in analyzing, applying, and tracking progress on the feedback. These organizations typically use a team structure for application development (standing or temporary category teams) in which senior leaders play key roles. Mercy, for example, used category teams, all led by senior leaders, to write the application and to address feedback, with Javon Bea responsible for Leadership, Category 1. The responsibility of the top leader for Category 1 is characteristic across the organizations we interviewed.

Through their personal, active involvement, they serve as role models to other leaders and the workforce—demonstrating themselves the level and type of engagement they expect of others. Their personal involvement also enables them to continually reinforce the focus on achieving organizational performance excellence, on the larger purpose served by using the Baldrige process.

These successful leaders engage personally in other ways, teaching and mentoring, for example. When Mercy Health System chose the Baldrige process to support and accelerate its performance excellence journey, the organization implemented an extensive organization-wide training effort, starting with 150 top leaders. Javon Bea gave Baldrige overviews to all four thousand employees. Leaders at other organizations took on personal responsibility for more focused efforts; at North Mississippi, for example, CEO John Heer provided personal mentoring to some one hundred people. Across organizations, successful leaders displayed varying levels of Baldrige expertise and used various methods to engage other leaders and the workforce. At Bronson, for example, leaders did not try to become experts in the Criteria but focused on "having people understand the framework," explained Frank Sardone. What was consistent across successful organizations was the active and personal engagement of leaders in building support for the process, understanding the framework, and applying the feedback.

Build Supportive Coalitions

Successful leaders build the supportive coalitions needed for the performance excellence journey. They look for and develop support within formal structures and committees but also among supportive leaders across the organization who can help them drive organizational change.[3,4] Because the focus of the journey is significantly improved performance, not "doing Baldrige," effective coalitions must include the individuals in the organization who are responsible for or have significant influence over organizational change and better performance. Successful leaders therefore pay particular attention to two key constituencies— other leaders and physicians.

First, the senior leadership team is responsible for performance excellence, so the senior leadership team must take responsibility for leading the assessment process to drive performance excellence. The assessment process is not delegated to lower-level staff or treated as an add-on to senior leader work (although it sometimes starts that way). All the successful leaders explain that just as senior leaders own the organization's performance, they must own the feedback and action on the feedback. When senior leaders take responsibility for the assessment process as central to their work, the pace of change increases dramatically. Sherry Marshall said that after the first Saint Luke's application, they "decided to assign senior leaders to lead category writing teams in areas of their responsibility. When we did this, things began to click and they could see their responsibility and accountability." According to Frank Sardone, the "process blossomed" at Bronson when he assigned senior leaders to categories, integrated Baldrige with performance goals, and made changes based on feedback part of weekly meetings.

Second, physicians must be engaged and actively involved in planning for performance improvement. Chuck Stokes, former president of North Mississippi Medical Center, emphasized, "Doctors have to have a voice at the table and must participate in planning. Each time [they are involved], the bottom line goes up and results improve." Successful organizations, therefore, involve physicians early in planning to address feedback; in some, physician leaders participate actively throughout the assessment process. Mercy involved physicians in application writing. At Saint Luke's, every category team has a physician co-chair dedicated by the medical staff for three years. Compensated for their participation by equal contributions from the hospital and the medical staff, "they are integral to working the feedback into improvement initiatives," said Hastings.

Successful leaders recognize the importance of using both push and pull strategies to build support and create engagement. Physicians, observed Bronson's Frank Sardone, "are motivated by results and seeing a difference. We have converts. You can't push them; they have to see results and that pulls them in." Paula Friedman, corporate vice president of strategy and systems improvement, SSM Health Care, concurred, noting that "one of the reasons physicians work with SSM process improvement teams is because they see a difference in the work system as a result of what we're doing."

In building effective coalitions, successful leaders inevitably are required to confront and manage skeptics and resisters. They clearly communicate and model their expectations of others and provide personal coaching as well as other learning opportunities. At Sharp, for example, the Baldrige Criteria and discipline are part of the leadership development curriculum. At the same time, successful leaders make commitment to the performance excellence journey and the process to support it non-negotiable. As a result, skeptics and resisters become engaged participants, or find it necessary to step aside. Sister Mary Jean Ryan, president and CEO, SSM Health Care, explained that "anyone who works at SSM and doesn't get on board, they 'stick out like a sore thumb.' If you're not engaged at SSM, you can't work here." At North Mississippi, the CEO made it clear that using Baldrige was his means to change the culture, says Ken Davis, MD, who served as chief medical officer. "People understood that you had to 'catch the vision or catch the bus.'"

Establish Strategic Line of Sight

Successful leaders align people in support of performance excellence by establishing the foundation for a line of sight from strategic goals to individual behavior to measured results. They lead development of a measurement framework that aligns with the organization's mission, vision, and values, such as the pillar frameworks of Sharp, Mercy, and Saint Luke's.

Three of these organizations refer to the elements in their framework as "pillars." Saint Luke's calls them their "strategic focus areas" and North

Mississippi calls them their "critical success factors." Regardless of the name applied to the elements, the critical factor is how these leaders built alignment, measurement, and performance expectations that drive organizational results using the framework. All of these organizations put the elements in different order for very specific reasons (see Figure 4.1) that they explain in their application summaries. For example, both Saint Luke's and North Mississippi believe that excellence of all kinds begins with people; the framework, therefore, focuses first on their people.

Successful leaders identify specific indicators that measure the organization's performance meeting key requirements in each dimension. For these indicators, they set overall goals and a timeframe to guide their workforce. A measurement framework, key performance indicators, and clear and measurable performance expectations aligned with the focus areas set the stage for the development and alignment of goals and action plans at lower levels of the organization, all the way down to individual members of the workforce. SSM leaders developed the SSM Passport to engage and align the SSM workforce (Figure 4.2). The Passport, a health-care industry best practice, is a tool for performance planning and annual appraisal that documents business-unit, department, and individual-contributor objectives and plans to support the system's vision, values, and strategy. The annual development of individual action plans that support larger organizational goals is a method to ensure alignment at every level of the organization. All recipient organizations had some method to establish line of sight in order to align the workforce to their key strategies.

Ensure ongoing communication

Successful leaders build and maintain mechanisms for ongoing communication— broad, open, and two-way—about the organization's performance and the journey to performance excellence. Rigorous attention to leadership communication enables leaders to reinforce organizational focus and alignment. At North Mississippi, for example, John Heer sends a weekly email message to everyone in the workforce

St. Luke's	North Mississippi	Mercy	Sharp
People	People	Quality	Quality
Clinical and Administrative Quality	Service	Service	Service
Growth and Development	Quality	Partnering	People
Customer Satisfaction	Financial	Cost	Finance
Finance	Growth	Growth	Community

Figure 4.1 Performance measurement areas.

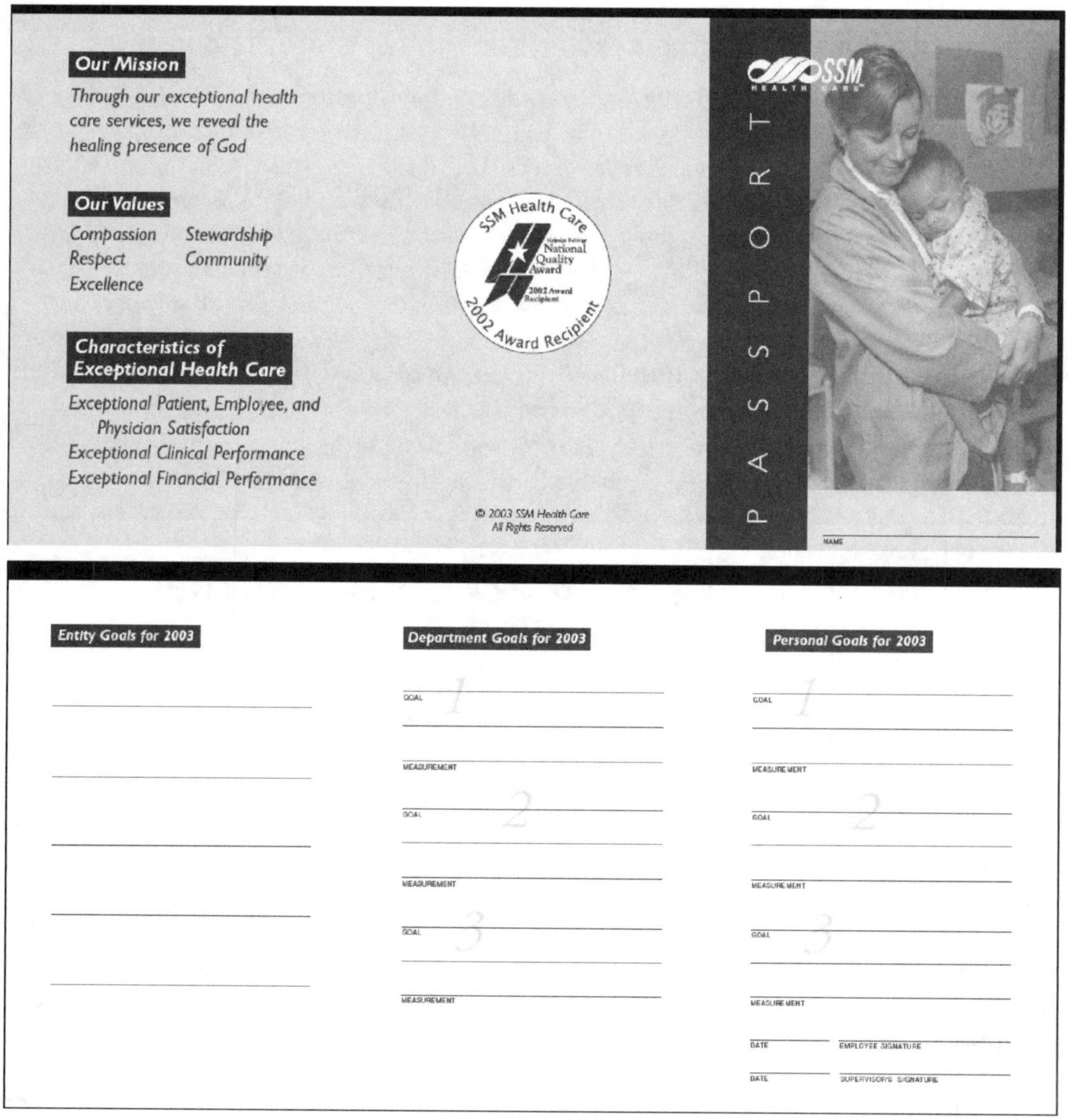

Figure 4.2 "Passport" method to align goals – SSM Health Care.[5]

detailing key data and information. "Here's what the board discussed today" might be a topic, for example. This communication approach enables leaders to reinforce the focus of the workforce on the performance excellence journey and promote alignment through clear and consistent messages from the top. This specific approach is one of several communication methods that are well deployed and contribute to workforce engagement and alignment.

Together, the four principal methods leaders use to create alignment, including personal involvement and visibility, coalitions, strategic line of sight, and ongoing communication, provide the focus necessary to accelerate improvement.

The Three-Cs Framework – Bronson Methodist Hospital

Bronson leaders define three critical success factors that represent the areas in which the organization must excel relative to its competitors: clinical excellence, corporate effectiveness, and customer and service excellence. This three-Cs framework represents the organizing framework for Bronson's strategic objectives and plans. Bronson leaders use the three-Cs framework in multiple ways to communicate the organization's direction and goals and to align key constituencies. The senior leadership structure includes three strategic oversight teams—one for each of the three Cs—that report to the hospital board. All employees receive a one-page Plan of Excellence with key initiatives organized by the three Cs. All leadership communications with the workforce are formatted according to the three Cs. The three Cs form the critical perspectives for the organization's balanced scorecard. As part of workforce performance management, every employee develops three personal goals that support the three Cs.

#3: BUILD AN ORGANIZATIONAL CULTURE OF LEARNING AND IMPROVEMENT

Seek the "truth" about the current reality. Management expert Jim Collins writes that "leadership does not begin just with vision. It begins with getting people to confront the brutal facts and to act on the implications."[6] Successful leaders of a performance excellence journey build an organizational culture of learning and improvement. They welcome "the brutal facts" of their current reality, actively and systematically seeking feedback to learn and improve. Leadership action in response to "truth" about the current reality gave rise to the Sharp Experience. This organization-wide performance improvement initiative was launched in 2001 after one hundred focus groups of staff, physicians, and patients related that the experience of working, giving, and getting care at Sharp was not what it could be— then no different from that available at any of Sharp's competitors.

Personal, active involvement in the assessment process is a systematic method for confronting "the brutal truth" and taking action in response to move to a higher level of performance. It also enables leaders to demonstrate their commitment to creating a culture of openness and truth-telling throughout the organization. Sister Mary Jean sets the expectation that all SSM hospital presidents will systematically confront and act on "the brutal facts" by requiring them to lead hospital-wide assessment at the state level. In addition to the assessment process, these leaders use a variety of other systematic methods to ensure that they understand the brutal facts about the current reality. These methods include focus groups, executive rounds, and patient feedback. At Mercy, for example, senior leaders "cruise and connect" weekly, rounding with staff to understand and find ways to better meet their needs. They also weekly review patient complaints. Sharp leaders perform "Rounding with Reason" to validate values and direction, solicit two-way communication, provide recognition, build personal relationships, and ensure customer/partner satisfaction.

Senior Leader Rounding – Baptist Hospital

As practiced by Baldrige leaders, senior leader rounding is not a spontaneous drop-in visit but a well-defined, systematic approach. The Baptist Hospital approach goes like this:

- Determine the best time to round based on the department's function and team member responsibilities (for example, avoid shift change on patient care units)

- Determine specific objectives for the visit

- Become familiar with the department's role, services/products, and performance, including individuals or work groups deserving recognition

- Develop a script to ensure that messages reflect the organization's culture, values, and goals and that key questions are asked consistently

- Conduct the rounding visit, communicating and, as appropriate, facilitating on-the-spot joint problem-solving

- Follow up after the visit to express thanks, and for problems recap the solution reached during the visit or outline actions planned to address a more complicated issue

While president of Baptist Hospital, John Heer spent some time rounding every day. "It's important to demonstrate to staff that you support their efforts and that their feedback will be used to make the organization better," he said. "Rounding is a great tool to reward and acknowledge your staff's performance or discover areas for improvement. This is your time to engage staff and find out what they need. Rounding is not a program—it is a *best practice* to impact the culture of the organization and create positive results."[7]

Conduct Objective, Data-based Performance Review

The performance measurement framework, with indicators, goals, and timeframe, promotes alignment of people around the goals of the of the performance excellence journey. It also supports periodic data-based performance review, another powerful mechanism for truth-telling and action for improvement. Successful leaders use these performance reviews to explore and understand both gaps and gains, in order to learn and adjust plans to increase improvement. Progress on goals and action plans to address gaps identified through the assessment process are a key part of these reviews. Measurable changes in results allow leaders to gauge the impact of changes being made in key organizational processes.

Develop Process Knowledge and Demonstrate a Process Focus

Successful leaders recognize that all work is a process and understand the key work systems and processes of their organizations.[8] This knowledge is fundamental to their ability to confront "the brutal facts." They understand that process failures—

not bad people—are the source of most poor performance; because they understand what the organization's key work systems and processes are, and have led the establishment of a measurement system, they can effectively analyze performance gaps and identify key leverage points for change. Their process focus is evident in their attention to the leadership processes they own. At Bronson, for example, senior leaders manage the leadership communication process (Figure 4.3) and measure the effectiveness of key communications so as to identify the need for alternative delivery mechanisms to reach their intended audiences.

Nurture Improvement and Innovation Capability

Finally, these successful leaders build and nurture the organization's capability to improve and innovate. Successful leaders lead improvement and innovation: they serve as role models to others throughout the organization, personally leading new approaches to organization design and care delivery and finding methods to fully engage the workforce. At Mercy, Javon Bea led the development of a physician partnership employment model that resolves economic competition, eliminates legal barriers, and creates a culture of cooperation. Some 80 percent of Mercy physicians participate. The model provides physicians with economic incentives similar to those of private practice while it relieves them of the administrative burdens of private practice. The partnership model is a contributing factor to Mercy's achievement of physician satisfaction scores above the AMGA 95th percentile.

At North Mississippi, John Heer and Chuck Stokes redesigned the care delivery system into six service lines reporting to Stokes. Each service line includes a small group of physicians, an administrator, nurse managers, and appropriate finance, outcomes measurement and ancillary staff. Service lines have responsibility for strategic planning, operational performance, and outcomes improvement to

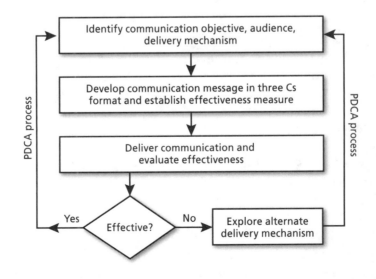

Figure 4.3 Leadership communication process – Bronson Methodist Hospital.[9]

support medical center and system goals. Flattening the organization through elimination of vice presidents and empowering front-line teams has resulted in cost reduction, patient satisfaction, market share growth, and clinical outcomes improvement.

Leaders provide the conditions and resources to engage not only those in the workforce, but key stakeholders beyond, and tap their creative energy for innovation and improvement. Poudre Valley Health System and its rural hospital partner Regional West Medical Center collaborated to open a new hospital. Design teams formed to research, develop, and test key processes for the new facility conducted benchmark visits to world-class organizations, created mock-ups of critical spaces planned for the new facility, and piloted various approaches in typical scenarios with key stakeholders. During one scenario, city transportation officials checked out proposed ambulance routes to the new hospital while riding as "patients." Physicians, community members, and other key stakeholders served on all the design teams.

Leaders of award recipient organizations actively built a culture of learning and improvement by welcoming the "brutal truth," conducting objective organization-wide performance reviews, developing a process focus, and nurturing improvement and innovation.

#4: CONTINUALLY MOTIVATE, INSPIRE, AND ENGAGE THE WORKFORCE

Successful leaders of a performance excellence journey continually motivate, inspire, and engage others throughout the organization.

Reinforce the Link of Organizational Purpose and Individual Values

Leaders find ways to link people in the workforce to a larger and ennobling vision and purpose aligned with their personal values. Typically, the mission and vision are key tools. To continually motivate and inspire the workforce, leaders find ways to incorporate them in a meaningful way into leadership communication and the rituals of the organization. At Sharp HealthCare, Mike Murphy compressed the organization's long vision statement into three memorable phrases: "best place to work, best place to practice medicine, best place to receive care." He uses these regularly in internal and external conversations, a recurring reminder of the organization's purpose and goals. Sharp adopted a flame to symbolize the Sharp Experience, and the appearance of this graphic symbol instantly telegraphs a deeper message to the workforce wherever it appears. The flame metaphor has become embedded in Sharp's culture and language. "Firestarters," for example, are "volunteer leaders who provide enthusiastic leadership within their entity to implement the Sharp Experience." Every meeting at Sharp begins with a group reflection on a brief quotation that uses the flame metaphor, and Murphy models this behavior in every meeting he leads. Sharp's reflections have become a simple but powerful mechanism to reinforce engagement (Figure 4.4).

Reflections

- Your SPARK can become a FLAME and change EVERYTHING. *(Edgar D. Nixon)*

- Life is no brief candle to me. It is a sort of splendid TORCH which I have got a hold of for the moment, and I want to make it BURN as brightly as possible before handing it on to future generations. *(George Bernard Shaw)*

- I believe a bit of the reason we're here is to throw little TORCHES out to lead people through the dark. *(Whoopi Goldberg)*

- The energy, the faith, the devotion which we bring this endeavor will LIGHT our bounty and all who serve it, and the glow from that FIRE can truly LIGHT the world. *(John F. Kennedy)*

Figure 4.4   Some reflections used at Sharp HealthCare.[10]

Involve People in Designing and Making Change

Successful leaders foster motivation and engagement by involving people in decision-making about how to achieve the vision.

Rulon Stacey explained that his leadership team at Poudre Valley "has changed significantly over time, and now includes some front-line staff who can provide top leaders with the perspective of front-line and director levels," a particular asset when the leadership team is deciding how to deploy new approaches to the rest of the organization. Workforce participation on design and improvement teams (for example, Sharp's 100 action teams focused on creating The Sharp Experience and Poudre Valley's new hospital design teams with employee, partner, supplier and community representation) and employee suggestion programs (for example, Bright Ideas at Baptist) are other key mechanisms leaders use to enable the workforce to bring their creative energy and ideas to the transformation.

Seek Out and Recognize Successes

These leaders take an active personal role in rewarding and recognizing success, building individuals' self-esteem and a sense that they are valued by the organization. At some organizations, the CEO and other senior leaders have established the practice of writing personal thank-you notes to employees. At Sharp, Mike Murphy said, thank-you notes have become a standard practice reflecting the organization's Attitude of Gratitude. At Baptist, where he first established the practice, John Heer required his subordinates to share names and notes on recognition-worthy events so that he could write thank-you notes to employees, which he sent to their home addresses. By this approach, Heer not only inspired, motivated, and engaged the employees he thanked, but he modeled the leadership behavior he expected from his reports, ensured they would seek out successes, and made clear to everyone the culture change he was working to bring about. This simple practice contributes to building a supportive coalition throughout the organization.

All-Staff Assembly – Sharp HealthCare

Inspiration, education, and celebration are the objectives of Sharp's annual All-Staff Assembly. This daylong event, repeated in three sessions so more than 11,000 members of the Sharp workforce can attend, allows leaders to bring together large numbers of Sharp employees, physicians, volunteers, and other partners to celebrate success and renew their commitment to Sharp's mission, vision, and core values. The agenda for the assembly traditionally includes a state-of-Sharp address by the CEO, educational sessions highlighting best practices, and presentation of Sharp's Pillar of Excellence Awards. There are special topics as well, such as the preview one year of a television documentary on the Sharp Experience. The All-Staff Assembly is also lots of fun. Employee action teams choose the theme, design the agenda, schedule special events, and, like Sharp's employee gospel choir, a regular performer, they participate throughout. At a recent assembly with a Love Boat theme, the CEO gave his state-of-Sharp address in a Hawaiian shirt and crepe paper lei, the costume of the day. What most differentiates Sharp's approach from other organizations' staff retreats, however, is not the keynote speech, the teaching, the awards, or the fun. It's the focus on creating an *experience* that reflects the purpose and the power of Sharp's people and the joy they can find in worthwhile work and making a difference. It inspires, motivates, and engages employees to recommit.

#5: BUILD A RESULTS FOCUS AND PROCESSES FOR PERSONAL AND ORGANIZATIONAL ACCOUNTABILITY

Since ultimately it is all about the results, it is no surprise that successful leaders create a focus on results. They understand and capitalize on the use of results to create and balance value for key stakeholders—patients and families, the community, the workforce, suppliers and partners, payers, and the public, for example.

Lead Development of a Measurement Framework

They guide development of a measurement framework that aligns key elements in the organization's mission and vision, and the requirements of key stakeholder groups, with key performance metrics that represent the organization's "measures of success." This "balanced scorecard" approach is evident in the pillar framework used by many Baldrige recipients and other high performers in health care (Figure 4.1). Second, they guide selection of a set of high-level, strategically important performance indicators representing all dimensions of the measurement framework. These key indicators are the measures that senior leaders regularly review to inform themselves on needed action.

Create a Focus on Action and Results

Leaders in Baldrige recipient organizations typically use the following methods to create a focus on action. First, successful leaders set clear and aspirational goals—goals that represent a significant stretch for the organization. Leaders of successful organizational transformations cite this more than any other factor as key to their organization's success.[11] At North Mississippi, according to Ken Davis, MD, Baldrige forced the leadership team "to look at benchmarks outside, on a national scale. How do you know who's best in the world? How do you do compared to them?" Leaders set North Mississippi goals to be "top 10 percent in every area."

Successful leaders not only set stretch goals. They systematically review progress on performance to achieve those goals. This means that performance review occurs predictably and consistently involves key decision makers with the responsibility and authority to act. Performance review is based on objective data, but goes beyond looking at numbers to analysis (frequently performed ahead of the review session) so that leaders have the information required for the most appropriate response. To promote action, accountability and timelines are assigned. Successful leaders enhance their responsiveness with methods that help them focus on performance areas in need of action. They establish performance thresholds, for example, and mechanisms to alert them when performance goes out of range. An example is the color-coding system used by Poudre Valley Health System (Figure 4.5), which enables leaders to see at a glance the performance range of each metric represented on the scorecard. Goals and ranges are set for each measure based on comparative data for the top 10 percent of U.S. organizations or an internal stretch goal.

Successful leaders further promote a focus on action and results throughout the organization by promoting effective performance review and alignment of measures at all levels. They ensure that the tools, knowledge, and skills are available at lower

Color	Interpretation
Blue	Best practice or world-class stretch goal
Green	Acceptable performance
Yellow	Performance is in transition and warrants monitoring
Red	Performance falls outside the acceptable range and warrants immediate action

Figure 4.5 Performance results color coding scheme – Poudre Valley Health System.[12]

levels of the organization to support systematic performance review and action. They ensure that the key measures tracked are aligned, both vertically from organizational goal (for example, overall patient satisfaction) to departmental goals (for example, patient satisfaction with surgical ICU pain management) to individual employee action (for example, my patient's satisfaction with pain control) and horizontally, across similar units. Figure 4.6 shows one example of plan deployment and measurement that links the top level of the organization to the front line. Such alignment promotes engagement of everyone's actions in support of the organization's overall direction and strategy and sets the stage for internal performance comparisons, benchmarking, and knowledge transfer among like units. Recipient organizations typically support this measurement and improvement capability through a cascading set of performance scorecards or dashboards, for example, organized by pillar and made available electronically on internal Web sites or in hard copy for posting on organizational knowledge boards.

Finally, successful leaders reinforce the focus on action by linking rewards and recognition to results and high performance. These reinforcements take a wide range of forms, from simple personal thank-you notes to organization-wide gain-sharing programs tied to key performance results.

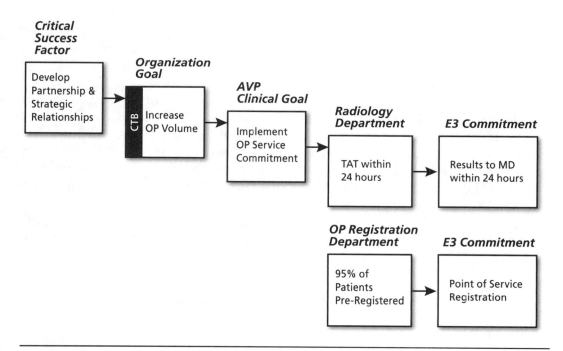

Figure 4.6   Plan deployment and measurement cascade – Robert Wood Johnson University Hospital at Hamilton.[13]

Establish Norms Around Performance Transparency

Successful leaders establish a results-focused culture in which transparency around performance becomes the norm. They do this by making performance results broadly available throughout the organization, by serving as role models in their own focus on performance review and follow-through, and finally by relentlessly communicating, in multiple ways to multiple audiences, about the organization's goals, results, and progress being made. These include leader messages distributed in material shared at daily huddles, top leader podcasts beamed to workforce PCs, and "state-of-the union" addresses such as the state-of-Sharp keynote Mike Murphy delivers annually at the All-Staff Assembly. "When you are on the journey," said North Mississippi's Chuck Stokes, "when progress is measured and improved, and publicly reported, it improves faster." Moreover, said Stokes, "health care is going to have to deal with public reporting," so building electronic capability to share results and an organizational culture of openness about performance are ways leaders prepare their organizations for the future.

Make It Safe to Talk About Performance

Relentless communication about performance is one way leaders create a safe environment to talk about results and encourage truth-telling. More important, however, are two specific ways in which they communicate. When they communicate about performance, successful leaders emphasize areas of opportunity and areas of strength equally. They recognize and encourage building on successes as much as they focus on identifying and addressing failures. A balanced focus on successes and problems appears key to engaging the workforce in making change.[14]

Second, when successful leaders do focus on poor performance and explore how to improve it, their questions reflect a process focus and a deep awareness that almost invariably poor performance results from bad processes, not from bad people. They are careful to demand accountability for action, yet while they recognize people for successes, they avoid placing blame for unfavorable results.

Successful leaders track their effectiveness achieving an environment in which employees feel safe to talk about performance. Key questions on workforce engagement and satisfaction surveys provide feedback. At Poudre Valley Health System, leaders monitor employee responses to the statement "It's OK to report errors or mistakes in my department."

THE FIVE CRITICAL LEADERSHIP BEHAVIORS AND THE LEADERSHIP SYSTEM

"The most pernicious half-truth about leadership," writes Kotter, "is that it's just a matter of charisma and vision—you either have it or you don't. The fact of the matter is that leadership skills are not innate. They can be acquired and honed."[15] In fact, the Baldrige Criteria and systematic organizational assessment offer a method for leaders to design, implement, and improve approaches that foster the five critical leadership behaviors evident in leaders of a successful performance excellence journey. The five critical behaviors are not a prerequisite for a successful journey, rather they are the *product* of leaders' thoughtful efforts to understand and apply the Criteria to their own leadership work.

Specific questions in the Criteria focus leaders' attention on the processes that must be in place to support leaders in demonstrating each of the five critical behaviors.

During the assessment process, leaders examine how their leadership and organizational practices respond to or address key leadership Criteria questions such as those outlined in Figure 4.7. With respect to leadership communication and workforce engagement, for example—an essential approach to continually motivate, inspire, and engage the organization—they would determine the following:

- If the leadership communication approach is accomplished by an ordered and repeated set of steps (or happens essentially ad hoc, depending on the leader, the issue, or the day)

Leadership Behavior	Related Criteria Questions[16]
1. Make a personal commitment to organizational transformation to achieve performance excellence	How do senior leaders' personal actions reflect a commitment to the organization's values? How do senior leaders personally promote an organizational environment that fosters, requires, and results in legal and ethical behavior? How do senior leaders create and promote a culture of patient safety?
2. Align people in support of the destination and the journey to get there	How do senior leaders deploy the organization's vision and values through the leadership system to the workforce, to key suppliers and partners, and to patients and stakeholders?
3. Build a culture of organizational learning and improvement	How do senior leaders create an environment for organizational performance improvement, accomplishment of the mission and strategic objectives, innovation, competitive or role-model performance leadership, and organizational agility? How do they create an environment for organizational and workforce learning? How do they develop and enhance their personal leadership skills? How do they participate in organizational learning?
4. Continually motivate and inspire	How do senior leaders communicate with and engage the entire workforce? How do senior leaders encourage frank, two-way communication throughout the organization? How do they communication key decisions? How do they take an active role in reward and recognition programs to reinforce high performance and a focus on the organization, as well as on patients and stakeholders?
5. Build a results orientation and processes for personal and organizational accountability for results	How do senior leaders create a focus on action to accomplish the organization's objectives, improve performance, and attain its vision? What performance measures do senior leaders regularly review to identify needed actions?

Figure 4.7 Criteria foster leader behaviors.

- If the approach is used by all leaders, used consistently, and reaches all in the workforce

- If the approach is evaluated regularly and improved

- If the approach is designed and managed in a way that supports other organizational goals and processes, such as enhancing employee engagement and capturing employee input for planning purposes

In this way, assessment creates the opportunity for leaders to examine their leadership and organizational practices in light of the Criteria questions; then they address their findings by designing and implementing new leadership processes, or refining existing approaches. Assessment and action on the findings over time shift leadership practices from variable, person-dependent, and often individual actions to predictable organizational processes, capable of evaluation and improvement, that become embedded in the organizational culture and define leaders' way of work. These processes support leaders in demonstrating the five critical behaviors that characterize leaders of a successful performance excellence journey.

Over time, through repeated assessment cycles, successful leaders align and integrate the key responsibilities and processes of leaders into a leadership system for the organization. A leadership system can be viewed as the "structures and mechanisms for decision making; two-way communication; selection and development of leaders and managers; and reinforcement of values, ethical behavior, directions, and performance expectations. An effective leadership system...sets high expectations for performance and performance improvement. It builds loyalties and teamwork based on the organization's vision and values and the pursuit of shared goals."[17] In other words, a leadership system is the combination of effective leaders and effective processes that set direction, build culture, and drive improvement in an organization.

As an example, Sharp's senior leaders support the accomplishment of Sharp's mission and values, strategic objectives, and organizational performance improvement initiatives through the leadership system shown in Figure 4.8.

Sharp's leadership system is mission-centric; it is focused on the organization's central purpose and bringing value to its key stakeholders. Fulfilling their needs and expectations in a manner consistent with the organization's values is central to leaders' work. Leaders drive performance through five key processes (the ovals), starting with setting direction. At each step, they must ensure deployment. Setting direction requires communication and commitment. Planning requires deployment of resources.

Creating and deploying a model of the organization's leadership system is a method successful leaders use to clarify, communicate, and "hardwire" how leaders take action to drive performance excellence. Sharp's model depicts responsibilities of senior leaders (Category 1) and links them to other key organizational processes, including strategic planning (Category 2), performance measurement and review

(Category 4), workforce management (Category 5), and performance improvement (Category 6). The model provides leaders at every level of the organization with a high-level view of the interdependent processes and the continuous cycle of action they must lead in order to fulfill the mission and achieve performance excellence.

Leadership forms a critical foundation for a successful performance excellence journey. The five critical leadership behaviors—making *a personal commitment to transformation, aligning people in support, building a culture of learning and improvement, motivating and inspiring the workforce, and building a results orientation*—create an environment in which transformation is possible. This environment is characterized by the ability of leaders and others to look at the brutal truth necessary to change (Assessment) and use that truthful evaluation to begin to understand the organization as a system of processes that create results (Sensemaking). This environment is also characterized by the discipline to design and improve key processes essential to achieve results (Execution). Use of the Baldrige framework encourages and supports leaders in developing the leadership system that enables them to demonstrate these behaviors consistently. It is a hard journey, but one made possible through the commitment and actions of leaders ready for change.

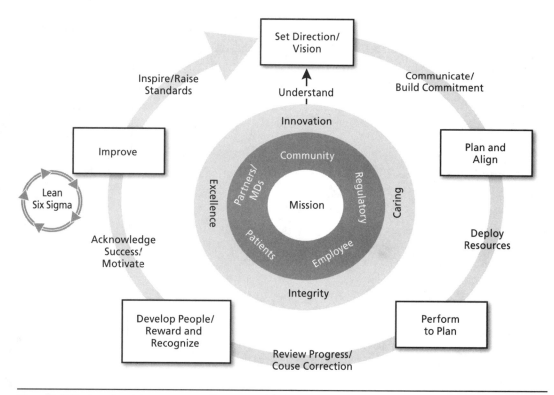

Figure 4.8 Leadership system – Sharp HealthCare.[18]

KEY POINTS IN THIS CHAPTER

- Five critical leadership behaviors are evident among leaders of a successful performance excellence journey:
  - Make a personal commitment to organizational transformation to achieve performance excellence.
  - Align people in support of the destination and the journey to get there.
  - Build a culture of organizational learning and improvement.
  - Continually motivate and inspire.
  - Build a results orientation and processes for personal and organizational accountability for results.

- Systematic organizational assessment using the Baldrige Criteria offers a method for leaders to learn and practice these critical behaviors as they design, implement, and improve the leadership system.

- Leaders of a successful journey build a leadership system that fosters workforce engagement and makes the organization capable of short-term gains, rapid adjustments in the face of change, and sustained high performance long-term.

5

Assessment

"If you had the opportunity to sit down and read...the good to great interviews, you'd be struck by the utter absence of talk about 'competitive strategy.' They talked in terms of what they were trying to create and how they were trying to improve relative to an absolute standard of excellence."

– Jim Collins, *Good to Great*[1]

Above all else, the Baldrige Criteria are an absolute standard of excellence. This book is not about winning an award, prestigious though it might be. Rather, it is about the journey that organizations took to achieve high levels of performance, using the Baldrige Criteria as a framework for defining and achieving excellence. Assessments are an essential part of the Baldrige approach for evaluating and improving performance.

WHAT IS AN ASSESSMENT?

As we use the term in this book, an assessment is a three-step process:

- Develop a description (the assessment document, or award application) that details the organization's operating environment, how it achieves its work and the results it obtains

- Evaluate that description against the Baldrige Criteria

- Learn from that evaluation the organization's strengths and opportunities for improvement

Effective Assessments are integral components of the LASER model, along with Sensemaking and Execution. Repeated assessments allow an organization to gain greater insight into its strengths and gaps, thus building Sensemaking. Execution addresses gaps in the organization's performance that are identified during the assessment process while fostering an awareness of the importance of assessments in driving the organization's strategy.

Assessments can take various forms. The most formal is the approach all the Baldrige health care recipients eventually took: submitting an application to the Baldrige Award program. A Baldrige application essentially is a formal version of the assessment document. However, an organization can start assessments in a less-structured manner, and many of the health care organizations we studied did so. For example, an organization might choose to do only an internal assessment, without any external support or analysis. This approach is very common for initial assessments. However, it rarely allows the organization to progress beyond the Projects stage because the organization's mental models of itself can result in blind spots that hinder asking—and answering—challenging Criteria questions. Another limitation to this approach is minimal understanding of the Criteria within the organization, which may lead to incomplete or inaccurate assessment conclusions. This approach can be helpful as an initial step, but before long successful users seek independent evaluation.

Some organizations elect to do an internal assessment, but with support from external experts. This approach tends to accelerate the learning, since the organization can build its internal understanding and expertise while at the same time receiving knowledgeable objective feedback and guidance. Because of this, these assessments can be effective in quickly moving the organization into the Traction stage and beyond. Most organizations that continue assessments eventually use the application process, either at the state or Baldrige Award level. Their reasoning, even if award seeking is not their motive, is simply that they receive objective feedback at a very low cost. This logic was echoed by most of the Baldrige health care award recipients we interviewed.

AN ASSESSMENT EXAMPLE

Assessment is a process: prepare an organizational description, evaluate the content of the document against the Baldrige Criteria, obtain and learn from feedback (either internally or externally developed or both). This process sets the stage for Execution, or taking appropriate action on the feedback. Figure 5.1 demonstrates, in an abbreviated form, how the assessment process flows from Criteria question through organization response and feedback to a potential improvement action. This example is based on a fictitious but altogether realistic community health center, Arroyo Fresco, the subject of a case study used to train Baldrige examiners.

An Assessment Self-Test

Many people believe the Baldrige Criteria questions are only strategic in nature. But the Criteria apply equally to the most common daily situations. See how well you can answer these questions that pertain to the work you do every day:

- What are the requirements and expectations for the health care services and operations in which I'm involved?
- How do I know what's expected of me in my job?
- How do I know if my patients and customers are satisfied or dissatisfied with my work?
- What measures do I use to track the quality of my work?
- How do I use these measures to make changes that will improve my work?
- How well do the people I work with cooperate and work as a team?

Note that there are two types of questions above:

- *"What"* questions seek specific information. These questions may be responded to with a brief list.
- *"How"* questions are more complex. These questions seek a description of the process used to accomplish the work in question. "How" questions are designed to understand whether the organization has systematic approaches in place (that is, the approaches are repeatable, use data to make decisions, and have the capability to be improved). Effective responses to "how" questions go beyond a list of activities; they include a clear description of the steps and people involved, the timeframe, and the measures used to evaluate the performance of the process. This understanding is the basis for what we term "process literacy."

In organizations that have progressed well into Traction (stage 2) and beyond, most employees can readily answer these questions. They also have a clear understanding of the processes they work in and recognize how their work fits into the "big picture" of the organization overall. On a large scale, this understanding produces organizational alignment and synergy. We'll explore this in greater detail in the next chapter on Sensemaking.

WHY DO ASSESSMENTS?

In the era of transparency, it is reasonable to expect leaders to review both their personal performance and that of their organizational systems. The 360-degree evaluation tool has become commonly used as a means to evaluate the performance of individuals in an organization, a tool that gathers input from peers,

Baldrige Criteria questions [abridged from 2006 Criteria 3.1a(2)]	How do you listen and learn to determine key patient and other customer requirements, needs, and changing expectations...and their relative importance...? How do your determination methods vary for different patients, other customers, or customer groups?
Applicant's partial response to the question	Arroyo Fresco uses a variety of methods to listen and learn to determine key patient, family and other stakeholder requirements. For patients and families, these include satisfaction surveys, complaint data (including requests to change the primary care provider) and information gathered through staff and volunteer interactions. Each facility has an eight-member Patient–Family Advisory Board that meets quarterly with Arroyo Fresco staff to give feedback on Arroyo Fresco's services and future needs and plans.
Feedback comment on the response	It is unclear how Arroyo Fresco's listening and learning methods vary for different customers and customer groups. This lack of clarity may affect the systematic evaluation and improvement of health care services.
Possible improvement action as a result of the feedback	Arroyo Fresco could review its patient and market segments to determine if there are unique requirements for any or all of these segments.[2] If so, Arroyo Fresco could revise its listening and learning methods to ensure that they were tailored to capture the key requirements for its varied patient and customer groups.

Figure 5.1 The flow of an assessment.

subordinates, and superiors. We expect individuals to be evaluated and to use the feedback from this process to improve their personal performance. Similarly, Baldrige assessments provide a 360-degree review of the performance of an entire organization.

Conducting objective assessments is critical for moving an organization first into the Traction stage of the journey and then beyond into the Integration stage. Assessments drive an introspective, disciplined approach to improvement, helping an organization to become less random and more focused in its thinking and actions. Assessments focus attention on leadership and management approaches, as well as on the daily work processes of clinical care or administrative functions. As the late management expert Peter Drucker stated, "Great leaders don't need to know all the answers. They just need to know what questions to ask."[3] The Baldrige Criteria, with its Socratic, question-based structure, provides nearly all the questions a leader ever needs to ask about the operations of his or her enterprise.

The self-learning that results as part of the development of the assessment document is important because it provides quick insights into the organization's strengths and areas for improvement. We call these "aha" moments, when assessment participants realize, by trying to respond to the questions in the Baldrige Criteria, some of their performance gaps and the important issues facing them. It is common in the early stages to realize you cannot answer many of the questions; the questions have never been asked before. Later on in the journey, leaders grow to anticipate their own gaps. Rich Hastings, president and CEO, Saint Luke's

Health System, said that at Saint Luke's "We wrote our own OFIs in the process of writing the application." Capitalizing on these "aha" moments requires involving the right people in the assessment and having a method to ensure the learnings are captured, shared within the organization, and acted upon. As we will see in the next chapter on Sensemaking, the learning builds over time and repeated assessments create increasing value to assessment participants. Timely use of these insights to redesign leadership and management processes helps drive improved performance for the organization.

The second type of learning from an assessment comes when the feedback report arrives. This report, polite in tone but brutally objective, adds insights through an external perspective of the organization's performance against the Baldrige Criteria. The feedback report can be as long as the application, with thorough analysis of the organization's strengths and OFIs. Organizations need to use both self learning and the feedback to get the greatest benefit from assessments. Just waiting for their feedback report to arrive—five or more months after the application has been written—means the organization will miss a timely opportunity to begin addressing obvious gaps identified during the application writing process. Such organizations are all too likely to use the delay in receiving the feedback as an excuse for moving slowly. In our experience, this is one of the major causes for slow progress in some organizations.

Successful organizations do not view an assessment as a one-time event. Instead, they make it an integral part—often the centerpiece—of their improvement agenda. This repetition and the ability to integrate the assessment process into the normal course of doing business are critical success factors that cannot be overemphasized. Javon Bea, president and CEO, Mercy Health System, tells other CEOs, "You have to stick with it."

THE VALUE OF AN ASSESSMENT

Baldrige Award recipients from all sectors state that they place very high value on the feedback they received from examiners. Many recipients say that while the Baldrige Award is the 'icing on the cake,' they saw a comparable or even greater benefit from feedback received through the application and review process. Recipients express solid support for, and belief in, the Baldrige approach. They describe the Criteria as unique, encompassing and well-founded, more than ample to address the performance needs of virtually any organization.[4]

Regardless of whether an applicant receives the award or not, a Baldrige assessment provides significant value. It identifies the gaps between "who we are" and "who we want to be." The Criteria evaluation factors help to shape an integrated, process-focused view of the organization. Leaders start to ask themselves "Do we have an approach? Is it deployed? Is it being reviewed and improved?" and "What is our current performance versus the long-term trends and external comparisons with best in class?" Knowing the questions to ask, posing them often, and searching for answers leads to identification of improvement opportunities.

How the Baldrige Approach Fosters Process Literacy

The first six categories of the Baldrige Criteria are known as the process categories. The questions in these categories mainly focus on *how* the organization does things. Even though, as W. Edwards Deming stated, "all work is a process," most organizations—both within and outside of health care—do not have a clear sense of how their work is accomplished, especially when that work spans several departments or locations. This results in errors and low efficiency, despite the best efforts of the people who labor in those processes every day.

The Baldrige approach drives process literacy in an organization—a clear understanding of *how* things work and why the organization gets the results it does. The constant focus on *how* in the Criteria questions forces an organization to think about its methods for developing, maintaining and improving its processes. Deborah Baehser, senior vice president of clinical services and chief nursing officer at Robert Wood Johnson University Hospital, Hamilton, said, "When you have to answer all those 'how' questions, you really do get insight into how your organization functions. That's how we benefited in the early years. We got a chance to look at what we were doing and that helped us understand our organization and see how to improve." This insight includes both the "hard" processes, such as service development and delivery, and the "soft" processes, including leadership and workforce development. In an assessment, the process evaluation factors—approach, deployment, learning, and integration—are taken into consideration to determine the maturity and effectiveness of the organization's processes. Whether done internally, with a consultant, or through an award program, the assessment reviews whether there are effective, systematic approaches in place that address the organization's needs, how well these approaches are deployed to all appropriate areas and used correctly, how these approaches are periodically reviewed and improved to keep pace with changing business needs, and how the inputs and outputs of the approaches integrate with other related processes to create a synergistic operational system.

The organizations we studied had a strikingly consistent view of the value of the assessment process. All cited getting the feedback itself as a valuable experience, providing insight they couldn't get elsewhere. "The feedback report provides a good external view of your performance. It has very specific details that you can use to direct improvements," according to Mercy's Javon Bea. Rich Hastings of Saint Luke's said, "Writing an application really helps to connect the dots. Where do we need to get stronger?" Sherry Marshall, vice president of quality, Saint Luke's Health System, offered this observation and advice: "Go ahead and write an application. Just by having to organize and tell your story, it draws staff together, but the writing process reveals the gaps. Application writing leads to identifying gaps. Gaps lead to performance improvement. Performance improvement leads to better results."

INTEGRATING BALDRIGE ASSESSMENTS INTO OPERATIONS

As we'll discuss in detail in the Execution chapter, linking feedback to strategic and operational planning moves the assessment from a "sideshow" to an integral tool for improvement. This is a critical step to enable moving from the Projects stage, that is, from viewing a Baldrige assessment as a new additional task for the organization, to gaining Traction (stage 2) and beyond. "Getting real traction eludes organizations that keep it a project," said Frank Sardone, president and CEO, Bronson Healthcare Group. Bronson incorporated the Baldrige assessment process as a means to support the organization's Critical Success Factors (Figure 5.2). Bronson recognized the value of embedding the Baldrige Criteria into its operations to improve its performance in those areas of focus that were most critical to the organization. Although Baldrige is mentioned in Figure 5.2 only in the context of Corporate Effectiveness, the holistic nature of the Criteria allowed Bronson to use the assessment process to identify and drive improvements across all facets of the hospital's operations, including clinical performance, patient satisfaction, and workforce engagement.

Similarly, North Mississippi viewed the Baldrige Criteria as an important driver for supporting its mission, vision, values, and critical success factors (Figure 5.3). North Mississippi translated its mission—"To continuously improve the health of the people of our region"— and *CARES* values (compassion, accountability, respect, excellence, and smile) into measurable actions through five Critical Success Factors intentionally arranged in the following order: people, service, quality, financial, and growth. The Baldrige Criteria were used as a means to prioritize and improve

Clinical Excellence (CE)
• Achieve national best practice performance in clinical outcomes.
• Use evidence-based medicine to achieve excellent patient outcomes.
• Be recognized as a safe environment for patients.
Customer & Service Excellence (CASE)
• Distinguished BMH as an employer of choice.
• Be recognized for a culture of service excellence.
• Foster a culture of excellence that values diversity while encouraging teamwork, learning, and innovation.
Corporate Effectiveness (CORE)
• Provide strong financial performance to allow for capital reinvestment, growth, and sustainability.
• Partner with physicians, the community, and others to achieve common objectives.
• Use the Baldrige Criteria for Performance Excellence to improve processes and organizational performance.

Figure 5.2 Critical success factors – Bronson Methodist Hospital.[5]

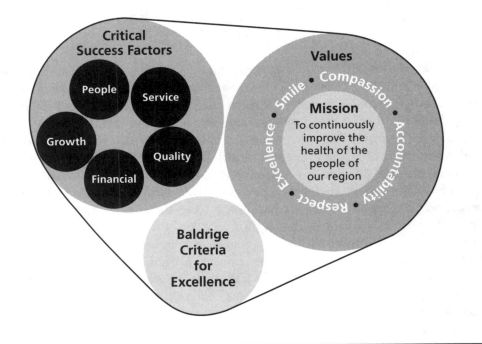

Figure 5.3 Integration of the Baldrige Criteria – North Mississippi Medical Center.[6]

all aspects of North Mississippi's operations. Note how the holistic Baldrige Criteria are used to address both the "hard" aspects of the operation, such as growth and financial performance, as well as the "soft side" of the business, such as people and service.

DEVELOPING THE ASSESSMENT DOCUMENT

Nothing beats the rigor of writing down how your organization works and getting from that an understanding of what and how to improve. "The discipline of writing an application is good discipline for management," Saint Luke's Rich Hastings told us. A Baldrige application is merely your organization's operations manual—documentation of how you do the broad array of work that's required to run your organization. Paula Friedman, corporate vice president of strategy and systems improvement, SSM Health Care, explained a lesson she learned as a result of combining her Baldrige experience and organizational insights: "If we can't explain clearly to someone outside, how can we expect line employees to understand? This insight led to clarification and simplification of several processes and messages." An assessment does take committed leadership and an effort to reach agreement on your organization's answers to questions such as "What are our strategic challenges?" and "Who are our customers?" and "How do we plan?" It also takes a willingness to be humble enough to learn from the process and feedback and to change based on that learning. This entails a readiness to continue the process even if the organization fails to win the award, not in continued pursuit of a prize, but because the process is the best way to move the organization along its journey.

There are several different approaches for conducting assessments, including the application-writing component. The starting points for the organizations we studied varied from self-assessments conducted internally or with the aid of an external consultant to just submitting a Baldrige or state program application directly.[7] In most cases, the Baldrige health care recipients used their state award program either in conjunction with a Baldrige application or as a precursor to applying for Baldrige. Most of these state programs include the option for an abbreviated application (10, 15, or 25 pages, compared to the 50 pages required by Baldrige), which allows for a gradual immersion in understanding the Criteria. According to SSM's Paula Friedman, "State quality awards help entities with specific information. And coaches and resources at the state level were helpful. Sister [Mary Jean Ryan] continues to encourage entities to participate in the state process for feedback, networking, and latest information on best practices of high performers." Poudre Valley Health System used their Colorado CPEX state award program for their initial assessments and was, in fact, a two-time recipient of their state award.

North Mississippi and Saint Luke's avoided reference to Baldrige as they began conducting assessments, at least for a time. Saint Luke's used its own name for the Baldrige Criteria Categories (see Saint Luke's *Commitment to Excellence* Assessment Model in Figure 5.8). These organizations positioned their approaches as a means for learning and improving performance, without reference to the Baldrige Award. Others, such as SSM, referred to Baldrige from the beginning by name, positioning it as the ultimate benchmark for overall performance. According to David Sjoberg, vice president of strategic services, Baptist was "very clear about adoption of the Baldrige Criteria" and "communicated that they were a platform to continue improving." At Poudre Valley Health System, Priscilla Nuwash, director of process improvement, cited a change in how their organization viewed the Baldrige process: "Probably early it was all about the award. Two years ago, after our third site visit, we were so disappointed, but we had an awakening that it was not about the award."

Developing an application for Baldrige or a state award program can be done in several ways. There is no clear right or wrong approach, and the method actually might change over time. Each method has its pros and cons, as shown in Figure 5.4. The decision on which approach to use should be predicated by several factors, including the size of the organization and the level of the application. For example, one, or a few, writers might be able to easily and quickly develop a 10-page application for a small organization. However, there is one approach that we, as consultants, strongly recommend against—the "ghostwriter" method. In this approach, the writer develops the assessment document with little or no input from the expertise within the organization. Having the Public Relations department or other internal resource write an application can result in a document that does not reflect reality if the writer does not have broad organizational knowledge.

This is not because these people are poor writers. Quite the opposite; it's why they get selected for the task in the first place. But they generally do not have a complete, detailed understanding of the complex workings of an organization to be able to respond fully and accurately to all of the Baldrige Criteria questions. As a result, the application will be incomplete or inaccurate and the outcome of that assessment will be feedback that is not fully useful or actionable. Using an external consultant to write an application can produce the same inaccurate outcome, but at a much higher cost. Alternatively, designating one person to coordinate and integrate the final draft helps with consistency. A number of the recipients used this approach.

Regardless of the approach used, the organization needs to understand that the content of the assessment document, not the format or writing style, is what is important. A first assessment document may be quite disjointed, reading as a collection from multiple authors, but the writing style is not a factor in the

Approach	Pros	Cons
"Ghostwriter" (either internal or external)	• Minimal organizational effort required	• Accuracy of the content is highly variable, which affects the value of the feedback • Extremely expensive when external resources are used
Solo author (that is, an individual with sufficient organizational knowledge to develop a complete, accurate application)	• Can result in an accurate application for small organizations or, in larger organizations, if the writer seeks and incorporates input from internal content experts • Possible to do this for an abbreviated state program application (10–25 pages), or for a full application, if input from internal content experts is included	• Misses detail in large organizations, especially in multi-site organizations, resulting in feedback of minimal value
Individual "Category champion" writers	• Can effectively address details if the writers are content experts for their assigned sections of the application • Can identify most obvious gaps in the organization	• Writers can take a narrow approach, focused on just their own category, missing important linkages across categories • May be difficult to validate content across categories
Category writing teams	• Allows greater, more valid input across the organization, which increases accuracy of the application and quality of the feedback • Quickly identifies obvious gaps in the organization	• Involves a large group of people, which may impact resources

Figure 5.4 Various approaches for developing a Baldrige application.

examiners' assessment. What counts is how well the responses in the document address the Criteria questions. Both the writing style and the content will improve over successive assessments. For a first assessment, the goals should not be to produce a polished document. Rather, the goals for a first assessment include the following:

- Have the assessment document provide a reasonably accurate reflection of the organization's current state, with no negative ramifications for accurately portraying that state

- Develop a collaborative learning environment through broad involvement in the assessment

- Have the assessment support and enhance improvement activities, and not take on a life of its own as a separate disconnected event

- Build some pride within the organization for its accomplishments and performance

It's simply not possible to delegate understanding of the Baldrige Criteria questions. SSM's Paula Friedman stated clearly, "For us, the learning comes from answering the hard questions. We didn't get that until we had been through it a number of times. That's why we write our own applications." Organizations that take the "ghostwriter" route to application development inevitably are disappointed with the outcome. Few go beyond viewing the Baldrige application as a task or continue on a successful journey that reaches Traction (stage 2) or beyond.

The most common—and generally most effective—application-writing approach, both by the organizations in our study and by many others, is the use of category teams. In this approach, senior leadership commissions a number of teams, each of which is responsible for developing the responses to the questions in one Baldrige category. There are several permutations for this approach. In a large organization, the structure might include the roles detailed in Figure 5.5. Of course, many of these roles can be combined for smaller organizations.

Although some organizations choose to have seven category writing teams—one for each Baldrige Category, including results—the most effective approach we have observed is to link the relevant results item to the process category, as shown in Figure 5.6. This reinforces the important relationship between processes and results and minimizes potential disconnects in the application. Figure 5.6 suggests one pairing approach, but there is no "right" way. Most important is that the team leaders and members are matched according to their organizational role and knowledge. Sometimes Health Care Outcomes (Item 7.1) are paired with Process Management (Category 6) or even Strategic Planning (Category 2). The key is to assign a portion of the results to each team and ask them to identify causal links between the process and results categories they describe in the assessment document.

Roles	Responsibilities
Senior Leaders	• Communicate the purpose of the application to the organization • Build shared understanding and commitment among the leadership • Support data gathering and application development by reviewing progress on the timeline and removing barriers, if necessary • Actively participate as a member of one Category Team • Review and give input to the application drafts • Own the feedback report and visibly lead improvement based on it
Application Lead Team	• Serve as a small steering group for the development process • Develop schedules and timeline for the application • Collaborate with all involved parties to ensure an effective and efficient process • Build knowledge to serve as internal Baldrige resources • Review drafts to ensure continuity across all categories

Category Team Leaders	• Identify and recruit their Category Team Members (typically 3 to 8), using the following selection criteria:
	    – Diverse representation (that is, cross-system, cross-functional, line, and staff)
	    – Broad knowledge and experience in the organization
	    – Appropriate subject matter expertise
	    – Opinion leaders
	    – Trusted and respected in the organization
	• Develop a Category Team work plan to help the team accomplish its application development tasks within the required timeframe
	• Convene and lead meetings and/or teleconferences as required for those application development steps requiring group interaction
	• Identify a Team Member (or self) to serve as the primary author on behalf of the entire Category Team
	• With the primary author, submit drafts for review by the Category and Lead Teams, review feedback on the drafts and set priorities
	• Review the final draft of all categories to ensure accuracy and alignment and to identify and address gaps
	• Sign off on final draft for the category

Category Teams	Organizational Profile Team: • Develop a description of the organization, the key influences on how it operates, and its key challenges and advantages (5 pages maximum) • Complete a draft of the Profile as the first step in the application development process; refine as required Category 1–6 Teams: • Develop descriptions of approaches related to the assigned Baldrige process Category (5–7 pages per category). • Identify and describe the most important results related to those approaches (2–3 pages per results item) • Ensure consistency of the application content with the facts stated in the Profile

Figure 5.5 Baldrige application development roles and responsibilities. *(Continued)*

(Continued)

Roles	Responsibilities
Category Teams *(continued)*	Category 7 Team (comprising one representative from each of the Category 1–6 Teams): • With the Technical Expert and Data Analyst, oversee the development of the results presentation (Category 7), in figures and narrative (15–20 pages)
Category Team Members	• Take part in orientation on the process (generally a half day) • Deepen personal understanding of the Baldrige Criteria • Gather input and/or draft Criteria responses for the assigned Category • Participate in reviewing and giving feedback on Category drafts
Measurement Expert	• Establish guidelines for content and style of results that address Baldrige evaluation factors • Offer guidance to Category Teams on how best to "tell a story" through graphics and data displays • Serve as an expert resource for the Data Analyst
Data Analyst	• With guidance from the Measurement Expert, establish and communicate guidelines for content and style of results presentation • Provide Category Teams with templates to support accurate and efficient data collection • Help Category Teams access and assemble data • Prepare results figures for Category 7
Designer	• Develop design for application components (graphics, cover, header/footer, headings, divider tabs) that conforms to Baldrige specifications • Provide support for printing and binding final document

Figure 5.5 Baldrige application development roles and responsibilities.

Baldrige Process Category	Related Baldrige Results Item
1. Leadership	7.6 Leadership Outcomes
2. Strategic Planning	7.3 Financial and Market Outcomes
3. Customer Focus	7.2 Customer-focused Outcomes
4. Measurement, Analysis, and Knowledge Management	7.1 Health Care Outcomes
5. Workforce Focus	7.4 Workforce-focused Outcomes
6. Process Management	7.5 Process Effectiveness Outcomes

Figure 5.6 Linking Baldrige process categories with results.

Several of the Baldrige health care recipients discussed their evolution in the use of category teams to write their applications. In some cases, these teams became standing, integral parts of their management approach. Initially at North Mississippi, the quality specialists developed their application. After the first year, this transitioned to their senior leadership team members, who then took full responsibility. As executives became more involved in leading the category teams and writing the application, they also took more interest in the feedback. Each category team had 10 members from different parts of the organization. Each was led by a senior leader and had a lead writer for their category. The teams met every two weeks, working backward from the results they had identified. For consistency, a single writer put the entire application together. When the feedback report was delivered, these teams reviewed it for improvement opportunities.

The experience at Baptist was similar. After their first application, they put together category teams, most of which were headed by senior leaders, along with a steering committee made up of the CEO, the category leaders, and a few other key people. The same structure and most of the same membership stayed in place for nearly five years. At Sharp, a senior leader led most of the category writing teams. SSM also used category teams for writing the application, but they were not standing teams; they convened only for the purpose of developing the application. Saint Luke's brought in their medical staff officers and partnered them with the category teams to get their insights.

At Robert Wood Johnson University Hospital at Hamilton, a person in the quality department was initially assigned the application writing. "That didn't work," said Deborah Baehser, "because she didn't have all the knowledge. So we assigned a leader for each category from the senior team. That person was responsible for writing the category. They worked with a team of content experts and all category leads met as a group to ensure we understood the linkages between the categories."

LEVERAGING THE ASSESSMENT PROCESS

Regardless of the approach used to develop an application, our interviews with the Baldrige health care recipients, as well as our experience with other organizations, has shown that there are some critical success factors for ensuring a successful assessment outcome.

Understand the Baldrige Criteria and Evaluation Process

The holistic nature of the Baldrige Criteria questions requires an ability to think in a systems perspective. Developing internal experts (nicknamed "Baldrige professors" by Mercy's Javon Bea) who have a deep understanding of the Criteria is common. All the health care award recipients, and most other organizations that commit to using the Baldrige framework, have one or more key senior people participate as examiners in either their state or the Baldrige program. For example, Sister Mary

Jean Ryan, president and CEO, SSM Health Care, encouraged building internal resources by having at least one staff member formally trained in the Criteria for every one thousand employees. Saint Luke's has had seven high-profile employees become examiners. Doing this combines expertise in the Criteria and the assessment process with organizational knowledge to provide a ready resource to drive improvement. It also limits the organization's need for external consultants. Such experts are widely recognized and regarded in their organizations as change agents, ultimately embedding their Baldrige expertise in the organization.

Beyond developing internal experts, the approaches used for training others in the organization about the Baldrige Criteria and assessment process varied. SSM focused on building a strong cadre of internal capacity but not broad workforce training in Baldrige. As Sister Mary Jean said, "You don't use the Criteria every day; you use the feedback every day." At Bronson, Michele Serbenski trained the senior team and other managers in Baldrige by means of a course she calls "Baldrige 101." They spent time at every weekly management team meeting discussing the "how" questions in the Baldrige Criteria. Saint Luke's leaders trained all managers in the Criteria. At Mercy, Javon Bea personally gave Baldrige overviews to all four thousand employees. Baptist uses its internal corporate university to educate five hundred leaders quarterly about various topics, including the Baldrige Criteria, and also developed its Baptist Leadership Institute as a way for people to learn about Baptist's Baldrige journey.

Engage Senior Leadership

We have already mentioned the vital importance of leadership involvement in the Baldrige process. Senior leaders' involvement and ownership in application development drove a transition in the way the leadership team functioned in the organizations we studied and moved them into the Traction and Integration stages (2 and 3) of the journey. Conversely, lack of active involvement by senior leaders is one of the main reasons organizations stay in the project mode and never progress beyond Projects (stage 1). According to John Heer, president and CEO, North Mississippi Health Services, "You cannot delegate knowledge and expertise." Leaders' delegation of Baldrige, both in writing and follow-up on the feedback, is the primary reason organizations either lose or never attain Traction, in our experience.

Get Started Early

One of the most common misconceptions about the Baldrige process is that you should wait until you are "ready" to apply. No organization is ever "ready" to do an assessment. Sister Mary Jean is emphatic about that. "No one is ever ready. You have to start somewhere and you can only get better by getting your feedback report." Waiting for the ideal time to conduct an assessment is like waiting to be in perfect health and fitness before going for a physical—it misses the point entirely and, in all likelihood, will only result in worse outcomes in the long run. Delaying an assessment means delaying receipt of feedback that can be used to drive improvement. David Sjoberg at Baptist said an organization "…can start any time, from any place. You can be learning a lot by using self-assessment." Javon Bea's advice to those just getting started is: "Get involved in your state program; attend Quest and the regional conferences; and have a senior person become a 'Baldrige professor' in order to teach others."[8] Saint Luke's Sherry Marshall recommended using the state program to begin: "Had we not had the state program, we would not have progressed as fast." Diane Grillo, senior vice president and chief learning and communications officer, Robert Wood Johnson University Hospital at Hamilton, concurred: "Feedback from the state program was helpful."

Ensure Adequate Support and Resources

While resources always will be an issue for any organization, that shouldn't be a valid excuse for not doing a Baldrige assessment. Frank Sardone of Bronson said, "[Baldrige] doesn't need to be added work. It increases the efficiency and effectiveness of current work." Saint Luke's Sherry Marshall observed, "You'll spend to get results anyway. So why not use a method to reduce waste and make processes work efficiently and effectively that's been proven across sectors?" Mercy's Javon Bea summed it up: "'We don't have the resources' probably means 'We don't have the commitment to do Baldrige.'" When questioned about how Poudre Valley can afford to pursue Baldrige, Sonja Wulff, performance excellence manager, responds this way: "We can't afford not to because of our Leadership Team's focus on sustained improvement. You can't think of it in terms of cost because it's about how you do your business."

Paula Friedman explained how SSM uses their state and Baldrige award examiners as resources by acting as a "coach and counsel at the entity level. They help senior leaders monitor, interpret, and apply the Baldrige Criteria; serve as resources to managers to talk about Baldrige and linkage among Categories; and help with writing entity-level state applications. We use the Baldrige framework picture to help people understand the 'map' as a 'You Are Here' diagram. Examiners are recognized at our May leadership conference and allowed to use work time for participation in state and national programs."

Using external resources also can help. Bronson's Michele Serbenski said, "Looking back, if we had tapped into resources available from the Baldrige National Quality Program, we could have moved faster. Also, we might have gone to more conferences where recipients presented and we might have used the Baldrige Web site more."

Use All Available Input

A broad, cross-functional group of knowledgeable leaders is important to understand the linkages across the various categories in the Baldrige Criteria. Conversely, having limited representation across the breadth of the organization in the development of the application can undermine its accuracy and completeness. Participation in the application development builds buy-in as well. Writing team members generally are process owners or subject matter experts in the processes addressed in each category, but even broader involvement can be beneficial. In particular, physician involvement can be critical. At Robert Wood Johnson University Hospital at Hamilton, a handful of physician leaders were engaged at the same time as the senior team in application writing. That was expanded in later years with more physicians becoming involved. Baptist involved physicians in writing responses to Categories 1, 2, 3, and 5 for their applications and also has them participate in their annual strategic planning process. Saint Luke's had medical staff officers partner with their category writing teams and physicians also were involved in application writing at Mercy. All of this input and participation helped build momentum for the transformational journey.

Commit to Telling the Truth

An effective assessment requires absolute "truth-telling." This is not so much about ethics as about value. An application depicting an accurate view of the organization against the Baldrige Criteria will yield accurate and useful feedback. Organizations that find it difficult to describe their actual, rather than imagined, reality in an application are unlikely to develop any significant insights or to accept whatever valid feedback they do receive. This is why a strictly internal self-assessment approach can produce limited return on investment—the lack of frank evaluation leads to an overoptimistic, distorted view of performance. While developing internal expertise on the Baldrige Criteria can help alleviate this, most high-performing organizations value the unbiased, objective feedback they receive through external eyes.

There are several possible types of feedback, as shown in Figure 5.7.[9] There are two common causes for receiving useless feedback. It can be the result of an application that has incorrect or misleading information. Useless feedback can also result if the application is not sufficiently clear to allow the examiners to understand the organization's environment, approaches, and performance. The latter frequently occurs when an applicant writes seven disconnected "short stories"—essentially independent Categories 1 through 7—as opposed to a novel comprising seven intertwined chapters. Having useless feedback is a concern for the award programs (after all, they take customer satisfaction seriously and know that even a few inaccurate or confusing comments can be frustrating for applicants), and it negatively affects an organization's view of the value of the assessment process. Leaders who remind the organization that it's about getting better, not about receiving an award, can help to ensure the application reflects reality. In turn, this helps to ensure an accurate and actionable feedback report that can be used to drive improvement. Like for so many other things, the old saying, "garbage in, garbage out" is true for an assessment as well.

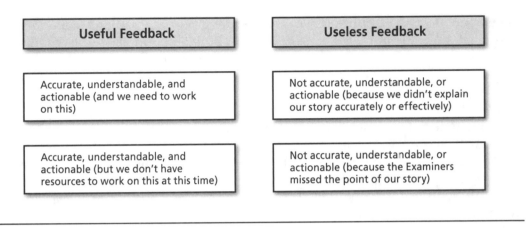

Figure 5.7 showing four types of feedback in a two-by-two arrangement:

Useful Feedback	Useless Feedback
Accurate, understandable, and actionable (and we need to work on this)	Not accurate, understandable, or actionable (because we didn't explain our story accurately or effectively)
Accurate, understandable, and actionable (but we don't have resources to work on this at this time)	Not accurate, understandable, or actionable (because the Examiners missed the point of our story)

Figure 5.7 Four types of feedback.

Take Action on the Insights and Feedback

The feedback report provides a good external view of your performance. It has very specific details that you can use to direct improvements," according to Mercy's Javon Bea. Rich Hastings of Saint Luke's says of his feedback reports, "OFIs are the best consulting I get all year." Priscilla Nuwash at Poudre Valley, observed, "When you ask for feedback, it's what you do with that information that gets you engagement." But it sometimes takes effort to understand the significance of the feedback because the report language is not prescriptive. It describes what the organization does well and not so well, but does not direct the organization toward any specific approach for improvement. SSM's Paula Friedman doesn't view this as a negative: "The non-prescriptive nature of the feedback is helpful. It provides for a strong dialogue in the organization. There's a fair amount of discussion about whether it's an application-writing deficit or an organizational deficit."

The Nature of Non-Prescriptive Feedback

The absence of prescriptive feedback is sometimes frustrating, but it is also liberating. The feedback tells you what to improve, but doesn't specifically direct you in how to do it. This leaves it up to the organization to decide the improvement approach that best meets their needs. For example, the feedback report may cite as a gap the absence of an approach to identify the requirements for all of the organization's key customer groups, including patients and the community. However, the feedback does not go beyond this to dictate how the organization should address this opportunity for improvement.

This is why the Baldrige Criteria are perfectly compatible with various improvement approaches ranging from Six Sigma to Lean to Plan-Do-Check-Act (PDCA). Any or all of these will be effective for improvement and problem solving within the Baldrige framework. For example, Sharp had a long history of using Lean Six Sigma before it began using Baldrige as a complement to its Sharp Experience initiative. Sharp also uses such tools as Rapid Action Project method, Kaizen Bursts, Change Acceleration Process, and Work-Out to drive improvement. Bronson uses PDCA as its primary improvement methodology, as does Mercy, which supplements that with Failure Modes and Effects Analysis to identify risks proactively. Along with PDCA, North Mississippi has long used the Care-Based Cost Management approach. Robert Wood Johnson University Hospital at Hamilton uses PDCA along with Six Sigma tools for root cause analyses and complex problems. Saint Luke's uses its own Design, Management, and Improvement Model, shown in Figure 5.8.

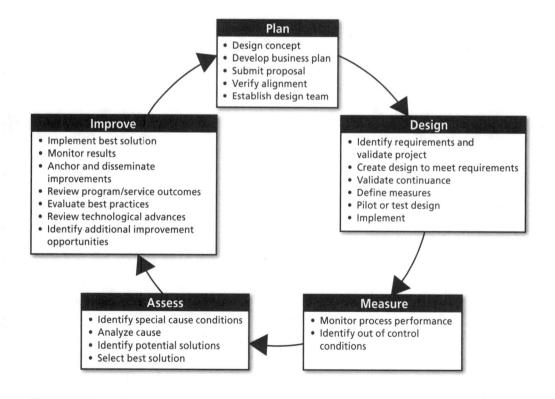

Figure 5.8 Design, management, and improvement model - Saint Luke's Hospital.[10]

KEY POINTS IN THIS CHAPTER

- Integrate the Baldrige assessment process into the leadership activities of the organization to create a learning and improvement culture.

- Perform repeated assessments to move from the Projects (stage 1) into Traction (stage 2) and beyond.

- Use both learning opportunities—"aha" moments during the writing of an application and the feedback report—to maximize the value of the assessment.

- The most common method for writing an application is to use category teams, but there are many ways to accomplish this.

- Develop internal expertise by sponsoring state or Baldrige examiners from within the organization.

- Assessments and feedback are most valuable if there is absolute "truth-telling."

6

Sensemaking

"What is necessary for sensemaking is a good story."

– Karl E. Weick, *Sensemaking in Organizations*[1]

Telling a "good story" through an accurate assessment document or application, capitalizing on learning during the assessment, analyzing and interpreting feedback, and implementing improvements based on the feedback can produce many benefits for any organization. A one-time assessment can be beneficial if the organization is prepared to accept and act upon some "brutal truth" observations about its operations and performance. The greatest value of assessments, however, comes from systematic repetition, typically in yearly cycles. This discipline enables organizational leaders to go deeper and deeper in making sense of their organization and the environment in which it operates. Combined with systematic execution on their insights and learning from feedback, this leads to higher performance and better results.

WHAT IS SENSEMAKING?

Organizations today are complex, and health care is certainly no exception. Leaders need a process to understand and manage the complexity—a way to view the organization, with all its interactions, priorities, and problems—as a holistic system. Sensemaking refers to the process of comprehending and interpreting this complexity. Sensemaking is the process by which leaders and others in the organization come to "understand and share understandings about such features of the organization as what it is about, what it does well and poorly, what the problems it faces are, and how it should resolve them."[2]

As the bridge between conducting assessments and execution of meaningful cultural change, sensemaking is essential for the assessment process to result in performance improvement and better results. All the organizations we interviewed experienced sensemaking as a step in the process. Some were keenly aware and realized exactly when and how they made sense of their organization. Others recognized sensemaking as a distinct senior leadership activity in hindsight, as they reflected back on critical success factors in their transformational journey.

THE OUTCOMES OF SENSEMAKING... WHAT DO WE MEAN BY "SENSE"?

Explaining the power and the value of the assessment process, the leaders we interviewed consistently reported these outcomes of sensemaking. Through repeated cycles of assessment, they achieved the following:

- They developed a clearer picture of what was most important for their organization, including its vision, values, and mission; its key customers, their needs and expectations; and its competitive situation, including its strategic challenges and advantages.

- They built a comprehensive understanding of their organization as a system of interdependent processes that they could design, manage, and improve to accomplish what was most important for their organization. They became process literate.

- They recognized that key processes in a health care organization include not only the processes required for delivery of health care services, but also leadership and management processes such as leadership communication, culture building, strategic and operational planning, customer and workforce engagement, and performance measurement. They understood that positive results come about as a direct consequence of the design, management, and improvement of the organization's processes, and they developed awareness of which processes offered them highest leverage to improve performance.

- They understood that by focusing, aligning, and integrating all the organization's processes and people, and managing the organization as a system, they could "hardwire" high-performance expectations so that high performance would inevitably result from system design and management.

Sherry Marshall, vice president of quality, Saint Luke's Health System, captured the essence of sensemaking when she explained why Saint Luke's chose Baldrige as a business model: "The Baldrige Categories focus on processes that every organization needs to perform extremely well to get the outcomes they want. If you perform these well, it drives results you want to achieve. So it made good common business sense."

ONE ASSESSMENT CYCLE, THREE OPPORTUNITIES FOR SENSEMAKING

Sensemaking begins with "a good story"—a clear and accurate statement describing the current state of your organization against the Baldrige framework. By "telling its story" through an assessment document, an organization sets the stage for an objective evaluation of its performance. Ken Davis, MD, former chief medical officer at North Mississippi Medical Center, observed that Baldrige is a "template for transforming an organization. What you learn can provide you the mechanism for change." The assessment process affords leaders and managers a broad and comprehensive view of their organization and its performance as a basis for decision making and action—a chance to look at their organization and it's performance in ways they never have before. The Criteria's Socratic format—more than 200 questions in all—fosters introspection and learning. The simple act of responding to the questions in the Criteria, putting facts on paper and organizing these facts into an assessment document, builds new understanding of the organization. Sensemaking is an ongoing process of deepening understanding, typically through repeated cycles of developing assessment documents, reviewing feedback, and implementing improvement initiatives that enable the organization to progress through the five stages of the journey.

Within one cycle of assessment, sensemaking occurs at three principal points:

1. When responding to Criteria questions while drafting the assessment document

2. When analyzing and interpreting the feedback, probing the meaning and relevance of each comment, as well as other components of the feedback report, and determining the implications for action

3. When designing and implementing process changes and measuring their impact on desired results

During the process of responding to the Criteria and drafting the assessment document, organization members repeatedly experience what we refer to as "aha" moments—sudden insights into improvement opportunities as they recognized that their organization was unable to respond appropriately to the Criteria questions, or in some cases at all. Michele Serbenski, vice president of performance excellence, Bronson Healthcare Group, recommends starting assessments with the questions in the Organizational Profile. "The key first step," says Serbenski," is to fill in the Organizational Profile. If leaders can't agree on who the customers are, there's probably not a process for determining the organization's customers in Category 3." Right away, the organization has an improvement opportunity—design of a process to identify key customers—with significance for other key decision-making processes in the organization such as marketing, business development, and resource allocation. Rich Hastings, president and CEO, Saint

Luke's Health System, describes the experience of sensemaking during Saint Luke's first assessment cycle this way. "We essentially wrote our own OFIs [opportunities for improvement] in the process of writing the application." Likewise, Sister Mary Jean Ryan, president and CEO, SSM Health Care, says they "got results just by going through the Criteria. Just looking at the questions, we learned from that."

The second principal opportunity for sensemaking comes with the feedback report. Leaders and others analyze and interpret the feedback to gain insight into strengths and, in particular, gaps that point to needed process improvements. The feedback report helps leaders and others in two somewhat different ways. It may validate insights that developed during drafting of the assessment document, confirming what leaders and others already know or suspect. Second, it generates new and actionable insights, opportunities that leaders and others have not been aware of or whose significance they have not understood. Sister Mary Jean recalled the impact of on SSM leaders when they received feedback on the mission statement that essentially said, "This is what you say about yourself, but we can't find any evidence of it in your documents, which we studied for hundreds of hours."' One SSM feedback report described "inconsistencies in communication and complaint management," says Sister Mary Jean, "and we developed a consistent approach to both of these." Another gap, she recalls, related to the workforce: "You say that human resources are your most important asset, but you don't cover them in your strategic plan." She saw the disconnect—the organization's failure to link its vision and values with the processes of strategy development and human resource management—and the organization took action. By making sense of her organization in this way, she was able to lead her team to a major breakthrough in their performance.

The third principal opportunity for sensemaking occurs when leaders and others address opportunities identified through assessment by developing and implementing process changes and measuring the impact of those changes on performance. According to Sherry Marshall of Saint Luke's, "The feedback is what we have tangibly to provide better care, function more efficiently, succeed in our market with payers (since payers want to send their patients where satisfaction and outcomes are best). Feedback is a blueprint for success." Marshall said that for Saint Luke's, feedback was a key mechanism to gain insight because it enabled them "to reaffirm that we were improving annually from the changes we were making."

HOW THE ASSESSMENT PROCESS FOSTERS SENSEMAKING

Understanding and Applying the Criteria and Evaluation Factors

Sensemaking begins for Baldrige applicants when they seek to understand and respond appropriately to the various questions in the Criteria. It develops as they perceive "aha" moments in terms of their gaps against the Criteria questions and again as they begin to understand the meaning of the various comments within their feedback report. At the simplest level, the Criteria questions help leaders identify critical gaps—by revealing processes, for example, that the organization lacks and must design. To illustrate, the Criteria question "How do you select, collect, and ensure the effective use of key comparative data and information to support operational and strategic decision making?" may trigger recognition of the gap in the organization's knowledge of competitive performance and signal the need for process development or improvement. Diane Grillo, senior vice president and chief learning and communications officer, Robert Wood Johnson University Hospital at Hamilton, explained, "Once we really understood the Criteria, we used them to establish processes and structures, for example, for determining and listening to all our customer groups."

Understanding the evaluation factors used by Examiners as their basis for evaluation and feedback contributes to sensemaking. Figure 6.1 shows a representative feedback comment related to deployment, a process evaluation factor.[3] The feedback comment makes the point that the organization's process for identifying skills and building competencies is not fully deployed across all key segments of the workforce. It further indicates why this is important, given the key role volunteers play in the delivery of services in this particular organization.

Understanding the evaluation factors, and applying that understanding in reviewing feedback and planning action, helps leaders gain a deeper and more precise understanding of their organization's process and results strengths and gaps, and appreciate specific leverage points for change. Over time, leaders familiar with the evaluation factors consider them explicitly during preparation of the assessment document, a practice that enables them to recognize improvement opportunities right away and drive change.

There are four evaluation factors each for processes and for results (Figure 6.2). As organizations mature, they move from putting systematic processes in place, to

Evaluation Factor	Key Questions Used in Evaluation	Sample Feedback Comment	Implications of the Feedback Comment
Deployment	• Is the approach used in all locations? • Is it used by all appropriate personnel, work units, departments? • Is it used consistently?	While Arroyo Fresco identifies skills and characteristics for its staff in four competency areas, it is not evident how skills and characteristics are identified for its volunteer workforce, who are closely integrated members of the clinical microsystem delivery model and whose actions contribute to Arroyo Fresco's performance achievement of its vision, mission, and values.	Volunteers perform significant work functions for the applicant in health care delivery, but the applicant has not deployed its tools for evaluating and developing its workforce to these volunteers. The action Arroyo Fresco should consider is to apply its tools for identifying and developing skills in its four competency areas to its volunteers.

Figure 6.1 Evaluation factor reveals improvement opportunity.

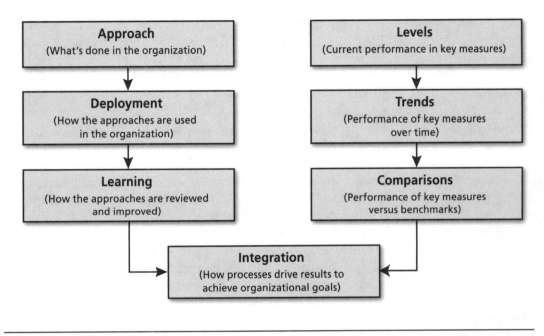

Figure 6.2 Integration: The intersection of process and results.

deploying them, to reviewing them (and formulating ideas and action plans for improvement). Similarly, as organizations mature, they move from establishing performance levels, to accumulating performance data that demonstrates trends, to realizing the importance of comparing their levels and trends to the performance of others. Approaches become more systematic; deployment becomes more widespread; and more organizational learning and improvement of processes occurs. At the same time, more positive results are achieved, with improved performance relative to the past and to others. Integration marks the point at which these improved results represent a direct outcome of process development, deployment, and improvement driven by deep knowledge of the organization's performance.

The Assessment Cycle Drives Alignment and Integration

Over time, cycles of assessment provide focus and drive alignment and integration across the organization. Organizations in the early stages of the journey (that is, Reaction, stage 0, or Projects, stage 1) are generally struggling to address short-term issues, many of which are recurring problems, and typically fail to appreciate the importance of these concepts. As organizations begin assessments and enter the Traction stage, they realize the importance of ensuring that what is most important to their organization is reflected in key organizational goals and objectives, and that these goals and objectives are addressed in the actions of everyone in the workforce. When the strategic plan is driven by and supports the organization's vision and values, and when the plan is deployed to lower levels and tied to employee performance expectations, then strategic plans become more than binders on a shelf. They become the glue that holds everyone accountable for progress toward the vision. That represents alignment—an intertwining of objectives and actions across and throughout the organization. For example, Priscilla Nuwash, director of process improvement, Poudre Valley Health System, explained how Poudre Valley used its Baldrige feedback to ensure that all other plans linked to and flowed from its strategic planning process: "This was something that changed after our first site visit. If you have an annual planning cycle, set it up and arrange it so all steps are in sync. It took us about eighteen months to get everything rearranged so that it would cascade. This was a big OFI from our site visit."

High-performing organizations go beyond alignment to integration, linking all major processes and their related measures together to form a holistic system; for example, the outputs of one process are used as an input to others. This linkage is fostered by a high degree of collaboration across departments, locations, and work units (often including outsourced partners) that in turn drives knowledge sharing and innovation. For example, the Baldrige health care recipients are able to demonstrate how their work is organized around their most important processes, how employee performance is evaluated based on clearly defined measures that link to and support strategic objectives, and how leaders regularly review progress against these measures. Priscilla Nuwash summarized Poudre Valley's learning in this regard: "The Baldrige Criteria challenge you to look at the entire system."

Understanding Critical Linkages

Feedback comments focus not only on the Criteria and evaluation factors. They also highlight critical linkages, and such feedback, OFIs in particular, helps leaders drive alignment and integration. For example, Paula Friedman, corporate vice president of strategy and systems improvement, SSM Health Care, said that the Baldrige process helped SSM clarify and explain to people about the mission and how it was deployed. Typically, feedback that highlights critical linkages—whether the comment presents an opportunity or a strength—focuses on the importance of linking such elements as the organization's strategic objectives, the requirements of patients and other stakeholders, and the design, deployment, and management of key processes.

Mercy Health System's 2007 Feedback Report contained the following comment on the organization's strength related to workforce support and engagement: "Job sharing for partners, work-to-retire option, flexible work scheduling, and compressed work week options provide benefits to partners that contribute to exceptional partner satisfaction and low turnover rates."[4] The comment showcases how the organization has effectively linked the following elements to drive superior performance:

- Who makes up the workforce

- What the workforce expects of the organization

- How the organization determines what drives workforce satisfaction and engagement

- How it addresses those drivers through its approaches

- What performance it achieves in key areas as a result

Figure 6.3 outlines how the Criteria questions lead to feedback about linkages and can help leaders, during assessment or in feedback review, to recognize those linkages.

Baldrige Criteria Question	Mercy Health System's Response (partial)[5]
What is your workforce profile? (from the Organizational Profile Criteria, P.1a)	Mercy Health System (MHS) employs a diverse workforce of over 3,700 staff partners as summarized in Figure P-3. The average age of MHS partners is 42 years and the average length of employment is 7.5 years. The employee composition is 7% minority, which reflects community demographics. MHS has a bargaining unit located at one clinic, which was in place at acquisition, and its members comprise 4% of the workforce.

Figure P-3, Staff Breakdown by Groups/Segments

Groups/Segments	Number (Percent)			
Staff Partners/LG	3,605 (97%)		111 (3%)	
Male/Female	595 (16%)		3,121 (84%)	
Union/Non Union	165 (4%)		3,551 (96%)	
Education	High School 1,349 (36%)	College 1,770 (48%)		Graduate 597 (16%)
Positions	RNs 711 (19%)	MDs/DOs 275 (7%)	Tech/Prof 1,153 (31%)	Other 1,577 (43%)
Ethnicity	Causasian 3,447 (93%)	Black 57 (2%)	Hispanic 84 (2%)	Other 128 (3%)

As needed, MHS contracts for temporary staff with staffing agencies. A number of contract labor service agreements are ongoing, such as those for select housekeeping and security services. Mercy Health also has an association of volunteers serving Mercy Hospital Janeville and Mercy Harvard Hospital with 905 active members. The key requirements and expectations of the MHS workforce include: a safe and healthy work place; competitive compensation and benefits; development and career mobility; effective communication; and involvement and recognition.

Physicians are essential MHS collaborators in improving clinical outcomes. A key MHS strategy is partnering with physicians through its employment model. MHS employs 275 physicians, 78% of its medical staff. MHS collaborates with non-employed, privileged physicians through its medical staff committee structure and credentialing process.

Figure 6.3   The Criteria uncover key linkages.   *(Continued)*

Baldrige Criteria Question	Mercy Health System's Response (partial)[5]
How do you determine the factors that affect workforce engagement? (from Item 5.1a)	The Culture of Excellence Steering Committee and the Human Resource (HR) Planning Committee perform analyses, such as correlation and salience, on system-level partner feedback and indicators to determine factors affecting partner engagement and satisfaction. Requirements and processes to meet and exceed requirements are incorporated into the HR Plan and approved by Executive Council.
	While the factors may vary in importance for different workforce groups and segments, the process used to determine them is the same. Key partner feedback data and indicators are segmented by job type, core service, and demographics to support improvement efforts for various workforce groups and segments. The annual partner survey, a primary formal feedback tool, is segmented by length of service, service category, age, gender, ethnicity, location, and position type. Analysis is prioritized in the HR Plan.
	Since 2004, MHS has participated in the Great Place to Work Institute survey (100 BEST) to identify and benchmark key factors of staff engagement, satisfaction, and motivation. Participation in this process provides MHS additional segmented feedback. In 2006, MHS began administering an American Medical Group Association (AMGA) satisfaction survey for employed physician partners. MHS informally collects additional inputs to validate factors affecting workforce engagement and satisfaction through two-way communication processes, such as partner forums and VP luncheons. HR committees also evaluate and monitor specific factors identified to affect engagement and satisfaction. These HR committees use various tools, such as tailored surveys, exit and stay interviews, focus groups, and work teams to collect, analyze, and improve workforce engagement and satisfaction.
How do you support your workforce via policies, services and benefits? How are these tailored to the needs of a diverse workforce and different workforce groups and segments? 5.2b(2)	MHS offers comprehensive policies, services and benefits to: support partners from the day of hire to retirement; meet individual and family needs; and assist partners while at work and home. The HR department analyzes feedback from formal and informal sources, including surveys, idea programs, and focus groups to support diverse workforce needs. These analyses help determine system-wide and tailored policy, services, and benefit opportunities. Also, the HR staff visit departments through monthly House Calls to assess the value of these programs and to solicit suggestions. Customized benefits developed as results of these processes have included: on-site concierge services; adoption assistance; a lactation accommodation policy; and wellness fairs tailored for female partners. Policies include flexible work arrangements, work-to-retire program, and leave sharing donation for ill partners. Tailored services include the Safe Handling Program, childcare resource and referral service and the Employee Assistance Program. These policies, service, and benefits cater to a diverse workforce, particularly women, who represent over 80% of partners and mature workers, a growing percentage of the workforce. In 2006, MHS was recognized by Working Mothers and by AARP for its efforts to meet the varying needs of its workforce.

Figure 6.3 The Criteria uncover key linkages.   *(Continued)*

(Continued)

Baldrige Criteria Question	Mercy Health System's Response (partial)[5]
What are your current levels and trends in key measures of workforce engagement...? (from Item 7.4a)	MHS ranks in the 96th percentile for *Feeling Valued* and 95th percentile for *Overall Satisfaction*. AMGA benchmarking data provides percentile raking based on top-box responses only. Physician satisfaction ranks above the AMGA 95th percentile. Culture of Excellence improvements, benefit enhancements, and leadership development have enabled MHS to maintain top-decile levels in partner satisfaction.

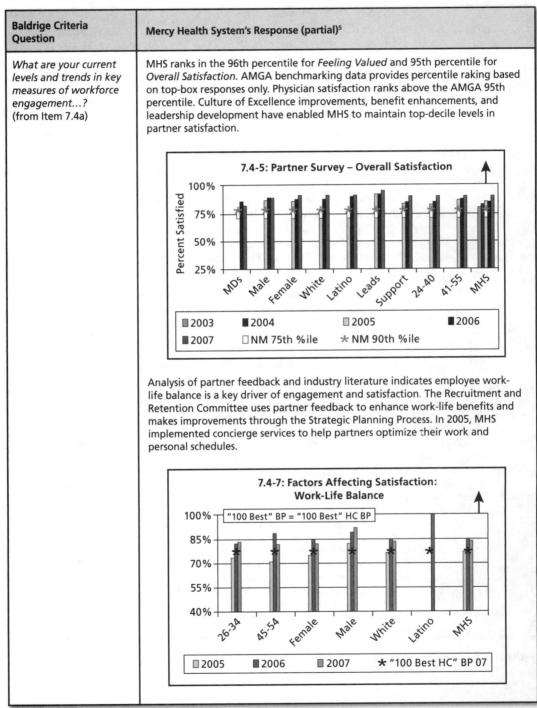

Analysis of partner feedback and industry literature indicates employee work-life balance is a key driver of engagement and satisfaction. The Recruitment and Retention Committee uses partner feedback to enhance work-life benefits and makes improvements through the Strategic Planning Process. In 2005, MHS implemented concierge services to help partners optimize their work and personal schedules.

Figure 6.3 The Criteria uncover key linkages.

SENSEMAKING AND THE JOURNEY: THE VALUE OF REPEATED ASSESSMENTS

Understanding the Criteria and using them to gain insight into and then improve the organization as a system, while beneficial from the start, typically requires repeated assessments. According to John Heer, president and CEO, North Mississippi Health Services, "It took a while to learn the lingo and understand how to use non-prescriptive Criteria. At first, we were clueless until we got the feedback. Once we started getting feedback, wow, maybe we're not as good as we thought. Once we had a site visit, we started looking at the tiny details. It took about three applications to get to this point." While the first assessment generates insights that point to obvious gaps and can be used for immediate improvement, systematic repetition of assessment over several cycles is required to achieve maximum value from the process. At SSM Health Care Paula Friedman related, "It took until we were close to receiving the award before we really understood" how the Criteria and process could transform the organization. David Sjoberg, Baptist Hospital's vice president of strategic services, also confirmed that for Baptist "the year before winning (the award) was the biggest light bulb year. By then we had listened and understood."

Repeated assessments and a multi-year journey are typical. First, the opportunities recognized during assessment and feedback review cannot be accomplished at once, since many require sequencing or staging. Faced with a process design opportunity, the organization has to design the process and test it first, then deploy it and link it to other processes. In addition, there's a limit to what an organization can address at once time. Resources, including organizational time, energy, and attention, are limited. Effective leaders set priorities to focus the organizations on the most critical gaps and opportunities. As CEO, David Spong led two Boeing divisions to become Baldrige recipients—Boeing Global Mobility Division (formerly Airlift and Tankers) in 1998 and Logistics Support Systems (formerly Aerospace Support) in 2003. He reported that Baldrige feedback reports are rich with accurate, important, and useful feedback, and organizational leaders must determine what parts of the feedback represent a "priority now."

Sensemaking Develops Process Literacy

One of the most important outcomes of sensemaking is the development of process literacy. A critical business competency, process literacy involves the following:

- Understanding the full scope of processes required to deliver value to patients and stakeholders

- Appreciating how these processes are linked or interdependent (and managing them as a system)

- Recognizing the causal relationship between processes—their development, deployment, management, and improvement—and the organization's results

The Baldrige Criteria, specifically the questions in the process Criteria (Categories 1-6), bring to leaders' attention some thirty high-level processes required for high performance (Figure 6.4). The non-prescriptive "how" questions that predominate in Categories 1-6 help leaders determine what processes are in place in their organization, and what must be designed, deployed, and linked.

Process Categories	High-Level Critical Processes
Category 1: Leadership	Senior Leader Direction-Setting and Culture Development Senior Leader Creation of Organizational Sustainability Senior Leader Communication with and Engagement of Workforce Senior Leader Review of Organizational Performance Organizational Accountability Leadership and Governance Improvement Legal and Ethical Behavior Societal Responsibilities Support of Key Communities and Community Health
Category 2: Strategic Planning	Strategy Development Strategy Deployment
Category 3: Customer Focus	Determination of Service Offerings and Support Patient and Stakeholder Culture Development Patient and Stakeholder Listening Complaint Management Determination of Patient and Stakeholder Satisfaction/Dissatisfaction and Engagement Analysis and Use of Patient and Stakeholder Data
Category 4: Measurement, Analysis, and Knowledge Management	Performance Measurement Performance Analysis and Review Performance Improvement Data/Information Quality and Availability Knowledge Management Information Resources and Technology Management
Category 5: Workforce Focus	Motivation and Engagement Workforce and Leader Development Workforce Engagement/Satisfaction Determination Workforce Capability and Capacity Workplace Health, Safety, and Security Workforce Support
Category 6: Process Management	Work System Design Determination of Key Processes Work Process Design Work Process Management Work Process Improvement

Figure 6.4 The scope of key organizational processes.

The Enterprise Model of Sharp HealthCare illustrates process literacy in a high-performing organization (Figure 6.5). Central to Sharp's performance are the organization's Enterprise Work Systems, the ten key work systems that deliver value to patients. Sharp's key work systems span the continuum of care, providing all basic patient care services. The Enterprise Model captures and reflects the understanding of Sharp leaders that the performance of these work systems is influenced by suppliers and inputs, as well as by other linked organizational processes on which the key work systems depend. Sharp's key support processes are shown as "enabling" processes that underpin the core work of clinical care. The governance, leadership, and planning Systems frame the enterprise model from above. The Enterprise Model can be viewed as a high-level picture of the organizational system Sharp leaders manage and improve to move the organization toward its vision of being the "best place to work, practice medicine, and receive care, and ultimately the best health system in the universe."

Though not shown in the diagram, Sharp leaders have further defined the key processes that make up each work system and must be measured, managed, and improved for each system: screening, admission/registration, assessment/diagnosis, discharge/education.

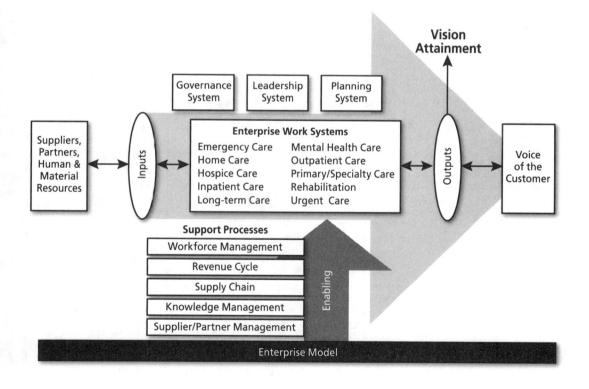

Figure 6.5 Enterprise model – Sharp HealthCare.[6]

Sensemaking Drives Organizational Maturity

Figure 6.6 depicts how organizations that effectively use assessments over multiple cycles might progress in terms of the Baldrige evaluation factors for processes (that is, approach, deployment, learning, and integration) or results. As an organization matures, an evolution in culture takes place: the questions leaders ask and the conversations that occur change. Leaders shift from attributing blame (asking, for example, "Who messed up?") to focusing on performance of their operational processes (asking, for example, "Why did this process not perform as expected?"). Conversations transform from the tactical (for example, "What do we do to fix the problems we have today?") to a long-term view (for example, "How do these initiatives fit with our long-term strategy?").

Evaluation Factor	Stages 0 and 1 "Early Efforts"	Stage 2 "Developing Efforts"	Stages 3 and 4 "Advanced Efforts"
Approach	The organization's approaches are not repeatable, nor are they based on use of reliable data and information (that is, approaches are random, not systematic). In other cases, approaches are not in place.	There is evidence of some systematic approaches that address basic organizational needs (that is, approaches are linked to the factors presented in the Organizational Profile).	Approaches are systematic (that is, they are managed using data and information, are repeatable and have the opportunity for evaluation, improvement, and learning built-in) and their inputs and/or outputs are integrated with other work units and processes.
Deployment	Not all work units use the approaches or use them consistently, hindering progress towards goals.	All appropriate work units use the approach, although some work units are in early stages of use.	All work units that need to use the approach use it consistently, resulting in the opportunity for improvement of the approach and for organizational learning.
Learning	The organization generally reacts to problems, with no proactive identification of improvement opportunities.	There is evidence of the beginning of a systematic approach used to evaluate and improve key processes and some sharing of organizational learning.	Innovations, best practices, and learning identified externally or developed in one process are used to improve other processes. Learning is embedded as a regular part of the daily work.
Integration	There is no alignment of approaches (that is, no consistency of plans and approaches across the organization to support its overall goals), or alignment primarily is achieved through joint problem solving.	Approaches are in the early stages of alignment with basic organizational needs (that is, linked to and addressing the factors presented in the Organizational Profile).	All of the individual components of the organization's performance management system operate as a fully interconnected unit (that is, are integrated).

Figure 6.6 The continuum of progress: How organizations mature. *(Continued)*

(Continued)

Evaluation Factor	Stages 0 and 1 "Early Efforts"	Stage 2 "Developing Efforts"	Stages 3 and 4 "Advanced Efforts"
Results	Levels and some trends are tracked for some key indicators, with widely varying outcomes.	Levels and trends (over several years) demonstrate positive performance in some key areas; some external comparisons are used and performance may be favorable against some of these.	Levels and trends (3 to 5 years or more) demonstrate high and sustained performance in many key areas; comparisons indicate performance leadership in many areas within the industry and some benchmark performance as well; valid performance projections indicate sustainability of the results.
Overall Perspective of Performance	The organization can provide responses to many, but not all, Criteria questions. There is an early indication of some positive results, but many gaps in approaches and results are evident.	The organization clearly demonstrates how it addresses the Criteria evaluation factors (ADLI and LeTCI), including alignment and some integration, with some positive results derived from its approaches.	The organization clearly demonstrates systematic, effectively deployed and integrated processes that have been subjected to cycles of review and improvement. Benchmark leadership in many processes and related results is evident.

Figure 6.6 The continuum of progress: How organizations mature.

Baldrige and state feedback reports provide leaders with insight into their organization's maturity by means of the scoring band descriptors. The 1,000-point scoring scale for the Baldrige Criteria is divided into eight scoring bands. Each of these has a paragraph—the scoring band descriptor—that provides a high-level view of the applicant's overall performance. State and Baldrige feedback reports begin with the scoring band descriptor to provide an overall context for the feedback that follows. The scoring bands serve as a maturity index, enabling organizations to plot their progress from assessment to assessment. Some organizations proactively use the scoring band descriptors to identify broad improvement initiatives and targets for their next assessment cycle. Although scores are not published for recipients of the Baldrige Award, data from the Baldrige program indicate that award recipients typically fall in the upper range of band 5 or higher.[7]

		Sensemaking on a Macro Scale – The Baldrige Scoring Band Descriptors[8]
Band Score	**Band Number**	**PROCESS Scoring Band Descriptors**
0–150	1	The organization demonstrates early stages of developing and implementing approaches to the basic Criteria requirements, with deployment lagging and inhibiting progress. Improvement efforts are a combination of problem solving and an early general improvement orientation.
151–200	2	The organization demonstrates effective, systematic approaches responsive to the basic requirements of the Criteria, but some areas or work units are in the early stages of deployment. The organization has developed a general improvement orientation that is forward-looking.
201–260	3	The organization demonstrates effective, systematic approaches responsive to the basic requirements of most Criteria Items, although there are still areas or work units in the early stages of deployment. Key processes are beginning to be systematically evaluated and improved.
261–320	4	The organization demonstrates effective, systematic approaches responsive to the overall requirements of the Criteria, but deployment may vary in some areas or work units. Key processes benefit from fact-based evaluation and improvement, and approaches are being aligned with organizational needs.
321–370	5	The organization demonstrates effective, systematic, well-deployed approaches responsive to the overall requirements of most Criteria Items. The organization demonstrates a fact-based, systematic evaluation and improvement process and organizational learning, including innovation, that result in improving the effectiveness and efficiency of key processes.
371–430	6	The organization demonstrates refined approaches responsive to the multiple requirements of the Criteria. These approaches are characterized by the use of key measures, good deployment, and evidence of innovation in most areas. Organizational learning, including innovation and sharing of best practices, is a key management tool, and integration of approaches with organizational needs is evident.
431–480	7	The organization demonstrates refined approaches responsive to the multiple requirements of the Criteria Items. It also demonstrates innovation, excellent deployment, and good-to-excellent use of measures in most areas. Good-to-excellent integration is evident, with organizational analysis, learning through innovation, and sharing of best practices as key management strategies.
481–550	8	The organization demonstrates outstanding approaches focused on innovation. Approaches are fully deployed and demonstrate excellent, sustained use of measures. There is excellent integration of approaches with organizational needs. Organizational analysis, learning through innovation, and sharing of best practices are pervasive.

Sensemaking on a Macro Scale – The Baldrige Scoring Band Descriptors[8]		
Band Score	**Band Number**	**RESULTS Scoring Band Descriptors**
0–125	1	Results are reported for a few areas of importance to the accomplishment of the organization's mission, but they generally lack trend and comparative data.
126–170	2	Results are reported for several areas of importance to the Criteria requirements and the accomplishment of the organization's mission. Some of these results demonstrate good performance levels. The use of comparative and trend data is in the early stages.
171–210	3	Results address many areas of importance to the accomplishment of the organization's mission, with good performance being achieved. Comparative and trend data are available for some of these important results areas, and some beneficial trends are evident.
211–255	4	Results address some key customer/stakeholder, market, and process requirements, and they demonstrate good relative performance against relevant comparisons. There are no patterns of adverse trends or poor performance in areas of importance to the Criteria requirements and the accomplishment of the organization's mission.
256–300	5	Results address most key customer/stakeholder, market, and process requirements, and they demonstrate areas of strength against relevant comparisons and/or benchmarks. Improvement trends and/or good performance are reported for most areas of importance to the Criteria requirements and the accomplishment of the organization's mission.
301–345	6	Results address most key customer/stakeholder, market, and process requirements, as well as many action plan requirements. Results demonstrate beneficial trends in most areas of importance to the Criteria requirements and the accomplishment of the organization's mission, and the organization is an industry* leader in some results areas.
346–390	7	Results address most key customer/stakeholder, market, process, and action plan requirements and include projections of future performance. Results demonstrate excellent organizational performance levels and some industry[1] leadership. Results demonstrate sustained beneficial trends in most areas of importance to the Criteria requirements and the accomplishment of the organization's mission.
391–450	8	Results fully address key customer/stakeholder, market, process, and action plan requirements and include projections of future performance. Results demonstrate excellent organizational performance levels, as well as national and world leadership. Results demonstrate sustained beneficial trends in all areas of importance to the Criteria requirements and the accomplishment of the organization's mission.

* Industry refers to other organizations performing substantially the same functions, thereby facilitating direct comparisons.

Sensemaking Fosters System Thinking

Sensemaking focuses on the interdependencies in an organization, so it requires seeing the organization as a system, which is the basis for the Baldrige framework. It goes well beyond just interpretation of the feedback report. It includes comprehending the connections between processes ("integration" in the language of Baldrige evaluation factors). As organizations mature, assessment team members responding to the questions in the Criteria realize more and more the interrelationships that exist across the Baldrige categories. This is a form of systems thinking—"a conceptual framework…to make the full patterns clearer, and to help us see how to change them effectively."[9] As stated by Saint Luke's Rich Hastings, "You don't take one particular issue or finding; it's how well a system is working."

Organizations generally start developing process literacy at lower-level (usually functional) processes. This helps to get the organization beyond the "doing projects" Stage. But systems thinking demands more—it requires an understanding of how all the organization's core processes link together to produce results. Process focus and literacy therefore are important factors in "connecting the dots." The Key Themes section within a Baldrige feedback report—two or three pages of bullet-point statements at the beginning of the report—is an important tool for understanding linkages and the patterns in an organization's performance, for promoting a system view. The "executive summary" of the feedback report, the Key Themes represent the most important strengths or gaps in the applicant's processes and results. Themes are high-level comments that consolidate and incorporate observations from feedback about specific processes. Cross-cutting observations, they provide evidence of patterns—both positive and negative—in the organization's performance.

Sensemaking Builds Team Learning

A strong culture differentiates recipients of the Baldrige Award from most other organizations. Sensemaking can build organizational culture—knowledge, beliefs, and behaviors—if a critical mass of employees from all functions, locations, and levels is involved. Together these employees build, communicate, and live a common, consistent understanding of the organization and its culture. There is a palpable, common sense of mission, vision, and values that permeates throughout the organization that drives decisions and actions by all employees. The interaction to build this mutual understanding can be considered a form of "team learning," one of Peter Senge's core disciplines for building a learning organization.[10] Senge identified three critical dimensions for team learning that also apply to building organizational understanding in the context of the Baldrige process:

1. *The need to think insightfully about complex issues* – The complex interrelationships in any organization are reflected both in the Baldrige Criteria questions and in the feedback report. Staff involved in writing the assessment must be able to listen to opinions and insights from others, as well as express their own views and understanding, so that they use the feedback and their own observations to develop common agreement on improving all facets of the organization's performance.

Gaps in Planning: A Key Theme

The following Key Theme from the Arroyo Fresco case study describes the multiple gaps evident in the organization's plans to address areas of strategic importance. Although the feedback comment gives credit for the fact that Arroyo Fresco's planning processes addresses some of its key strategic challenges, it points out areas of strategic concern, listed in the Organizational Profile, that do not appear to be addressed in the application. Like all Baldrige feedback, it is not prescriptive. It's left up to the applicant to decide how—or if—it will address the issue:

"Although Arroyo Fresco focuses on several key strategic challenges through its Strategic Planning Process, action plan deployment, and performance reviews, there is little evidence of approaches to address other key challenges, success factors, changes, and customer/market segments. These include identifying additional sources of revenue, competing for key staff, and meeting the unique needs of certain populations (that is, Native Americans, veterans, and patients from all income strata). Without systematic approaches to articulate and address all the important factors, challenges, and segments described in the Organizational Profile, it may be difficult for Arroyo Fresco to ensure that it creates and balances value for all patients, customers, and stakeholders."

2. *The need for innovative, coordinated action* – Before execution on the feedback can take place, the organization needs to develop a rationale for why the action is needed. By building on their common insight, participants in the assessment process can construct meaning to help identify possible improvement actions.

3. *The role that team members play on other teams* – Assessment team members involved in application development and subsequent activities typically also have responsibility for communicating information about the Baldrige process within their sphere of action and influence. This provides reinforcement of the assessment process, helping to move it beyond the Projects stage.

The Baldrige recipients used various techniques to build understanding in their organizations. Several provided overviews of the Baldrige Criteria and process to the organization. Others trained managers in the Baldrige Criteria and had them in turn cascade this learning down throughout the organization. Poudre Valley's Learn and Lead program for all managers is a good example of this approach. Most ensured their communications regarding Baldrige and the motivations for developing an application were clear. All used some form of category teams—usually cross-functional—to help develop the application. In most cases these teams also were involved in subsequent execution. Gradually, these initiatives helped build a common understanding of why the organization was using Baldrige and how the assessment process was driving change.

HOW TO MAXIMIZE THE VALUE OF ASSESSMENTS

While short-term gains are in themselves valuable, it generally takes repeated cycles for organizations to understand the Criteria and their feedback fully, and to recognize and take action on all the implications for improvement. This leads to a critical question: How can an organization speed up the sensemaking process to make the most progress in the shortest time? The Baldrige health care recipients we interviewed and other applicant organizations provided some "if we had to start over again" insights:

- Understand the Criteria and the evaluation factors

- Explore and address surprises and unexpected feedback

- Understand the role of experts and build internal capabilities

- Build knowledge of recipient practices

- Use all the learning and (relevant and accurate) feedback

- Seek additional feedback cycles

Understand the Criteria and Evaluation Factors

It takes time to understand the Criteria, the evaluation factors, and the linkages across categories that are as important as the category questions themselves. "Connecting the dots"—understanding the linkages across categories—is an ability that differentiates high-performing organizations, and typically results from several cycles of assessment. Frank Sardone, Bronson Healthcare Group president and CEO, advises, "Don't be intimidated by the Criteria. People read them and throw their hands up. The Criteria seem esoteric at first. Look at other applications. It took me several applications and rounds of feedback to 'get' it." Saint Luke's Sherry Marshall described her top three challenges this way: "First, understanding the Criteria. We had to drown leaders in their categories, then teach about linkages, then back to categories. Second is understanding the concept of alignment. It took a couple years to get this, moving from customer requirements and using alignment in the planning process, then linking to process design and setting up performance measurement feedback. Third, writing and organizing the application."

Explore and Address Surprises and Unexpected Feedback

Organizations get better and better at predicting their feedback. Ken Davis, MD, formerly at North Mississippi, noted, "As we got more sophisticated, we could anticipate where the OFIs would be." Sometimes, however, comments are a surprise. Some are positive (for example, comments about the strength approaches that the applicant might take for granted). Others may describe gaps or opportunities the organization is not aware of. Surprises of this kind commonly result from (1) incomplete understanding of the Baldrige Criteria questions, resulting in vague or inaccurate responses in the application, or from (2) an overly positive sense of the organization's actual performance. The first is relatively easy to overcome, by developing internal expertise in the Baldrige Criteria and assessment process, for example. The second is more complicated. Organizations with an inflated view of their overall performance—fostered by a top leader's ego or naïveté or by an organizational culture focused on perfection—may reject the feedback out of hand. Organizations in the Traction and Sustaining stages of the journey rarely have this problem; indeed, they are more often over-critical. Figure 6.7 demonstrates the shift in self-perception that occurs for many organizations over several cycles as they compare their performance against an objective external assessment.[11] Organizations often are surprised by lower-than-expected performance on their first assessment; below 300 points on a scale of 1,000 is not uncommon. As an organization matures through repeated assessments, its perception of its performance begins to mirror its actual state.

Understand the Role of Experts and Build Internal Capabilities

The availability of experts, internal or external, contributes to sensemaking. They play an important role in clarifying the meaning of the Criteria and stimulating insights during the assessment process—the "aha" moments—by their questions; they also help the organization understand the feedback and set priorities for improvement. Although external experts—consultants as well as staff and other resources from state award programs—are particularly helpful for organizations early in the assessment process, effective leaders, over time, build internal expert resources as well, typically through participation in the Baldrige or state award

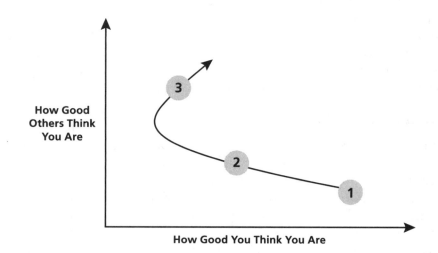

Figure 6.7 Actual versus perceived reality.

programs. All the health care recipients accelerated their journey by having some leaders become Baldrige or state award examiners. Internal experts helped coach and mentor others, expanding Baldrige knowledge within the organization. Many organizations use both internal and external expertise. External experts bring less ego and more objectivity, while internal experts can use their organizational knowledge to help translate the Criteria and feedback throughout the organization.

Build Knowledge of Recipient Practices

Effective methods for building knowledge of the Baldrige process and the best practices of recipients include the following: attending national and regional Quest for Excellence conferences, which showcase the journey and accomplishments of the most recent recipients from all sectors; reviewing recipients' applications posted on the Baldrige Web site, and attending sharing days sponsored by recipient organizations, typically on-site day-long sessions that provide an opportunity for interaction with leaders and others. In all cases, it's important not just to learn, but also to make sure that the learning is widely shared throughout the organization.

Use All the Learning and Feedback

Effective use of the assessment process requires capturing and addressing all insights and making maximum use of the feedback report. The value of the assessment process can begin immediately, with the generation of "aha" moments as people get new insights into their performance gaps. Issues identified in this manner are sometimes relatively easy to address, even before the application is completed. It is important not to lose track of these opportunities in the pressure to produce an application. "Aha" moments occur also when the feedback report arrives and the organization reviews it, as well as periodically during day-to-day interactions and problem solving when leaders and others see the interconnections and their impact on managing the organization. As organizations mature, their focus on the feedback shifts, from a focus on immediate opportunities in specific processes, which is typical early in Traction (stage 2), to a focus on all elements of the feedback report as a source of priorities for improvement, including the Key Themes and scores, as they move forward in the Traction stage and beyond.

Seek Additional Feedback Cycles

Repetition of the assessment cycle builds and deepens organizational learning and understanding. While there is only one annual assessment cycle for Baldrige, most states have parallel programs, and many are on a different calendar from Baldrige. Since the state programs use the same Criteria as Baldrige, developing a state-level application can provide some additional feedback in advance of a Baldrige report with minimum additional effort. Award recipients are precluded from applying again for five years after receiving the award, and most health care recipients use some form of assessment, for some a state program, to generate additional feedback cycles.

As organizations mature and can demonstrate effective processes and strong results, they will receive a site visit by examiners, the final step before preparation of the feedback report. The site visit provides additional opportunities for learning, both in preparing the organization for the visit (in particular, gaps in deployment become evident as employees are briefed on the application content and what to expect) and during the site visit itself.[12] This adds an additional "learning loop" as shown in Figure 6.8. Poudre Valley's Priscilla Nuwash said that during their most recent site visit, they realized that the examiners' questions were "pushing us to the next level." Following the site visit, leaders wrote their own feedback report to capture the OFIs they identified during the site visit and begin to take action. "When you can write your own feedback report," says Nuwash, "that was a good site visit."

Even award recipients, however, receive an official feedback report, which is typically even more accurate and useful when examiners have seen the organization firsthand.

SENSEMAKING AND EXECUTION

Thoughtfully conducted, with the engagement of senior leaders, assessments result in Sensemaking for the organization. But high performance results only when sensemaking is followed by effective Execution—taking action based on the self-developed learning and feedback. As Weick observed, it takes a compelling story for an organization to begin making sense of its situation and performance. The Baldrige application is the "story" of an organization. According to Weick, "Sensemaking is about authoring as well as reading."[13] That is why we say that senior leaders' involvement is necessary both in developing an accurate application that reflects the depth and breadth of an organization's reality, and also in leading improvement initiatives based on the learning from the assessment.

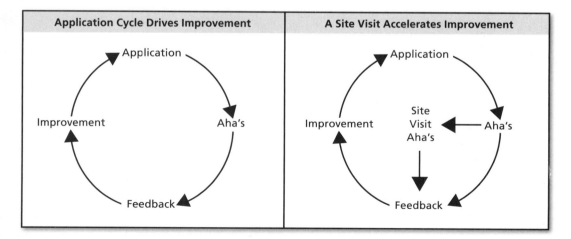

Figure 6.8 Site visits add another learning loop in assessments.

KEY POINTS IN THIS CHAPTER

- Sensemaking is the process of comprehending an organization's complexity, how it is performing, and how it can improve—developing a view of the organization as a holistic system.

- Sensemaking occurs at three points within one assessment cycle: during development of the assessment document as leaders and others respond to the Criteria, during analysis and interpretation of the feedback, and during implementation and evaluation of improvements based on learning and feedback.

- Systematic reassessment, typically annual cycles, enables leaders and others to go deeper in sense-making and contributes to organizational maturity, system thinking, and team learning.

- Sensemaking builds from effective execution and repeated assessments and through development of process literacy in the organization.

- Many organizations experience a breakthrough after two to three assessment cycles when they fully appreciate the power of the assessment process to drive higher performance and better results.

- Sensemaking is the work of senior leaders that brings about systems thinking, process literacy, organizational learning, and maturity as a team overseeing a high-performance enterprise.

7

Execution

"Execution is not just tactics—it is a discipline and a system. It has to be built into a company's strategy, its goals, and its culture. And the leader of the organization must be deeply engaged in it."

– Larry Bossidy and Ram Charan, *Execution*[1]

Execution is the step in the LASER model that focuses on action to deliver better results. It is the critical work of changing *how* your organization runs in order to produce higher overall performance. Clark American, 2001 Baldrige Award recipient in the manufacturing sector, popularized the notion that every organization must pursue two activities in parallel: *Run the Business* and *Change the Business.* The Execution step describes the *Change the Business* activities that lead to a more effective organization, an organization capable of executing its strategy. Clark American claimed that as they grew more and more capable as an organization, senior leaders spent more of their time changing the organization and less of their time running it.

Building a process-literate enterprise is the ultimate approach to delegation. An organization that understands the cause-and-effect relationship between how work gets done (its work processes) and the results it gets, and then intentionally designs, manages, and improves those processes, is far likelier to get the results it desires. The organization becomes more focused and less reactive. Well-developed leadership, management, and daily work processes can be managed by other people, making the organization less dependent on individuals and more able to operate efficiently and effectively. Leaders are freed up to focus on strategy and improvement. Execution boils down to a set of actions that transform the learning from Assessment and Sensemaking into improved processes so that the organization is capable of doing its daily work, executing strategy, and achieving critical results. As we studied the health care Baldrige recipients, a common set of actions emerged as the essential elements used to convert these organizations into high-performance cultures, capable of executing on strategy with discipline and success.

EXECUTING ON BALDRIGE INSIGHTS AND FEEDBACK

Leaders of a successful performance excellence journey execute on their Baldrige insights and feedback in the following ways:

- Make changes from day one

- Set clear priorities

- Establish accountability and plan actions

- Benchmark, measure, and improve key processes

- Review progress and drive change

- Spread improvement and transfer knowledge

This chapter describes these activities in detail, with examples of how they were applied in our study organizations.

MAKE CHANGES FROM DAY ONE

A common misconception about Baldrige is that it is very slow and leaders must wait long periods of time before seeing any benefit. Clearly, fundamental learning and cultural transformation come over time, but several recipients cited early important changes to key processes that produced tangible benefits. They described insights gained while developing their early assessments and concrete changes from the very beginning of their journeys. This is important because any change strategy needs to achieve early tangible successes to build credibility; short-term visible improvements in performance can be cited as proof of efficacy of the journey.[2]

Some early changes came when these leaders struggled to answer a Criteria question about a specific process. Leaders at Robert Wood Johnson University Hospital at Hamilton described a fundamental change that came early on, before they even started an application. Diane Grillo, senior vice president and chief learning and communications officer, recalled that her organization realized they did not have a process to determine their key customers and had not defined their approaches to listen to and learn from customers: "We hadn't addressed these issues before. The Criteria prompted us to design these processes in a systematic way. We recognized the need for a complaint management process just from reading the Criteria." Others found the process of writing an application helpful for similar reasons. Michele Serbenski, vice president of performance excellence, Bronson Healthcare Group, noted that the initial writing process was valuable: "It helped us to 'formalize the informal.' By writing the application, we formalized what we had been doing in a more informal way. This was very valuable to us." Bronson Healthcare Group president and CEO Frank Sardone was quick to add, "Our reason for writing the application was to develop our approaches, not just to apply for the award. We improved our strategic planning process just by writing about it." Through grappling with the Criteria questions, they made important improvements to this fundamental leadership process.

Sister Mary Jean Ryan, president and CEO, SSM Health Care, described how SSM's first feedback report gave them a list of relatively simple things that needed attention. It identified specific processes they needed to design or improve: "The feedback talked about inconsistencies between our communication to staff and our complaint management process. The feedback was right. So we developed a consistent approach to both of these." But she also noted, "After a year or so, there was nothing *easy* to do in the feedback."

Another area of early gains was in growing an understanding of process thinking applied to leadership and management processes. Even for organizations experienced with quality improvement methods applied to clinical care or revenue cycle processes, the idea of designing and improving the communications process can be an "aha" moment. Bronson developed and refined their leadership communication process (Figure 4.3). Leaders recognized that "effective communication, alignment, and deployment are essential for achievement of organizational strategy. Using the Leadership Communication Process...the Executive Team communicates values, plans, and expectations...throughout the organization and to the community."[3] This example illustrates the point made by Bronson's Michele Serbenski about formalizing what had otherwise been done informally. The Baldrige process also prompted them to design an approach they could learn from and improve: a specific step in the process ensures that when messages go out from leadership to the workforce, the effectiveness of the process is evaluated and steps are taken as appropriate to address ineffective messaging.

Improvements in strategic planning and deployment came early in the journey for several recipients. It is often among the first processes redesigned during Traction (stage 2). Baptist Hospital's vice president of strategic services, David Sjoberg, explained: "Early on, Baldrige helped us to develop and deploy our strategy. In response to feedback, we made a number of changes to strategic planning. We were one of the early adopters in health care of 90-day action plans, before we started with Baldrige, but the feedback really helped us refine our process and deploy it more fully throughout our organization." At Poudre Valley Health System, after their first site visit and feedback, they realized that the elements of their strategic planning process were not in sync with operations. They revised their capital planning, operational planning, balanced scorecard, and other components to make them consistent and ensure that the planning process was logical, efficient, and effective.

Early on, each recipient organization took actions to address "low-hanging fruit"; that is, gaps discovered through attempting to answer Criteria questions, completing an application, or receiving feedback. We have seen organizations fail to progress because they don't take early action to address their feedback. Sometimes these "slow starters" get going after additional rounds of feedback. Early action that leads to meaningful improvement is critical to developing the momentum required to continue the Journey. Capitalizing on the low-hanging fruit is necessary but not sufficient. It builds trust in the process, but once the low-hanging fruit is gone, it takes planning and execution to gain Traction, build Integration, and achieve sustainable high levels of performance.

SET CLEAR PRIORITIES

Some improvement happens almost by osmosis as those working with the Criteria began to understand their gaps and look for ways to improve. But major improvement needs to be systematic and prioritized. This is the job of senior leaders. Informed by Assessments (Chapter 5) and Sensemaking (Chapter 6), only senior leaders can re-align the organization around priorities for action. Senior leaders can connect the Baldrige feedback with analysis of the performance of key organizational processes and the critical causal link between those processes and organizational results. Choosing what to improve, and when, is a critical strategic decision. Focusing organizational attention and resources on the high-leverage priorities to achieve critical results creates the opportunity for meaningful improvement and ultimately determines the long term success of the enterprise.

Several of the award recipients took their feedback report directly to their senior leadership team. "The year we got the award, we had forty-seven OFIs. We took the feedback report and pulled it apart. We sort and prioritize the feedback through a nominal group process. We decide what are short-term and long-term priorities and how to resource the necessary work," explained Sherry Marshall, vice president of quality, Saint Luke's Health System. After Poudre Valley Health System's fourth site visit, Priscilla Nuwash, director of process improvement, concluded, "A great site visit is when you can write your own feedback." They did just that, with their Leadership Team beginning to work on the expected OFIs even before the feedback report was delivered.

John Heer, president and CEO, North Mississippi Health Services, took charge of the process himself. He went to the annual Quest for Excellence conference, at which prior year Baldrige recipients detail their approaches and results. He came back with a list of high-performance practices he wanted to adopt: "I would tell my team, 'Here is what we need to do.' I prioritized the OFIs myself. I knew them and understood them thoroughly. I understood that there were systematic processes lacking in our organization." Ultimately, North Mississippi aligned their action plans with their critical success factors, goals, and key performance indicators.

Criteria for Priority Setting on Feedback

Organizations often create a simple process for selecting the high-leverage feedback to work on. Typical criteria for selecting priorities include the following:

- Feedback is straightforward, highlighting "low-hanging fruit" that someone wants to work on

- Resources are available to address the feedback

- Topic is critical, addresses key organizational strategic challenges

- The opportunity supports current organizational strategic objectives and goals

- Topic with potential for near-term impact

Setting clear priorities is critical because in health care, resources almost inevitably are scarce. Without clear priorities, important work languishes. Senior leaders must align resources—both financial and human—to priorities. Stopping activities and delaying non-critical work can be just as important as or even more important than adding new initiatives. The feedback will point out where activities are *not* aligned with overall organizational goals or priorities. It sends a great message when leaders take action to stop non-value-added meetings, committees, and initiatives as a part of the journey to performance excellence. The point is to become more effective, aligned, and results oriented.[4] Stopping activity that is not aligned can make room for more productive work and provide a great morale boost to overworked staff as well. Collins found this in the *Good to Great* study as well. The good-to-great organizations are as focused on what *not* to do as they are on what is critical to do.[5]

Sooner or later, each award recipient developed an approach that tied addressing feedback directly to the strategic planning process, thus addressing feedback routinely as an input to their planning. Saint Luke's integrated their Baldrige feedback with their system strategic planning process the first years of their journey. They tied addressing the feedback to employee performance and their performance metrics, said Rich Hastings, president and CEO, Saint Luke's Health System. Baptist made similar use of their feedback. "The first thing we did for strategic planning and goal-setting every year was look at the feedback report and integrate the OFIs into our priorities and plans," said David Sjoberg.

In setting priorities, our study organizations focused on celebrating and building upon strengths along with addressing OFIs. A balanced approach is critical to engaging the workforce around the Journey, to building momentum and enthusiasm for change. We asked recipients how they sustained interest and commitment for several cycles of assessment and feedback. Paula Friedman, corporate vice president of strategy and system improvement, SSM Health Care, was straightforward about the answer for SSM: "We celebrate successes wherever we have them. We celebrated successes at the entity level as well as at the system level." Taking advantage of strengths and core competencies helps an organization compete. Baldrige provides just as much feedback on strengths as it does on opportunities. This feedback can increase an organization's understanding of how to enhance and leverage their critical advantages.

Balancing the focus on strengths as well as gaps has been shown by others to be a critical success factor in transformational change. In a recent survey by McKinsey and Company, more than 3,000 executives from industries and regions around the world responded to questions about creating transformations. Only one-third reported that their organizations were successful. Companies deemed successful by their leaders were far likelier to communicate the need for change in a positive manner, encouraging staff to build on success in balance with focusing on closing gaps, and fixing problems.[6]

Ultimately, Baldrige provided these organizations with a framework to focus on key priorities to *change the business*. Award recipients shared common approaches to set priorities so that resources and attention were channeled effectively to improve the enterprise. They brought OFIs directly to the senior leadership team, applied a basic process for setting clear priorities, and linked their feedback into their strategy and operational planning.

ESTABLISH ACCOUNTABILITY AND PLAN ACTIONS

After recipients set their priorities for change, they were methodical about establishing accountability. They developed action plans and measures to execute changes and track their progress. They identified who, what, and by when key processes would be formalized, benchmarked, and improved. They divided up the feedback among senior leaders who took accountability for changing the organization's operations. These responsible individuals led the efforts to address the strengths and OFIs by:

- Building more systematic *approaches* and processes

- Developing methods to *deploy* their approaches and processes

- Creating a means to *learn* how to improve the approaches

- *Integrating* with other key processes

Saint Luke's took a very straightforward approach to accountability. The Baldrige feedback report goes directly to the CEO. He reviews it with two others in his senior leader triad, the vice president of quality and the vice president/medical director of quality. After the triad analyzes it, they present it to their full leadership team. After the leadership team prioritizes the OFIs, a specific leader's name is assigned to address each OFI.

Poudre Valley went through an interesting evolution in the role of their category teams over the years. Early on, they called them their "Malcolm Baldrige Teams" or "MB Teams." They had one team for each Baldrige category: "MB2," "MB3," and so on. Initially, these teams only met for a few months each year to write the application. But after their third site visit, and their "tipping point" lesson about the proper positioning for the award in their transformational journey, this changed, explained Sonya Wulff, Poudre Valley performance excellence manager: "When we didn't win after our third site visit, we realized we really weren't doing this for the award. We were doing it to be a better organization. The teams changed their names to be Performance Excellence Teams. They started meeting year round. They became system-wide steering committees responsible for key processes in various areas, and they set priorities and serve as the clearinghouse for all initiatives and performance data in their areas. Now we have a Strategy Team, Knowledge Management Team, and Customer Service Team, and so on. These teams will continue in their role even now, after we were named a recipient." Today these teams oversee their category of processes and monitor health care and other industries for better approaches to achieving the culture of excellence and results Poudre Valley strives to build.

Bronson took a slightly different approach. They created category teams only when no other team existed to take responsibility for the process categories and feedback. "Category 2 (Strategic Planning) is handled by the group of leaders responsible for planning. Category 3 (Customer Focus) goes to five individuals with responsibility for customer research and relationships. The Human Resources leadership team is the Category 5 team," described Michele Serbenski. Frank Sardone added, "This is example of integrating Baldrige into how we work." They discovered that Baldrige is the work of improving how the organization does its work, not additional projects or initiatives.

The journey is a means to focus and align activity around a disciplined agenda of continual improvement in operations. It's more about stopping wasted activity and working more effectively, while holding the organization to the highest performance standards for the results. Robert Wood Johnson University Hospital at Hamilton assigned owners to each strategic objective and the associated short-term and long-term action plans. They identified the key changes expected, resource requirements, measures, and goals. Figure 7.1 shows this alignment. Recipient organizations all have some way to align their action plans with strategy and results. This helps ensure that activity is focused and easy to monitor.

Action plans include resource commitments (people, funds, special skill sets) and time horizons for accomplishment. It is the stage in planning when strategic objectives and goals are made specific so organization-wide understanding and deployment are possible. Without clear action plans, it is difficult to know what resources are required. Deployment of action plans includes creating aligned measures for all departments and work units. Over time, these Baldrige recipients linked strategic objectives to action plans to measures reviewed at appropriate levels of leadership throughout their organizations.

These organizations found that effective measurement was essential to improving performance. They deliberately selected measures that would allow them to review:

- Overall organizational performance

- Key process capability and outcomes

- Action plan success

Objective	Owner	Short- and long-term action plans	Key Changes	HR/Staffing Plans	KPI	Goals 04-05	Goals 06-09	Benchmark & Proj
1. Finance Margin Management	CFO COO	POS Cash Collection team to develop new process. Evaluate Margin by Product Line monthly. Implement suggestions from "Front-Line" committee. Reduce Red-bag waste. Implement reusable/recyclable program.	New contract initiated with United Health Care. RWJ Center for Health & Wellness. Shift in revenue generating Services out of hospital.	Provide education for MT on margin management	Operating Margins • Overall Hospital • Inpatient • Outpatient • Emergency Dept. • Ambulatory-Surg	• x% • x% • x% • x% • x%	Overall Hospital x%	Overall Hospital
2. Quality Length of Stay	COO	Initiate Multi-Disciplinary Rounds on all units. One-on-one meetings with high-variance MDs. Quarterly report cards to medical staff section chiefs. Reduce avoidably days through Patient Management.	Day observation status. Clinical observation unit. Physician incentives to decrease length of stay. Outpatient care management.	Patient Management in ED	All Payor LOS Medicare LOS % patients > 10 days	x x x	x	
3. Quality Patient Safety	VPPCS AVPQO AVPN	Develop comprehensive plan based on NQF, AHRQ, JCAHO Guidelines & Internal Goals. Increase volume of incident reporting including increase in near-misses. JCAHO mock survey and tracer methodology training.	Increased use of technology to decrease errors. NJ mandatory error reporting.	Designation of patient safety leader. JCAHO tracer methodology training with System & Network	JCAHO Safety Indicators	100% safety goals, Veri-5 Barcoding Cil Safe	EMR CPOE 100% safety goals	100% Safety Goals
4. Quality Clinical Outcomes	AVPQO	Use PDCA to improve order sets to be more user-friendly. Increase use of evidence-based order sets. Link with Disease Management Committee to improve overall outcomes. Education plan for staff on NQF standards.	Increased public acceptance and importance of Quality Reporting organizations. Reimbursement based on quality outcomes.	Staff and MD education on quality indicators and compliance.	Core Measures Mortality Rates AHA NVHQI	Clinical Outcome measures above the 90th percentile nationally	Clinical Outcome measures above the 95th percentile nationally	Clinical Outcome measures above 95th percentile nationally
5. Service Outpatient Service Growth	AVPCAS	Develop Outpatient Service Commitment. Advertisements for Commitment. Monitor 24-hour results reporting. Monitor appointment timeliness	Competitor with new OP facility one mile from RWJUHH, MD SurgiCenters, and Endoscopic Centers. Increased Physician competition	Hire additional staff to cover additional am/pm hours and volume	OP Volume Growth	x%	x%	

Legend:
CFO – Chief Financial Officer; COO – Chief Operating Officer; VPPCS-VP, Patient Care Services; AVPQO-AVP, Quality Outcomes; AVPCAS-AVP, Clinical & Ambulatory Services; AVPN-AVP, Nursing

Figure 7.1 Key action plans – Robert Wood Johnson University Hospital at Hamilton.[7]

They focus on a broad range of performance measures that go well beyond financial, quality, and satisfaction measures. They balance in-process and outcome measures and use strong approaches to measurement including tracking trends, comparing to benchmarks, and segmenting results by meaningful groupings to facilitate analysis. Award recipients gave careful consideration to how progress is measured and where progress is reviewed for action.

Poudre Valley Health System demonstrated several role model practices in the use of their data to drive excellence. On a monthly basis, Poudre Valley collects and analyzes input from various customer groups and multiple listening methods for use in strategy development, measuring performance, and identifying opportunities for improvement. Care units utilize patient feedback for goal setting and performance measurement and post action plans on the Poudre Valley intranet to engage the entire workforce. Poudre Valley patient loyalty ranks in the top one percent of U.S. hospitals, according to the Centers for Medicare and Medicaid Services.

Clear accountability for organizational change priorities, action plans that identify how the organization is going to accomplish the change, and measures of success are essential to create a structure for improvement. Award recipients developed effective approaches over time. Strong approaches in this area were essential to formalize improvement, increase focus, and accelerate progress.

Mercy Health System wrote ten Baldrige applications and had five Baldrige Award site visits before being named a recipient in 2007. Their results are strong across multiple dimensions of performance. Since 1989, Mercy's revenue has increased from about $33 million to $847 million, demonstrating significant growth. During the same period, while many health care systems have seen declining bond ratings, Mercy's Moody bond rating remained stable at A2 from 1996 to 2007 and increased to positive long-term outlook in 2007. Their overall mortality rates matched the best practice benchmark based on data from the CareScience adjusted rate for the top 15 percent of hospitals in the United States. Mercy results for community acquired pneumonia mortality decreased steadily from 2003, achieving 1.2 percent—significantly below the benchmark of 4.0 percent. In 2006, overall satisfaction with Mercy multi-specialty outpatient centers was 96 percent; overall satisfaction with Mercy hospitals was 95.2 percent. Staff turnover at Mercy Health System declined from 13.5 percent in 2002 to 7.5 percent in 2007.[8]

Mercy's leadership approaches and processes evolved significantly over the years of their journey. The Mercy Health System Leadership Excellence Model, displayed in Figure 7.2, illustrates their current approach to accountability and action planning. Their board of directors reviews the mission, vision, and values, sets long-term strategy and objectives, and refines action plans. Senior leaders provide data and information, including their Baldrige feedback, for strategic decision making by the board.

The Mercy Executive Council identifies shorter-term action plans to achieve the strategies. They review system-level performance data and best-practice measures and determine goals, indicators, and targets to include in the system and department dashboards. Mercy uses an array of processes to engage their employees and medical staff partners, including departmental performance reviews using the

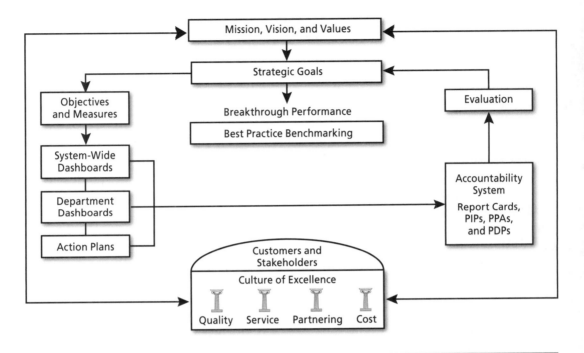

Figure 7.2 Leadership excellence model – Mercy Health System.[9]

dashboards, Partner Performance Appraisals (PPAs), Personal Development Plans (PDPs), and Physician Incentive Program (PIP) goals. Underpinning the entire Leadership Excellence Model is the Culture of Excellence, developed by senior leaders to communicate and create a common understanding of Mercy's values and goals. The key principles of the four pillars supporting the Culture of Excellence (Quality, Service, Partnering, Cost) are communicated to employees and medical staff through a two-day formal training program and annual in-services.

Some organizations may recognize these elements and believe they have many of them in place. What distinguishes Mercy (and any Baldrige recipient) is that each element is fully developed with clear steps, timing, participants, owners, and outputs and is deployed to all appropriate areas throughout the organization. Each element is well linked to the other elements with clear inputs, outputs, and timing. Further, the workforce and key stakeholders know that this system of integrated leadership, management, and measurement approaches is in place. This sets the stage for successful strategy deployment including linking each individual's efforts to strategy. The most effective organizations engage and align the entire workforce toward achieving its goals.

An effective approach is essential to move into Traction (stage 2), and a robust process that links and aligns the whole organization is critical for Integration (stage 3).

John Heer made improving strategy development and deployment a high priority at both Baptist Hospital and North Mississippi to provide alignment and create a focus on action. "Our action plans were not as effective as they needed to be. We aligned them with overall goals and changed how we deployed them, renaming them 90-day action plans. This proved very effective," he explained.

Poudre Valley's Strategy Development and Deployment Process ensures active participation of key stakeholders in driving organizational change and achieving targeted results. Displayed in Figure 7.3, the process incorporates the Baldrige evaluation factors—approach, deployment and learning—into its design. In steps 1 through 4, it provides a systematic *approach* to developing strategies, goals and action items. Then the process moves into *deployment* in steps 5 and 6 when leaders focus on allocation of necessary resources to accomplish strategic objectives and communicating and aligning goals with funded action items. The final step addresses *learning* through organizational performance reviews conducted at the system and department levels. The Strategy Development and Deployment Process itself addresses the final evaluation factor, *integration*, through its comprehensive inclusion of all major initiatives, budgeting, and key measures into a single approach and plan.

Poudre Valley's process follows an annual calendar, starting with the Senior Management Group's winter retreat where they assess the progress on the previous year's strategic plan as well as the effectiveness of the prior year planning process. Each year, the assessment leads to changes to improve planning and execution. Then the group analyzes market and industry trends using defined criteria to determine current Poudre Valley's strategic advantages and challenges and evaluate new service proposals.

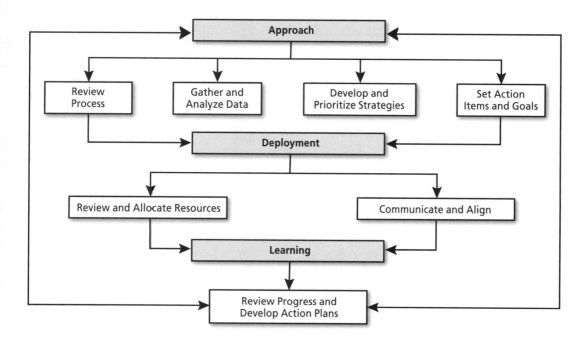

Figure 7.3 Strategy development and deployment process – Poudre Valley Health System.[10]

The third step occurs in April when the Senior Management Group and Board retreat to plan the future of the organization. Poudre Valley Health System has six standing strategic objectives displayed prominently in their leadership model, called the Global Path to Success (Figure 7.4). Based on a thorough analysis of organizational, market, and industry information, senior leaders determine major new directions. They identify goals aligned with each of their six strategic objectives along with specific action plans and resource requirements. Their balanced score-card, the key mechanism for measuring and tracking organizational performance relative to the Strategic objectives, serves as the basis for aligned cascading score-cards with goals, benchmarks through the system and departments.

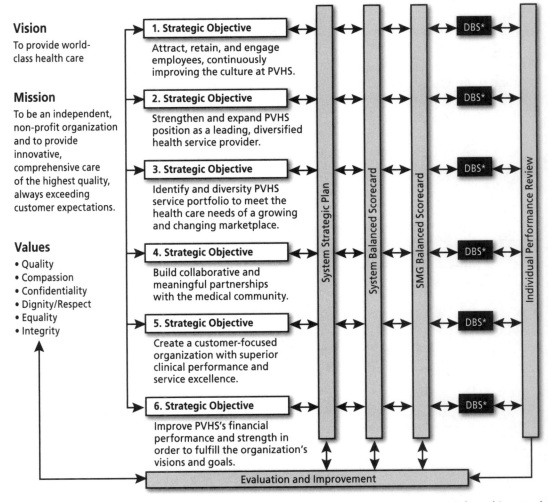

*DBS = Department Balanced Scorecard

Figure 7.4 Global path to success – Poudre Valley Health System.[11]

The planning process steps 5 and 6 address goal deployment to all relevant staff and departments. Step 5 determines budget parameters for capital, revenue, expenses, and FTEs. Step 6 matches the resources required to carry out the strategic objectives with available resources and adjusting the goals to accommodate action items that are not funded. Once the budget is final, directors make department adjustments to account for items that did not receive budget support. Step 7 entails senior leadership and departmental review of the scorecards relative to goals specific to each strategic objective. If results fall short of the goal, the individual accountable for the action item develops an action plan that is approved and monitored by the Senior Management Group. All action items are reviewed by the Senior Management Group every ninety days to ensure system-wide deployment of goals.

This level of discipline was not built in a year or two. The Strategy Development and Deployment Process and all of its component processes grew over several cycles of improvement, fostered by eight Baldrige applications and feedback reports. With this sustained effort at refining their execution capabilities, Poudre Valley has achieved significant results in multiple dimensions of performance.

A strong leadership system deploys expectations from the governance bodies to the front line. The main mechanism for doing this, as shown in the earlier examples from Poudre Valley and from Sharp, is the strategic planning process. The Baldrige Criteria for strategic planning look not only at the planning process itself, but how the outcomes of the process—the strategic objectives and organizational goals—are deployed throughout the organization. This is the essence of alignment—"consistency of plans, processes, information, resource decisions, actions, results, and analyses to support key organization-wide goals."[12]

Deploying strategic plans down from the organizational level to entities and departments can be a tricky task in itself. The Baldrige health care recipients all developed effective mechanisms to go well beyond this. They build and maintain what they often call "line of sight" from organizational goals right down to the individual level, using both formal and informal communication methods. For example, Baptist deploys its strategic objectives through 90-day action plans that frequently extend involvement to the people on the hospital floor. SSM Health Care's Passport—a card carried by all employees that lists both the organization's objectives and the actions the employee personally will take to impact the objectives—is another example that has been widely emulated by organizations, both inside and outside of health care, that want to build alignment. (See the Passport in Figure 4.2.) SSM's Baldrige application summary explains how this approach fosters line of sight: "Through the Passport program employees identify personal goals that are linked to organizational goals and are then evaluated on their performance in achieving these goals."[13]

Another example of vertical deployment is North Mississippi's approach that aligns the individual's performance plans with the corporate goals and the organization's mission, vision, and values (Figure 7.5). The concept also includes coaching and reward and recognition policies based on both achievement of results and exhibition of the desired behaviors. Note how North Mississippi has embedded the Baldrige evaluation factors—approach, deployment, learning, and integration—into the structure of the process.

Health care recipient leaders were typically open about the feedback they received from the Baldrige program and the subsequent actions they planned to take as a result. This transparency tends to foster organizational buy-in to the Baldrige process and supports building clear lines of sight. The vertical transfer of knowledge and facts about the organization's challenges and initiatives also helps build a common, clear sense of purpose.

BENCHMARK AND IMPROVE KEY PROCESSES

For organizations to excel, they must find out how they are performing relative to others. How would athletes know that they were good unless they competed against others? The same is true in health care. While we have begun to benchmark clinical outcomes, there is still tremendous opportunity to benchmark a broad array of processes and results both within and beyond the bounds of health care. Benchmarking provides insight into relative levels of performance and also provides a tremendous opportunity to learn and apply best practices to achieve higher performance. Benchmarking both processes and results is an essential practice to improve health care.

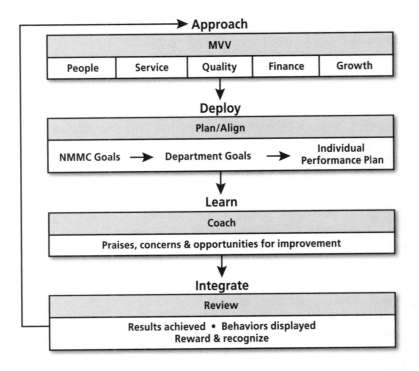

Figure 7.5 Performance management process – North Mississippi Medical Center.[14]

Better practices need to come from both internal and external sources. External sources are plentiful, as the recipient organizations demonstrate. The Criteria drive benchmarking throughout the seven categories, and Baldrige assessments specifically look for evidence that throughout the organization people are encouraged to seek out new approaches and processes to adopt. There is an expectation that you certainly will stay abreast of best practices within health care but also develop an appetite for innovations across industries as well. The Baldrige framework readily facilitates cross-industry benchmarking. The Baldrige Program encourages adoption of practices and supports it by making available in the public domain the Criteria, recipient application summaries, and many other resources. There is evidence in almost every Baldrige recipient's application of learning from the practices of others. Rich Hastings told us about how he took advantage of his visits to Boeing and mirrored their scorecard system at Saint Luke's. Baptist imitated Ritz Carlton Hotel's daily huddle practice. Sharp HealthCare's leadership system bears striking resemblance to Boeing's. These are just a few of the many examples of smart benchmarking that led to great results.

One noteworthy characteristic of external benchmarking among the award recipients is a strong tendency to adapt and rename practices, building ownership of their newly adopted approaches. They rename a practice modeled after another company or health care organization and adjust it to their culture and systems. They follow their own internal leadership direction rather than the direction of gurus or campaigns. If they use consultants, they are kept low on the organizational radar screen. While they are quick to "steal" a great idea, when they bring something home internally it's done in the name of their organization, using their terms and culturally appropriate ways. Arguably, this emphasis on internalizing new ideas from the outside is a critical factor for successful transformation using Baldrige.

The assessment process and the Criteria themselves enable successful benchmarking. A typical feedback report has some comments highlighting the need for more systematic approaches, for example, in succession planning or managing complaints. The application summaries of Baldrige Award recipients provide an obvious source of ideas. The numbering system of the Criteria is consistent across industry sectors promoting benchmarking across sectors; for example, you can look at recipient summaries in other industries to see how they manage complaints. Even more powerful is hearing the presentations at the annual Quest for Excellence conference in Washington D.C. each spring, at which award recipients present their approaches and processes. There are regional versions of the Quest for Excellence conference in two locations nationally every fall. Recipients host sharing events on-site that enable outsiders to visit and gain deeper understanding about how they lead and manage their organizations.

All recipient organizations aligned and extended their process improvement capabilities. They charter many improvement projects, but later in their Baldrige journey, projects are well aligned with strategic objectives and supported by clearly defined resources and methods to ensure success. These organizations developed effective performance improvement system for applying people, methods, and tools to improving key work systems and processes regularly throughout the enterprise to ensure results.

Baldrige is not prescriptive. The Criteria do not require specific improvement methods or tools. They ask that the approaches used be well defined, deployed across the organization, and applied as appropriate to the range of processes that need to be improved. For many in health care today, Plan-Do-Check-Act (PDCA), Six Sigma, Define-Measure-Analyze-Identify-Control (DMAIC), and lean methodologies are essential elements in their approach to improving performance. Baldrige integrates all the approaches that the organization embraces into a cohesive framework and evaluates the effectiveness and integration of the approaches with the culture and organization overall. Sharp uses a typical approach to improve their processes. Six Sigma provides an improvement framework with lean and Six Sigma events and tools (Figure 7.6). These tools enable continuous performance improvement driven by rapid responsiveness, rigorous data analysis, and reduction in variation and waste across the system. Ongoing assessments along with continuous performance improvement efforts ensure that key leadership, management, and work processes are evaluated and improved. Existing service lines use evidence-based guidelines and in-process metrics, outcomes analyses, and listening and learning tools to drive improvements, and improved health care service outcomes are achieved.

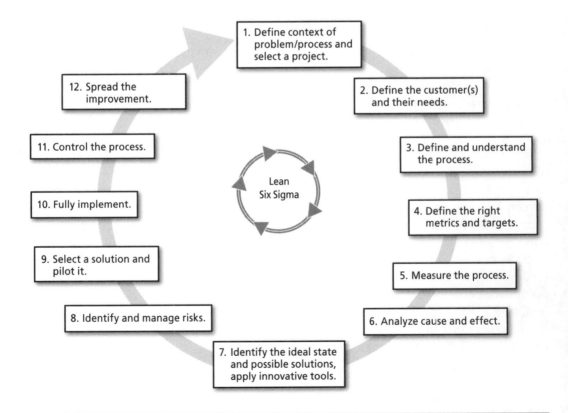

Figure 7.6   DMAIC 12-step improvement problem-solving process – Sharp HealthCare.[15]

Each award recipient benchmarked, measured, and improved the key processes that produce results. They focused on process. They used rigorous approaches to understand and define requirements, improve performance measurement, externally benchmark, and redesign key leadership systems and processes causally linked to measured results. They became more capable organizations.

REVIEW PROGRESS AND DRIVE CHANGE

Baldrige asks *how* an organization reviews its performance and capabilities to assess organizational success, performance relative to competitors, and comparable organization and progress relative to strategic objectives and action plans. These reviews are expected to support effective, fact-based decision making and help determine priorities for improvement. The following are three typical areas for review:

- Balanced scorecards—broad organizational metrics aligned with organizational critical success factors or pillars and reviewed at senior level and at the board. Entity, department, and subunit scorecard are reviewed at the appropriate level.

- Action plans—prioritized initiatives tracked and reviewed regularly (at least quarterly).

- Process scorecards—key in-process and outcome measures of key work systems and processes tracked and reviewed.

North Mississippi set up clear accountability and review structures to ensure their goals were effectively deployed and their medical staff leadership was fully engaged in driving performance excellence. Chuck Stokes, former president of North Mississippi Medical Center, led the effort to build a service structure that took charge of the change process: "Most organizations use service lines as a marketing ploy, to market 'integrated care, coordinated care.' But I knew that we had to create forums to make decisions. The service line leadership must have a true role with authority and responsibility." The North Mississippi service line management includes four to eight physicians, an administrator, case manager, nurse managers, finance and outcomes measurement specialists, and a representative ancillary person such as respiratory therapy, if appropriate. "These groups make their operating budget and capital budget, once approved, this team is responsible for managing that budget," Stokes explained. "When the distracting issues and conflicts come up, they get referred back to their service line administrative team to request new capital equipment. If you need a robot, go to your service line team. They have to get their peers to approve their investment proposal, their business plan. The service line is complementary, not competing, with the medical staff organization. The chief and vice chief of surgery sit on the service line for surgery, for example. Operating room committee or surgery department policies must go through the service line where policy compliance is managed. The operating and capital budget get set and managed by the service line administrative team. Six Sigma and PDCA projects, core measures, whatever is being set as performance goals, these are chartered by this team. Every service line has a strategic plan that is aligned with the medical center and system, all the way to the employee."

Stokes and Heer created a flat structure, further empowering the service line administrative teams to lead performance excellence. As of 2006, the six service lines administrators reported directly to Stokes. He had no chief operating officer or vice presidents between the service lines and himself. He had a chief nursing officer to support the service lines for nursing policy, the float pool, training, and similar responsibilities, but all nurse managers reported to the service line administrators. Each service line monitored its own report card of operational and quality metrics that it monitors. Keep in mind that Baldrige is non-prescriptive. Nothing in the Criteria say the North Mississippi way is the right way for every organization. But responding to the Criteria and feedback fosters building a systematic way that generates desired results, which for North Mississippi was a service line structure with delegated authority and oversight responsibilities.

Change is never easy and rarely welcome. Terry May, CEO of MESA Products, 2006 Baldrige recipient in the small business sector, talked about his view of this challenge.[16] He explained that early on in his organization's journey, everyone was convinced PDCA meant "Please Don't Change Anything!" Even in his small manufacturing business, managing change is difficult. The senior leader's ultimate challenge is driving change that motivates and engages the workforce to improve and achieve higher organizational performance.

With your priorities for change and accountabilities established, it's a matter of managing those accountabilities in parallel with running routine operations. Some leaders choose to add a "change the business" agenda item to their regular operational meetings. Others add it as a topic to a less frequent and more strategic leadership team meeting. Management consultant Patrick Lencioni lays out an approach to structuring meetings according to the type of agenda topic, ranging from tactical to strategic.[17] Regardless of when and where you choose to monitor the change effort, the key is to evaluate progress regularly and objectively.

The Baldrige score is useful in this regard. Bronson has a track record that clearly demonstrates a commitment to improvement using Baldrige as the measure of organizational progress. They chose to establish achieving award recipient status by 2010 in order to put a spot on the wall and focus the organization on excellence. "We had a goal of achieving the award by 2010. It gave everyone a goal to aspire toward," shared Frank Sardone. "Bronson Methodist Hospital was a recipient in 2005, ahead of schedule." Michele Serbenski added, "We achieved better results faster than we predicted. Almost every objective for 2010 was achieved by 2005 or 2006." Some recipients have reportedly used their Baldrige score as a key metric for organizational performance review. Other business award recipients have linked the score to senior leader compensation, though none of the health care recipients went this route. Although there are pitfalls to this approach (people may tend to "game" the system when performance ratings and salary increases are on the line), the attraction of this option is the simplicity of an overall score for the organization which is a simple score anywhere from band 1 to band 8 (see Chapter 2, Baldrige, for the details on scoring).

In a full assessment, each of the eighteen Criteria items also gets a score in a series of ranges from zero to 100 percent (of the total potential point score for that item). This can be useful in monitoring progress as well. If your most recent score for strategic planning (Category 2) was a 30–45 percentile, that team will focus on moving that score to the 50–65 percentile range on their next assessment. Having a numeric score to center on is one of the utilities of the Baldrige process. Each team has this score to measure their progress from assessment to assessment. The process evaluation criteria provide the basis for understanding the requirements for moving the score forward and monitoring progress, giving senior leaders the questions to ask:

- What is your approach?

- How is it deployed?

- How will you learn if the approach is successful?

- How your approach is integrated with other key leadership and management processes?

- How does it drive results?

The feedback comments from award programs are non-prescriptive, meaning they do not tell you what you should do to improve your score. But insightful leaders and skilled examiners figure out the necessary changes to improve the competence of the organization. At lower scoring levels, the needed actions often require defining processes and making them systematic, building in the capacity for measurement and improvement. Often, benchmarking leading-edge practices can help in redesign efforts. In other cases, the organization has a reasonable, systematic approach, but it is not fully deployed to all work units and staffs that need to use the process for the overall organization to be successful. At higher scoring levels, it may be that the approaches are sound and well deployed but need to go through a cycle of evaluation and improvement to stay up to speed with the current best management practices. At the highest scoring levels, the means to a improving may be ensuring that strategic planning is fully integrated and aligned with human resource practices and performance measurement systems. (Keep in mind that a 50–65 percentile score is a strong score, and a 70–85 percentile score is rare and very high.) These examples highlight the type of questions and analysis that can go on in a conversation about driving change and reviewing progress.

Priorities are set by senior leaders; however, transparency in communicating the feedback increased buy-in for change. While recipients varied in terms of how they communicated the feedback, generally, they chose to be highly transparent with it, sharing it widely or even posting it on their intranet for any internal person to view. This choice paralleled the overall commitment we saw to listening to the brutal facts and openly reflecting in an inclusive dialogue about what the feedback says. As Jim Collins said, "There is nothing wrong with pursuing a vision of greatness. After all, the good-to-great companies also set out to create greatness. But, unlike the comparison companies, the good-to-great companies continually refined the *path* to greatness with the brutal facts of reality."[18] The feedback with this level of scrutiny is going to be fairly accurate (though not always) and often profound. Hearing the feedback, accepting it when it's right, and acknowledging that it warrants action can only come from top leadership. We've seen significant disconnects that lead to cultural toxicity around the journey when middle managers recognize the OFIs in the feedback are accurate but their superiors reject the negative feedback. The recipient organizations studied the feedback, accepted the truth, rejected the inaccuracies, and went to work in a disciplined and focused way on making changes that could help them be more successful.

Driving change through a Baldrige journey can result in redesigning leadership structures and approaches and building systematic processes for setting expectations, assigning accountabilities, and monitoring results. The Criteria questions ask about your approaches to setting and communicating expectations. They specifically ask how senior leaders create a focus on action to accomplish the organization's goals, improve performance, and achieve your vision. They go on to ask for a description of how you review your organizational capabilities and performance and what analyses you perform to support your reviews. These questions apply to running your organization as well as changing it. Early on in a transformational journey, most organizations do not have systematic approaches to these activities. They may have informal ways of setting expectations and deploying them, but building a systematic approach to deploying expectations and ensuring that employees and staff members in fact know how they contribute to achieving organizational expectations is often an early OFI for most leaders.

All the Baldrige health care recipients developed their own internal expertise in the Baldrige Criteria and process by having one or more state or Baldrige examiners on staff. These individuals serve not just as content experts in the Criteria, transferring their knowledge and insights to others, but also help to drive cultural change in the organization. Several of the recipients also rely on others within the organization to serve in specific roles as change agents. For example, Sharp's Firestarters are front-line volunteers who help to lead implementation of the Sharp Experience within their entity. Poudre Valley's uses Customer Champions, a team of front-line staff that assist in deploying improvements system wide in patient-facing and customer-facing processes.

Most of the health care award recipients use public venues to recognize and share stories of outstanding performance within their organizations. SSM's primary method of recognizing teams as well as sharing results is through their annual Showcase for Sharing conference, a system wide recognition event. North Mississippi has an annual Outcomes and Safety Fair, which "allows each employee to see how he or she contributes to patient outcomes and to both patient and staff safety."[19] Poudre Valley's Annual Quality Festival attracts a large number of participants across all sectors of the organization. It allows "the workforce to highlight their quality improvement projects, and promotes and rewards sharing and implementation of innovations."[20] Sharp's presentation of its Pillar of Excellence awards at its All-Staff Assembly is another example of visible celebration of successes.

Systematic performance review to inform decision making and prioritize improvement combined with approaches to engage the organization and drive change help embed transformational change into the organizational DNA and set the stage for the final element of Execution, spreading improvement.

SPREAD IMPROVEMENT AND TRANSFER KNOWLEDGE

The final activity for leaders as they build execution practices that yield intended results is in the area of deploying best practices and transferring knowledge vertically and horizontally throughout the organization. Successful transformational change requires the adoption of new ways of working from the board to the leaders to the front line. It also requires transferring new knowledge across work units, horizontally within the organization across departments, locations, and settings.

Just as strategy alignment is important in creating a line of sight from leaders to individuals, communication and knowledge-sharing are essential to support progress throughout the organization. Widespread and consistent communication to the workforce about the organization's mission, vision, and objectives also is a consistent theme we heard among the Baldrige health care recipients as a means to develop strategic line of sight. For example, Poudre Valley uses a cascade learning approach to sharing information: each person is responsible for sharing their learning with others, who in turn, share with others, thus cascading the knowledge throughout the organization. Sharp has an annual All-Staff Assembly for all employees to provide "inspiration, education, and celebration. Three sessions, offered over two days, allow all Sharp employees to attend. Content includes the CEO's state-of-Sharp address, a keynote address, the annual Pillars of Excellence Awards, stories that highlight specific Sharp Experience learnings, and special features such as the preview of a television documentary about Sharp.[21]

Another example of a formal communication approach is the systematic, two-way Five-Pillar Communication Approach used at Robert Wood Johnson University Hospital at Hamilton, shown in Figure 7.7. The organization uses this approach not only for its own workforce but also to facilitate knowledge transfer horizontally, from patients, physicians, suppliers, and the community.

Horizontal Knowledge Transfer

Transfer of knowledge horizontally across an organization can be much more problematic than vertical transfer. Mechanisms exist in all organizations to encourage and facilitate communication and transfer of knowledge up and down the line. Placing people on a formal organizational chart with defined reporting

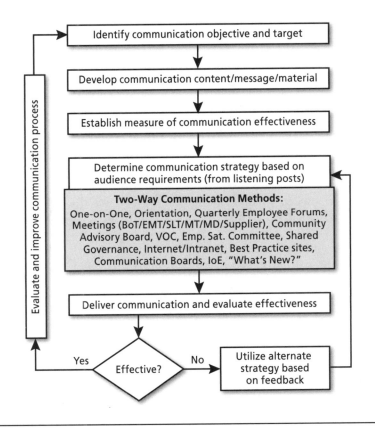

Figure 7.7 Five-pillar communication process – Robert Wood Johnson University Hospital at Hamilton.[22]

responsibilities and grouping functional specialists into departments and work units with common skills and interests provide natural incentives to communicate and share knowledge above and below. Effective managers also try to foster knowledge transfer horizontally within the limited reach of their departments.

But how does an organization preserve and build its knowledge assets horizontally? The functional specialization defined in the organization chart sets up vertical "silos" that hinder effective horizontal interaction. The challenge is to bridge all functions, locations, levels, entities, and all segments of the workforce, including physicians and volunteers. While that's not easy, the results are tangible. SSM's Paula Friedman said, "Now there is so much learning across functions that it's normal to work in that way. It's how we operate."

Even beyond that, high-performing organizations also recognize the value in the knowledge outside their walls, knowledge that resides in its other stakeholders, including patients, partners, suppliers, and the community. The Baldrige health care recipients used four primary methods to achieve horizontal communication and knowledge transfer—developing internal change agents; recognizing and rewarding appropriate behaviors and performance; implementing formal listening and learning approaches with external stakeholders; and identifying and transferring of best practices from both inside and outside of the organization.

The Baldrige Criteria set an expectation that a health care organization will have effective processes in place to listen and learn from its patients. The Criteria also stress the importance of understanding the needs and requirements of its other stakeholders. All of the Baldrige recipients have robust processes in place to listen, learn, and apply the learnings from their patients and stakeholders. Examples from two Baldrige recipients demonstrate how they build and transfer knowledge horizontally from outside the organization's boundaries.

Mercy Health System places great importance on its relationships with its physician partners. Their quarterly Physician Roundtables provide an opportunity for Mercy's Executive Committee members and physicians to discuss quality care initiatives and have two-way communication on current plans. Their annual CEO/Partner Forums also help to communicate Mercy's strategy and build partner engagement. Mercy also uses a formal relationship management model (Figure 7.8) to define its methods for gathering and using knowledge and information from its primary customer groups.

Transfer and Implementation of Best Practices

One method commonly used in all health care recipients to transfer and use knowledge is to identify best practices, either from inside or outside the organization, then ensure their effective implementation. Robert Wood Johnson University Hospital at Hamilton uses an intranet repository of best practices that have been vetted by the Executive Management Team. Mercy also maintains a best-practices repository on its intranet; uses a systematic process to facilitate rapid identification and sharing; standardizes best practices with system-wide applicability through

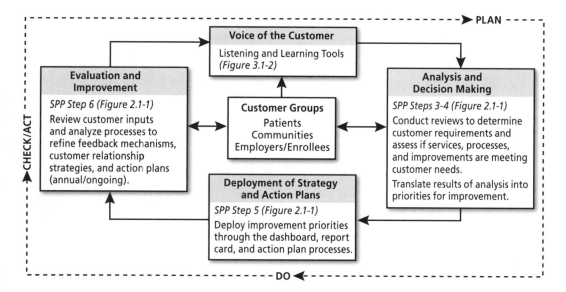

Figure 7.8 Customer relationship management model – Mercy Health System.[23]

action plans, programs, and policies; and reinforces the importance of developing and implementing best practices through several recognition approaches, including a Physician Incentive Program.

Poudre Valley has a formal process to ensure best practices are implemented throughout the organization. The appropriate oversight committee monitors implementation and effectiveness of best practices. The organization also has several other approaches targeted at sharing learning on particular issues for specific audiences. Poudre Valley looks at internal physician practice patterns to determine the local best practice. Changes are then incorporated into processes, protocols, and order sets and are shared with staff through several venues. Its Monday Afternoon Conference is a weekly meeting that allows regional speakers and Poudre Valley nurses and physicians to share best practices and evidence-based medicine. Poudre Valley also provides its leaders with a weekly informational email, "Turnover Tips," which describes best practices for decreasing workforce turnover.

These approaches range from the informal to highly structured. As they have become embedded as standard practices in the way the Baldrige health care recipients operate, it has become easier for them to build and improve the knowledge and skills of their workforces. In turn, this has increased the efficiency and effectiveness of these organizations.

SSM's Paula Friedman summed up the importance of using the Baldrige framework to drive effective execution. When asked, "What are your top three learnings that you share with those who ask, Why Baldrige?" she replied:

- "Clarity – (Baldrige) helped us clarify and explain what's important to us, our mission and how it connects to everything we do each day.

- Focus – It helped us identify and prioritize the vital few opportunities to improve and integrate our work to achieve the results we want to achieve.

- Discipline – To make sure that we know how to measure, evaluate systematically, achieve improvement and breakthrough."

Organizations that progress and excel using Baldrige use effective strategies to build and sustain momentum, including making meaningful changes from day one, effectively engaging their organizations, and driving change. They hardwire approaches to focus and take action on critical opportunities for improvement. They prioritize improvement and discontinue efforts that are not aligned with strategy so that the organization works smarter, not harder, even as they reinvent themselves. They establish accountability, develop action plans, and measure progress. They focus on process—taking advantage of the cause and effect relationship between how work gets done and the results that are achieved. They benchmark and improve their processes. They employ strong measurement and analysis approaches and systematically review key measures of progress, including a broad range of in-process and outcome measures to manage by fact. They transfer knowledge and spread best practices, becoming ever more agile and capable. They become organizations capable of achieving better results.

KEY POINTS IN THIS CHAPTER

- Executives need to develop and manage two agendas to be successful in their journey: (1) run the business and (2) change the business.

- Execution entails developing and implementing a set of actions that transform the learning from Assessment and Sensemaking into improved leadership and management processes.

- Elements of successful execution include the following: making changes from day one; setting clear priorities for changing the business; establishing accountability and developing action plans and measures to change the business; benchmarking, measuring, and improving key processes; reviewing progress and driving change; and spreading improvement.

- Determining what activities to stop doing can be just as important as, or even more important than, deciding which new initiatives to launch.

- Accountability plus action plans plus measurement create an essential structure for improvement.

- Benchmarking provides insight into relative levels of performance and also provides a tremendous opportunity to learn and apply best practices to achieve higher performance. Benchmarking both processes and results is an essential practice to improve health care.

- A focus on Execution leads to fundamental improvement of strategic planning, culture of accountability, line of sight, and process literacy throughout organizations.

8

Results

*"We do this [Baldrige]...for one simple
reason. We have found it saves lives."*

Rulon Stacey, President and CEO,
Poudre Valley Health System[1]

T he end game for transformational change is one thing: Results. Results are
the outcomes of an organization's strategy, key processes, and successfully
executed action plans. A Baldrige assessment of results provides an ideal
measure of overall organizational performance. In this final chapter, we analyze
the results of our study organizations to understand what health care performance
leadership looks like.

BALDRIGE AS A METHOD TO
DETERMINE HIGH PERFORMANCE

Ideally, superior performance is determined through methods blind to reputation
and personal opinion and based solely on unbiased evidence of high achievement
against a broad array of measures critical to an organization's success. Methods
should be *objective, results-focused,* and *comprehensive.* Several health care award
recipients looked for methods that would meet these requirements. There aren't
many options. As Rich Hastings, president and CEO, Saint Luke's Health System,
tells other organizations, "We had business practices in place, but no metrics to
demonstrate achievement. The Baldrige process provided an integrated a way to
demonstrate achievement." Rulon Stacey, president and CEO, Poudre Valley Health
System, told us that his organization reviewed the options for a cultural transformation approach ten years ago. They looked at various improvement methodologies, ISO 9000, and Baldrige: "We wanted a model for ongoing improvement
that would set our sights really high, get the organization unified toward one

common goal and provide an objective way to measure progress." Receiving the 2008 Baldrige Award will not change their commitment to using Baldrige. "Now that we have our processes and measurement system established, it will be easier to stay on the path," Stacey explained.

The Baldrige process and scoring methodology provide the *objectivity* in the score and feedback, as explained in detail in Chapter 2, Baldrige. The Criteria are nonprescriptive. Examiners are trained for consistency, use standard tools such as the evaluation factors linked to defined scoring ranges, and work as a consensus team. Policies requiring full disclosure of potential conflicts of interest and safeguarding confidentiality are strictly enforced for all examiners and judges.

The scoring system puts the focus on *results* by assigning 45 percent of the total point potential to the results category. An organization may score high in terms of the six process categories, demonstrating that it has systematic approaches to all areas of leadership, administrative, and patient care processes that are well deployed. But without results to prove those approaches are effective, the overall score is likely to be relatively low. The point distribution reinforces the importance of demonstrating excellence through rigorous quantitative evidence. The score is further weighted to emphasize the importance of health care outcomes, which receive a higher proportion of the results point total than the other five results items.

A Baldrige assessment is *comprehensive*. Baldrige is designed to identify high-performing organizations capable of addressing six aspects of an organization's performance, the six items of Category 7 in the Criteria:

- *Health care outcomes* – process, safety, and outcomes of care

- *Customer-focused outcomes* – satisfaction, dissatisfaction, engagement, and relationship building

- *Financial and market outcomes* – aggregate measures of financial return, financial viability, or budgetary performance; market share or position, growth, and new markets

- *Workforce-focused outcomes* – satisfaction, engagement, workforce and leader development, capability and capacity, climate

- *Process effectiveness outcomes* – operational performance of key work processes, productivity, cycle time, efficiency, and innovation

- *Leadership outcomes* – accomplishment of strategy and action plans, governance and fiscal accountability, regulatory and legal compliance, ethical behavior, and fulfillment of societal responsibilities

A Baldrige assessment is also comprehensive in that it examines all aspects of the organization leadership, management, and daily work processes, and how those processes contribute to results generated—how the organization functions as a system.

Results are judged as to their *importance*. This is determined by the unique circumstances of the particular organization. Important results address key factors for that organization; for example, they show fulfillment of the mission and vision, accomplishment of strategy and action plans, effective responses to strategic challenges, and success meeting and exceeding the needs and expectations of patients and stakeholders.

PERFORMANCE RESULTS OF BALDRIGE RECIPIENTS

So, using Baldrige as the method to determine high performance, what does high performance look like in terms of organizational results? We answer this question with a sampling of publicly available results from the four most recent recipient organizations: North Mississippi Medical Center, Mercy Health System, Sharp HealthCare, and Poudre Valley Health System. We focus on recipients from 2006 to 2008 because performance measurement in health care is in active and rapid evolution, and has changed substantially over the last decade since the Baldrige Award opened in the health care sector.

This is only a sampling intended to illustrate fundamental concepts in the evolving landscape of health care performance reporting and accountability. These examples were chosen not only to illustrate strong results, but also to show the kinds of data that applicants use to satisfy the results Criteria. Most of these results can be found in the publicly available application summaries and recipient profiles posted on the Baldrige Web site.

In general, the results of these four organizations share the following characteristics:

- Good to excellent organizational performance levels for most areas of importance to the organization

- Beneficial trends, sustained over time in areas of importance to the accomplishment of the organization's mission

- Some to most trends and current performance levels evaluated against relevant comparisons and/or benchmarks, with areas of good to excellent relative performance

- Results segmented by logical groupings, such as customer or workforce segments, location or service line, and so on to make analysis more meaningful

- Organizational performance results reported for most key patient, stakeholder, market, and process requirements

- A balanced mix of in-process and outcome measures

- Results demonstrate alignment/integration with key organizational strategies and goals

Award recipient organizations are very strong in most areas; in some areas they are industry leaders. But they are not the highest performers in every area.

Baldrige is not a perfection award, nor is it focused solely on quality or patient safety or any other single aspect of excellence. As an objective, results-focused, comprehensive evaluation, it looks at total operations and the organization's ability to excel in multiple dimensions in the areas most critical for success. It is perhaps best characterized as an "organizational culture of excellence" award or "total competency" award.

HEALTH CARE OUTCOMES

In health care, the highest priority for results is patient outcomes. This section of Category 7 is valued at 100 points out of the 450 points possible for results. Typically three types of results are included in this section:

- Publicly reported measures of quality and patient safety

- Measures available from large commercially available risk-adjusted data systems

- Measures critical to the specific organization's success and related to key factors such as its competitive situation and scope of services

Commonly reported results include mortality/morbidity rates, wound infection rates, functional status improvement, and use of restraints. Others may show the performance of critical pathways or results of efforts to improve patient safety, in areas such as handwashing practices and medication administration.

High-performing health care organizations demonstrate performance on measures tied to their unique mission, business objectives, and patient and community needs, endorsed and now frequently mandated by organizations such as CMS/Joint Commission, the Agency for Health Care Research and Quality, and the National Quality Forum. These and other standard-setting institutions create a "floor" for measurement reporting.

Summary of 2006-2008 Health Care Recipients' Health Care Results

Poudre Valley Health System (2008):

- With high levels of performance in many process measures for clinical assessments, care, and discharge, Poudre Valley is consistently at or near the top 10 percent of national performance standards for treating acute myocardial infarction, heart failure, and pneumonia.

- A community case management program that pairs advance practice nurses and social workers with high-risk, chronically ill patients decreased emergency visits annually by 50 percent.

(Continued)

Summary of 2006-2008 Health Care Recipients' Health Care Results *(continued)*

Sharp HealthCare (2007):

- The number of Sharp Health Plan patients with diabetes who have levels of low-density lipoprotein cholesterol—the so-called "bad cholesterol"—above 100 dropped by 44 percent in 2007.

- The incidence of breast and cervical cancer screening and blood sugar testing among members of Sharp's medical groups has increased steadily since 2003 and outperforms the top decile in the state of California's publicly reported database.

- A community case management program that pairs advance practice nurses and social workers with high-risk, chronically ill patients has decreased emergency visits annually by 50 percent and resulted in more than $850,000 savings for the past three years.

Mercy Health System (2007):

- Overall mortality rates for Mercy in 2007 match the best-practice benchmark based on data from the CareScience adjusted rate for the top 15 percent of U.S. hospitals. (CareScience is a provider of care management, clinical analysis, and clinical quality improvement solutions.)

- Results for community acquired pneumonia mortality have decreased steadily since 2003, with current results at 1.2 percent—significantly below the benchmark of 4 percent.

North Mississippi Medical Center (2006):

- Deep vein thrombosis (blood clot) rates were reduced 65 percent and pulmonary embolism rates were reduced 45 percent resulting in cost savings of more than $760,000.

- Physician "champions" working with service line leaders and clinical teams improved the care of patients requiring long term mechanical ventilation resulting in decreased mortality and length of stay in the intensive care unit and a reduction of $2 million in the cost of care.

- North Mississippi patients receiving coronary bypass surgery have fewer infections and postoperative stroke and pulmonary complications when benchmarked with the best (top 10–15 percent) in the Surgical Thoracic Society and the CareScience patient outcomes database.

North Mississippi Medical Center has powerful ways of presenting data that facilitate meaningful analysis and decision making. Their application includes twenty figures for their health care results. Eight include multiple variables in a single chart. North Mississippi integrates their measurement reporting of in-process (filled symbols) and outcome metrics (unfilled symbols) for a single diagnosis into one chart to show cause-and-effect relationships. These techniques make it easy to connect related information and draw conclusions.

North Mississippi uses benchmarks to set a high bar for performance. They use an internal system, the Cost Information Decision Support system, and an external database, CareScience, as the data sources for their analyses. In the Joint Commission's Core Measures program and measure themselves against the national 90th percentile.

Sharing comparative data engaged physicians in performance improvement and set the stage for the development of the Care-Based Cost Management approach. This approach links health care quality and cost containment by looking beyond traditional cost drivers (for example, people, equipment, supplies) to the care issues that have a much greater impact on the actual cost of care (such as practice variation, complications, and social issues). The approach has produced significant health care results, earning North Mississippi a place among Solucient's 100 Top Hospital Performance Improvement Leaders for three years running and in 2005 the American Hospital Association McKesson Quest for Quality Prize.

Figure 8.1 displays North Mississippi's results for Congestive Heart Failure (CHF). Cardiovascular disease is critical to the North Mississippi Medical Center; Mississippi has the highest cardiovascular disease death rate in the nation, and congestive heart failure is a high-volume chronic disease in North Mississippi's service area, so they focus on optimal management. They implemented the American Heart Association recommended processes and in 2006 approached the Joint Commission top decile. North Mississippi's comprehensive team approach extended optimal management to include home care, ambulatory care, and

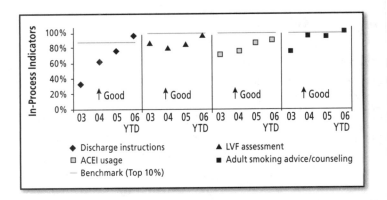

Figure 8.1 Cardiovascular/medicine service lines – congestive heart failure – North Mississippi Medical Center.[2]

long-term care settings with the goal to improve quality of life for this population. Figure 8.2 displays both in-process and outcome measures for acute myocardial infarction. Results were at or near the top 10 percent benchmark in 2006.

North Mississippi segments results along their service lines, since it is through this structure that all their clinical care is managed and improved. For the Cardio-vascular Service Line, North Mississippi reported on Acute Myocardial Infarction and Coronary Artery Bypass Graft with multiple variable charts, achieving bench-mark performance in both diagnoses.

For the Emergency Department/Surgical Service Lines, they presented outcomes for trauma, tracheotomy care, and craniotomy. In each area, multiple variable charts displaying in-process and outcomes measures showed benchmark performance. They achieved top 15 percent in trauma risk-adjusted outcomes, including morbidity and other complications, and approached this level with trauma mortality.

For the Medicine Service Line, North Mississippi reported on pneumonia proc-esses and outcomes, and ventilator guidelines compliance with outcomes. For the Behavioral Health Service Line, they reported on falls resulting in injury and restraint use, and set a target of zero restraint use with zero falls resulting in injury. Their Women/Children's Service Line was at or exceeded the top 10 percent on publicly reported quality measures related to pregnancy. Obstetricians led a focused performance improvement team to understand the causes and effects of third-degree and fourth-degree lacerations in vaginal delivery patients.

Sharp HealthCare makes extensive use of comparative and benchmark data to track and assess their relative performance. Sharp's health care outcomes include the following:

- Benchmark leadership related to average blood glucose levels among ICU patients with diabetes, breast and cervical cancer screening (Figures 8.7 and 8.8), blood sugar testing (Figure 8.9), and high-risk cholesterol LDL control.

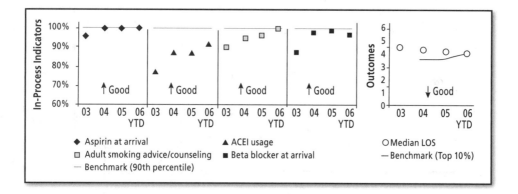

Figure 8.2 Cardiovascular service line – acute myocardial infarction – North Mississippi Medical Center.[3]

- Top decile results for appropriate antibiotic selection non-ICU, beta blockers at discharge.

- Top quartile results for skincare measures, surgical central line infections, and ventilator-associated pneumonia rates.

- Most other results better than national benchmarks, including commonly accepted patient safety indicators (Figure 8.3), mortality in patients with acute myocardial infarction, functional status in hip surgery and stroke patients, and transfer ability in home care patients.

Mercy's application includes results for many of the same measures. Like scores of health care organizations nationwide, Mercy has participated in the Joint Commission's Surgical Care Improvement Project. Mercy Hospital, Janesville, implemented a multi-disciplinary process in 2003 and created a protocol to administer prophylactic antibiotics sixty minutes before procedure start. Initial order sets with preoperative antibiotics listed aid the physician in timely ordering. Timeliness of postoperative antibiotic therapy is addressed through surgical nursing staff education (Figure 8.4). Mercy monitors and reports on mortality, segmented by procedure as well.

Sharp and Mercy, both integrated delivery systems, also reported results for outpatient quality of care. Sharp HealthCare includes affiliated medical groups as part of its system and considers both medical group and independent physicians as partners in delivering value to its patients. Sharp medical groups steadily improved breast and cervical cancer screening from 2003 to 2005, and they outperform the top decile in the Integrated Healthcare Association database publicly reported by the state (Figures 8.5 and 8.6).

Indicator Description (rates shown per 1,000 cases)	AHRQ Population Rate	Sharp 2006 Rate
Death in low mortality DRGs	0.66	0.10
Decubitus ulcer	22.71	17.70
Iatrogenic pneumothorax, secondary Dx	0.83	0.60
Selected infections due to medical care	1.99	1.50
Postoperative hip fracture	0.30	0.10
Postoperative hemorrhage or hematoma	2.03	1.90
Transfusion reaction, secondary Dx	0.01	0.00
Birth trauma – injury to neonate	6.34	0.70
OB trauma – vaginal delivery w/ instrument	217.09	172.00
OB trauma – vaginal delivery w/o instrument	81.98	38.30
OB trauma – cesarean section	5.93	2.70

Figure 8.3   Patient safety indicators – Sharp HealthCare.[4]

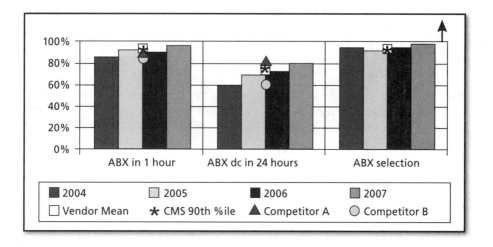

Figure 8.4 Surgical care improvement process measures – Mercy Hospital, Janesville.[5]

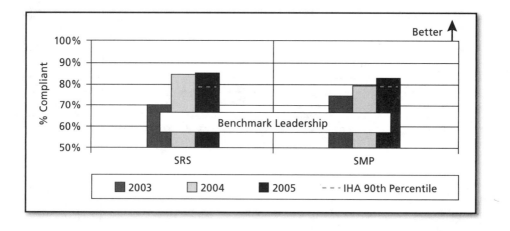

Figure 8.5 Breast cancer screening – Sharp Rees-Stealy and Mission Park Medical Clinics.[6]

Improvement in outpatient diabetes care is a statewide initiative and was set as a system target. Sharp's medical groups accelerated the rate of improvement year-over-year and, as a result, less than 8 percent of their patients need intensive management for diabetes. Sharp's medical groups lead the community in diabetes management (Figure 8.7).

A high score in Category 7 typically requires evidence of high performance across all business units and care settings. To illustrate, as an integrated delivery system, Mercy reported on its home health outcomes. Mercy Assisted Care participates in national projects to benchmark home health quality. Focus areas include improvement in pain, dyspnea, and ambulation. Through the performance measurement system, improvement opportunities in these areas were identified. A multi-disciplinary team made process improvements through staff education on appropriate assessment and documentation and created standardized patient assessment questions, and results are reviewed with staff at quarterly meetings.

Poudre Valley's performance on three CMS core measures—acute myocardial infarction, heart failure, and pneumonia—is consistently in or near the top 10 percent of national performance (Figure 8.9).

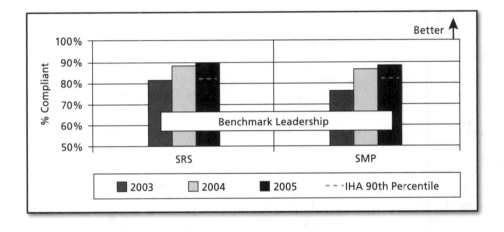

Figure 8.6   Cervical cancer screening – Sharp Rees-Stealy and Mission Park Medical Clinics.[7]

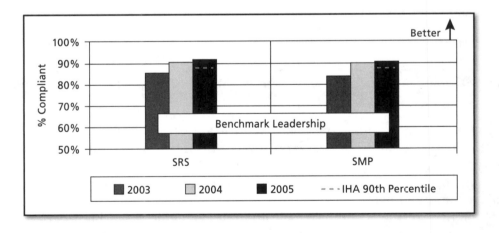

Figure 8.7   Compliance with blood sugar testing – Sharp Rees-Stealy and Mission Park Medical Clinics.[8]

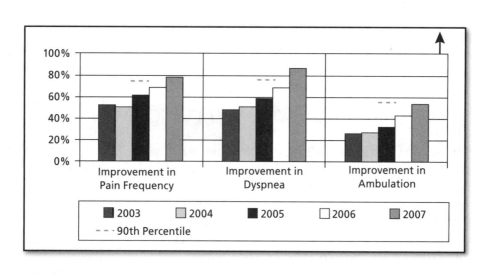

Figure 8.8 Home health outcomes – Mercy Assisted Care.[9]

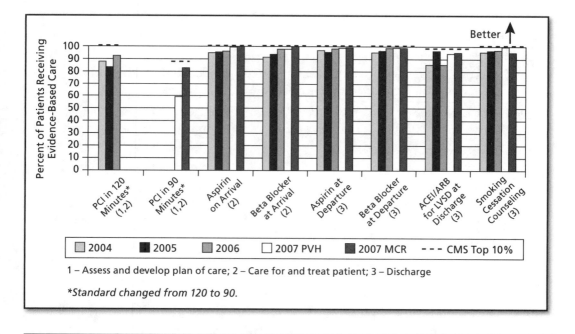

Figure 8.9 Process results for acute myocardial infarction – Poudre Valley Health System.[10]

Although no organization demonstrates the highest level of performance in every measure, health care award recipients demonstrate significant improvement with benchmark performance in many critical health care indicators.

CUSTOMER-FOCUSED OUTCOMES

Customer-focused outcomes demonstrate the satisfaction, dissatisfaction, and engagement of the organization's patients and stakeholders. In today's competitive health care environment, successful organizations take seriously the idea of patients as customers of a service who have a choice in their care. Commonly reported results include satisfaction and engagement survey data, complaints and grievances, and enrollment and retention data, as well as market perceptions and preferences.

In 2009, the Criteria place an increased emphasis on performance related to patient engagement, recognizing that patient and stakeholder investment in or commitment to the organization is key to success and long-term sustainability.

Summary of 2006-2008 Health Care Recipients' Customer-Focused Results

Poudre Valley Health System (2008):

- Poudre Valley's patient loyalty ranks in the top 1 percent of U.S. hospitals, according to the Centers for Medicare and Medicaid Services.

- In 2007, Avatar named the Medical Center of the Rockies as the Exemplary Service Overall Best Performer and ranked the hospital among the top twelve nationally for customer satisfaction.

- Poudre Valley Health System has consistently maintained competitive health care costs when compared to local competitors who have a similar patient base and to the average health care costs in the Denver metropolitan area, their secondary service area. In 2006, the average Poudre Valley charge was significantly lower than that of competitors.

Sharp HealthCare (2007):

- San Diego consumers have named Sharp as the best health care provider in the region, with top rankings for clinical quality, customer service, doctors, and nurses.

- Inpatient satisfaction with the nursing staff has improved more than 300 percent systemwide since 2002, while satisfaction with the discharge process has grown 200 percent during the same time span.

- Sharp Health Plan's grievance rates have been consistently low—fewer than 0.15 grievances per 1,000 members per month—since 2002, a measure that puts Sharp in the top quartile nationally for the entire period.

(Continued)

Summary of 2006-2008 Health Care Recipients' Customer-Focused Results *(continued)*

Mercy Health System (2007):

- In 2006, overall satisfaction with Mercy multi-specialty outpatient centers was 96 percent; overall satisfaction with Mercy hospitals was 95.2 percent.

- In 2006, about 84 percent of hospital customers and about 90 percent of multi-specialty outpatient center customers would recommend Mercy to others, a key indicator of customer loyalty and a reflection of overall satisfaction.

- Mercy's "Take the L.E.A.D." program—Listen to the customer; Empathize with the customer; Accept the customer's perspective, Apologize, Acknowledge concern and take Action to recover; Direct to the person able to recover the situation—is used to turn negative experiences into positive ones. Effectiveness in resolving patient and customer concerns has risen from about 90 percent in 2002 to 94 percent in 2007.

North Mississippi Medical Center (2006):

- Results for inpatient satisfaction demonstrate consistent improvement since 2004 and, in 2006, the Likelihood to Recommend scores approached Press Ganey's 90th percentile.

In support of its vision to provide world-class health care, Poudre Valley Health System monitors "top-box" results, meaning they track and manage to the top satisfaction grouping in their data, since only this highly loyal segment has been shown to actively refer other patients. This rigorous measure of customer retention and loyalty allows comparison across industries, surveys, and databases. Top box is the percentage of patients who give the highest customer satisfaction rating to a given aspect of their care. Driving improvement in top-box measurement is the same approach Disney has used for years. It demonstrates a commitment to achieving true customer engagement. Poudre Valley has shown strong improvement using this technique and consistently achieves superior top box results for patient satisfaction, as measured by the Avatar Patient Satisfaction Survey (Figure 8.10).

Poudre Valley continues to improve its top box results for the key customer requirements of Friendly Staff and Prompt Service (Figure 8.11).

Mercy Health System divides its market segments into customers within four core service areas: acute care patients, post-acute care/retail services, communities (counties); and employer/enrollees. Mercy has identified its patient satisfaction performance targets as the top quartiles of Press Ganey for hospitals; American Medical Group Association for clinics; and the National Committee on Quality Assurance for the MercyCare Insurance Company.

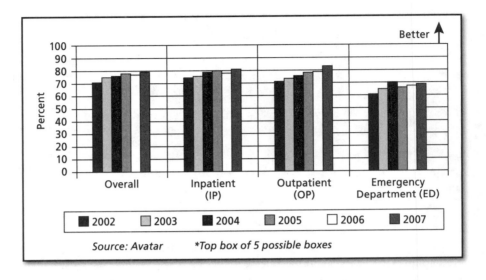

Figure 8.10   Top box scores for patient satisfaction – Poudre Valley Health System.[11]

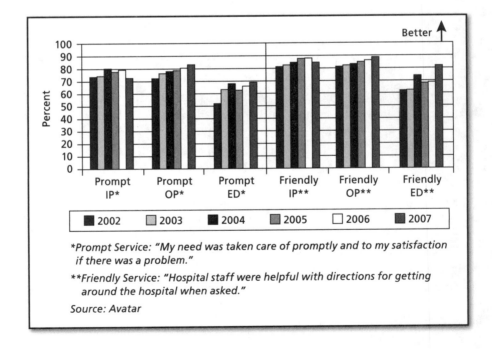

Figure 8.11   Top box scores for prompt service and friendly staff – Poudre Valley Health System.[12]

Since 2002, Mercy has used an internal, rapid-cycle surveying process for all four core service areas to measure percent satisfied, the top two ratings on each survey (satisfied and very satisfied combined) (Figure 8.12). The percent satisfied measure is a key factor used to determine the Mercy annual discretionary contribution to the Matched Savings Plan.

In fiscal year 2006, Mercy started requiring top quartile targets on dashboards, report cards, and their Physician Incentive Plan to increase focus on patient satisfaction and best-practice performance. Satisfaction with Press Ganey scales for Nursing Care and Personal Issues are key indicators, highly correlated with overall inpatient satisfaction. In 2006, Mercy Hospital, Janesville, chartered a team to improve inpatient satisfaction. Improvement initiatives implemented included increased nursing leadership rounds, addition of a patient representative, communication boards, discharge phone calls, and thank-you notes to patients after discharge. Inpatient Satisfaction for Mercy hospitals by location and key indicators are shown in Figure 8.13. Emergency Department Satisfaction on key indicators is shown in Figure 8.14.

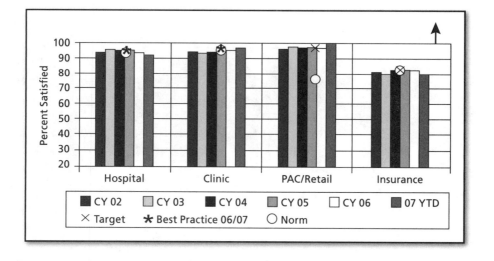

Figure 8.12   Patient satisfaction by core service – Mercy Health System.[13]

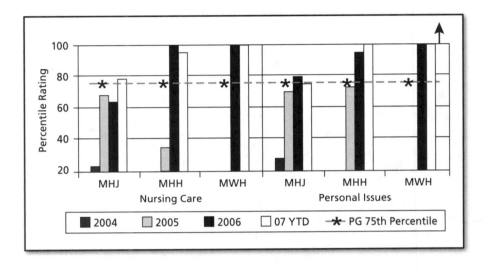

Figure 8.13   Inpatient satisfaction by hospital – Mercy Health System.[14]

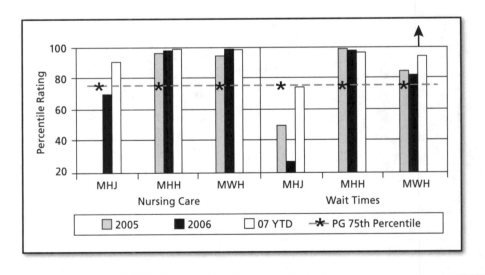

Figure 8.14   Emergency department satisfaction by hospital – Mercy Health System.[15]

Mercy measures clinic satisfaction and analyzes data by state, specialty, and key drivers of satisfaction, such as Personal Manner of Physician and Courtesy of Staff. Mercy charters improvement initiatives based on review of these analyses. Figure 8.15 displays clinic satisfaction with courtesy, segmented by staff role. Each exceeded the 75th percentile benchmark in 2007.

Like Mercy Health System, Sharp HealthCare evaluates patient satisfaction scores using Press Ganey with targets to outperform the Press Ganey 75th percentile level. All Sharp's patient satisfaction scores are evaluated at the system, department, and unit levels. These data are updated on a weekly basis and reviewed at all levels of the organization monthly to drive improvement. Sharp segments data by survey type and demographic characteristics to further understand the information and enhance their capacity to satisfy their customers.

Sharp's overall satisfaction scores for both inpatients and outpatients have improved 150 percent since 2002, with scores approaching the Press Ganey top quartile rankings. Results for Sharp's target market segments (Spanish speakers, seniors 65+, and women 25–54) are in the top quartile (Figure 8.16).

Medical group offices showed positive trends from 2002 through 2006. Although they did not achieve their goal of Press Ganey 75th percentile, their improvement is meaningful, particularly for urgent care patients (Figure 8.17).

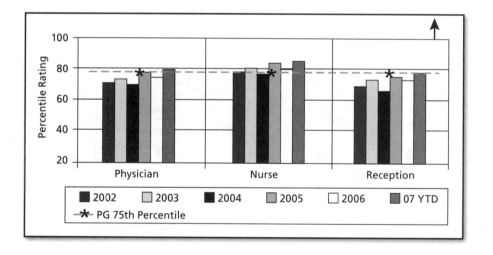

Figure 8.15 Clinic satisfaction with courtesy – Mercy Health System.[16]

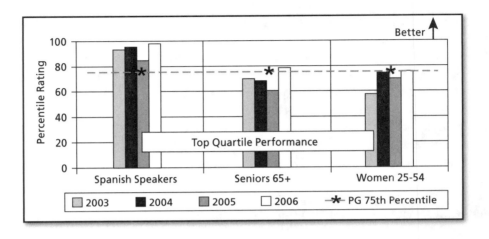

Figure 8.16   Overall inpatient satisfaction by target market segment – Sharp HealthCare.[17]

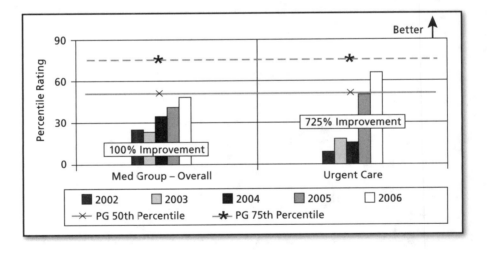

Figure 8.17   Medical group patient satisfaction – Sharp HealthCare.[18]

Sharp tracks the perception that San Diego residents have of Sharp's quality compared with other providers (Figure 8.18). These findings show a substantial increase in perception of clinical quality, customer service, best nurses, and best overall compared to Sharp's closest competitor.

FINANCIAL AND MARKET OUTCOMES

Strong financial and market performance is a critical outcome of an efficient and effective organization, and a key contributor to long-term sustainability. Financial performance is demonstrated by results for aggregate measures of financial return, such as return on investment, operating margin, and profitability, and by results for measures of financial viability, such as debt-to-equity ratio, days cash on hand, and bond ratings. Marketplace performance is demonstrated by results for such measures as market share or position, growth in market share, and new markets entered.

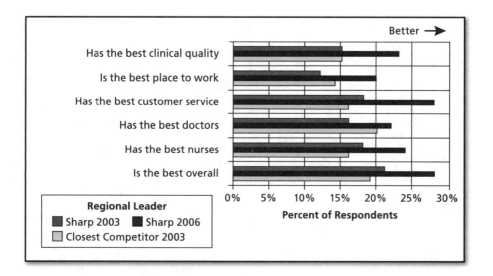

Figure 8.18   Perception of quality: Sharp and closest competitor, 2003 and 2006 – Sharp HealthCare.[19]

Summary of 2006-2008 Health Care Recipients' Financial and Market Results

Poudre Valley Health System (2008):

- The Poudre Valley score on the Financial Flexibility Index (a composite of seven financial ratios measuring financial stability) determined by Ingenix, a provider of comparative clinical and financial results, has approached or surpassed the top 10 percent nationally for six years.

Sharp HealthCare (2007):

- Between 2001 and 2006, Sharp HealthCare's net revenue increased by 56 percent.

- Between 1999 and 2005, Sharp gained more than four percentage points in market share, an unprecedented achievement in a mature health care marketplace.

- Sharp's market share in its target segments—women between 25 and 54 years of age, seniors ages 65 or older, and Hispanics—increased by 1.5 percent, 5 percent, and 5 percent, respectively, between 2002 and 2006. Sharp's improved performance enhances not only its financial health but also the breadth and quality of its health.

Mercy Health System (2007):

- Since 1989, Mercy's revenue has increased from about $33 million to $847 million, demonstrating significant growth.

- Mercy is the leader in market share for inpatient services and outpatient surgery in its Wisconsin service area. In addition, Mercy's physician clinic office visit captures 87 percent of the market in its Wisconsin service area.

- Since 1989, many health care systems have seen declining bond ratings while Mercy's Moody bond rating remained stable at A2 from 1996 to 2007, and increased to positive long-term outlook in 2007. This is a key measure of its commitment to financial stability and long-term viability.

Sharp's transformational journey, the Sharp Experience, began in 2001, and Sharp started to see revenue improvement in 2003. Net Revenue Results (Figure 8.19) shows an average growth rate of 14 percent, with a 56 percent increase from 2002 to 2006.

Sharp chose a common comparative, Moody's Investor Service, to demonstrate its assets to liabilities results. Sharp's 3.2 ratio compares favorably to the Moody's benchmark score of 2 for A-rated facilities (Figure 8.20). Though modest improvement occurred between 2001 and 2004, Sharp saw strong, continued improvement from 2004.

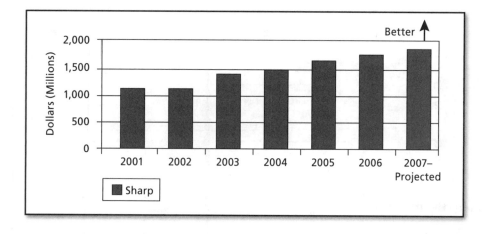

Figure 8.19   Net revenue results – Sharp HealthCare.[20]

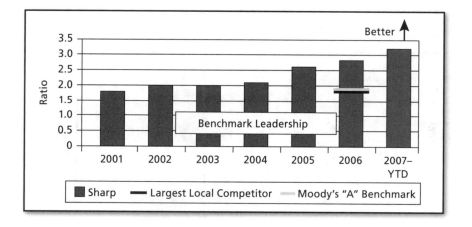

Figure 8.20   Current ratio of assets to liabilities – Sharp HealthCare.[21]

Sharp performs at the Advisory Board top quartile for Hospital Days in Accounts Receivable and Billing Cost per Dollar Earned, two key measures of overall financial performance. Sharp demonstrates strong marketplace performance as the market leader in San Diego County and the only one of five key service providers experiencing growth.

As evidence of marketplace performance, Sharp demonstrates its market position overall compared to key competitors (Figure 8.21) and its market share by target market segment (Figure 8.22).

Sharp has grown in each of its key target market segments over three years.

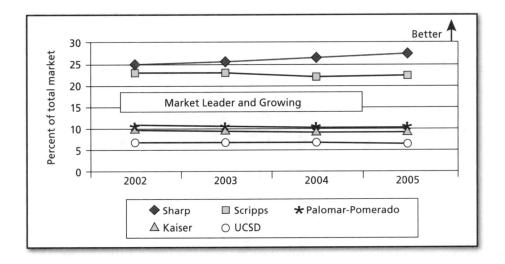

Figure 8.21 Market share results for San Diego County – Sharp HealthCare.[22]

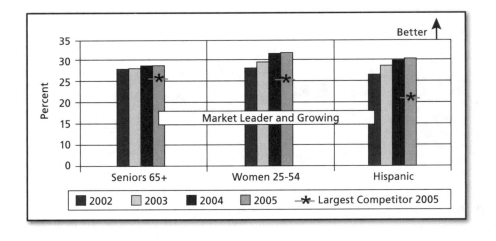

Figure 8.22 Market share by target market segment – Sharp HealthCare.[23]

Poudre Valley has consistently maintained an advantage in health care costs when compared to local competitors and to the Denver metropolitan area (Figure 8.23).

Poudre Valley measures financial performance and sustainability, key to its mission and non-for-profit status, with a composite measure. In addition to typical profit-per-discharge data, the Financial Flexibility Index, shown Figure 8.24, represents a composite of seven financial ratios measuring stability of funds flow, and is considered one of the most balanced measures of financial health. The score is calculated by Ingenix, a provider of comparative clinical and financial results. It shows Poudre Valley approaching or surpassing the top 10 percent nationally for six years. The application explains the dip in results in 2007 as expected with the impact of opening a new hospital, but notes that even within that disadvantage, Poudre Valley's score remained well above the U.S. top 25 percent.

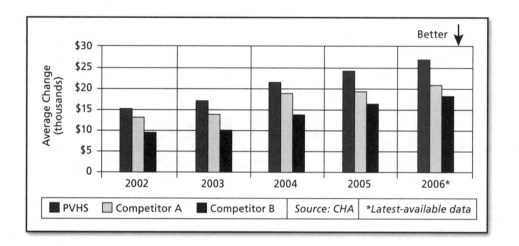

Figure 8.23 Low-cost provider – Poudre Valley Health System.[24]

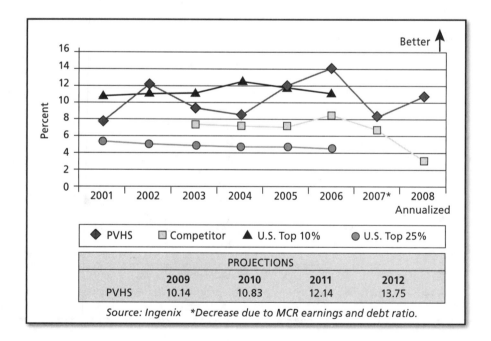

Figure 8.24 Financial flexibility index – Poudre Valley Health System.[25]

Mercy describes its financial successes as an outcome of an integrated delivery strategy and diversification to protect operations from revenue instability. Use of their own subsidiary, MercyCare Insurance Company, supports their strategy through direct contracts with employers and generation of system referrals, thereby increasing usage of their own provider network. Mercy has seen steady growth in net revenue is displayed below (Figure 8.25).

A compelling addition to their financial results story is the success in Physician Practice Measures, which are compared with results from the Medical Group Management Association (Figure 8.26). Mercy's physician partnership model seeks to enhance clinician engagement in productivity and efficiency improvement. With Mercy's management of the clinic practice, physicians can focus on patient load increases, supervision of nurses, and submission of charges. Engaging physicians in process improvement has resulted in increasingly favorable financial performance. These paired outcomes reflect the effectiveness of Mercy's alignment of workforce, process improvement, and financial performance.

North Mississippi Medical Center offers a similar set of outcomes to demonstrate how clinical quality management related to growth in financial gains. Targeted clinical improvements resulted in a 65 percent reduction in deep vein thrombosis and 45 percent reduction in pulmonary embolism, generating cost savings of more than $760,000.

In addition, North Mississippi addressed head-on the challenges of low or no compensation for care, identifying those diagnoses whose Medicare reimbursement is less than the cost of providing care as "DRG losers." Results of the focus on practice variation, complications, and social issues in North Mississippi's Care-Based Cost Management approach makes a strong business case for improved quality and reduced cost (Figure 8.27).

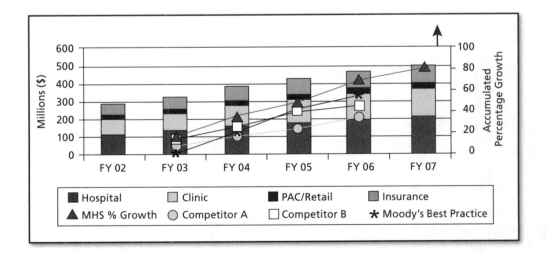

Figure 8.25 Growth in net revenue – Mercy Health System.[26]

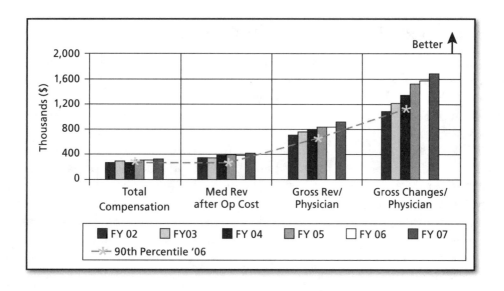

Figure 8.26 Physician practice measures – Mercy Health System.[27]

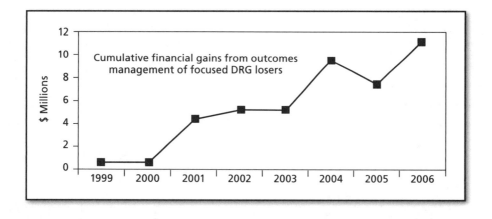

Figure 8.27 Care-based cost management relationship of quality to cost – North Mississippi Medical Center.[28]

In response to non-reimbursed care, North Mississippi targeted efforts toward reducing inappropriately long lengths of stay. The organization learned that even small avoidable delays in discharge have significant impacts on costs. Improving key work processes, such as discharge, resulted in increased financial health for the organization, which contributed to the organization's ability to serve the broader community and fulfill its mission.

WORKFORCE-FOCUSED OUTCOMES

Workforce-focused outcomes reflect the organization's ability to create and maintain a productive, engaged workforce capable of implementing the strategy and achieving high performance in a patient-focused culture. Successful organizations manage and develop their workforce and create a healthy, safe, secure, and supportive environment.

"Workforce" refers to everyone actively involved in achieving the work of the organization: all levels of employees paid by the organization, contract employees, independent practitioners (for example, the medical staff), volunteers, and students, as appropriate. Organizations segment their workforce-focused results by key factors, such as job type, level, and location, to demonstrate performance across the entire workforce. Workforce-focused results include the following:

- Workforce satisfaction and engagement (the extent of commitment to the organization's work, mission, and vision)

- Workforce capability and capacity (that is, evidence the organization has the knowledge, skills, and abilities, and in sufficient supply, to accomplish its work)

- Workforce safety (for example, needle stick incidents), security (for example, identification badge compliance), and benefits (for example, percentage of employees using health club membership)

- Workforce and leadership development

Summary of 2006-2008 Health Care Recipients' Workforce-Focused Results

Poudre Valley Health System (2008):

- Overall physician satisfaction ranks in the national 99th percentile, according to Gallup.

Sharp HealthCare (2007):

- Physician satisfaction surveys show that the majority of the organization's 2,600 affiliated physicians consistently feel Sharp is the best place to practice medicine. Sharp's physician satisfaction scores exceed industry benchmarks at almost every hospital in the system. Eighty percent of those ratings are in the top quartile.

(Continued)

Summary of 2006-2008 Health Care Recipients' Workforce-Focused Results *(continued)*

Mercy Health System (2007):

- For the last two years, Mercy has been ranked number one and number two in the nation on the American Association of Retired Persons "Best Employers for Workers Over Age 50" list. This year, Mercy was the only organization to receive AARP's "Bernard Nash Award" in the flexible work options category for its innovative age-neutral policies. Mercy also was named one of the "100 Best Companies to Work" by Working Mother magazine.

- To determine workforce engagement, Mercy uses surveys as well as informal methods such as CEO partner forums and lunch with leaders. Mercy ranks in the 96th percentile for "feeling valued" and in the 95th percentile for overall satisfaction. Physician satisfaction ranks above the American Medical Group Association 95th percentile.

- Staff turnover at Mercy has declined from 13.5 percent in 2002 to 7.5 percent in 2007.

North Mississippi Medical Center (2006):

- Through tuition reimbursement and other activities, North Mississippi allocates more than $1.4 million annually to help employees upgrade skills and advance their careers.

- Since 2000, overall employee satisfaction has exceeded the 90th percentile benchmark levels from Human Resources, Inc.

- Employee satisfaction is demonstrated with an employee retention rate of more than 89 percent since 2001.

Poudre Valley Health System considers workforce engagement one of its organizational core competencies, critical to achieving the strategic plan. Their strong approaches to workforce focus are complemented by strong approaches to measurement of workforce-focused outcomes. This link between what is important (from the organizational profile), how it is done, and how it is measured (process categories) with the actual results achieved (results categories) is characteristic of organizations in Integration (stage 3) in the journey to performance excellence. Poudre Valley's Employee Culture Survey Results shows strong improvement trends in Staff Requirements, a key culture dimension (Figure 8.28).

Figure 8.29 demonstrates Poudre Valley's improvement trends over four years achieving or surpassing the Management Science Association's 90th percentile national benchmark across four employee statements.

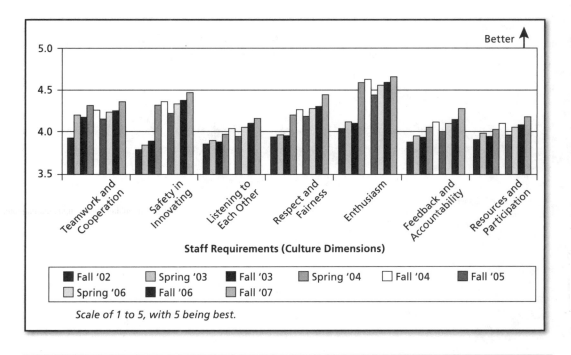

Figure 8.28   Employee culture survey – Poudre Valley Health System.[29]

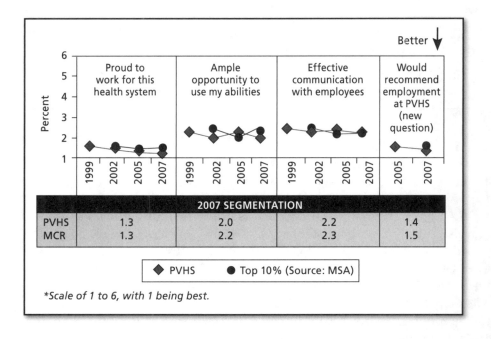

Figure 8.29   Employee engagement survey – Poudre Valley Health System.[30]

Poudre Valley exceeds the national top 10 percent in 11 out of 16 key "attitude areas" associated with employee satisfaction and engagement. They exceed the national top 20 percent in 14 of the 16 (Figure 8.30).

Like others at the leading edge of workforce focus, Poudre Valley found that more frequent sampling of employee engagement allowed the organization to better maintain its culture and achieve related goals.

Poudre Valley's systematic improvements to workforce satisfaction and engagement have resulted in dramatic improvements in Staff Voluntary Turnover (Figure 8.31). Poudre Valley's rate in 2006 is better than the American Society for Health Care Human Resources Administration top 10 percent and the rate reported by Colorado Health Care, which includes local competitors, and is less than half the 2001 rate. The figure demonstrates the strong connection between process and results with annual improvements indicated.

The American Nurses' Credentialing Center, which sponsors Magnet Recognition for Nursing Excellence, asserts that higher skill levels of caregivers correlate with improved patient outcomes. With this alignment in mind, Poudre Valley tracks the number of nurses holding national certifications. Based on its National

Attitude Areas of Measurement	U.S. Top 10%	U.S. Top 20%	Above National Norm
Job satisfaction	•	•	•
Senior management group	•	•	•
Department director	•	•	•
Immediate supervision			•
Communications	•	•	•
Human resources		•	•
Pay	•	•	•
Benefits	•	•	•
Job security	•	•	•
Development		•	•
Physical work environment	•	•	•
Teamwork		•	•
Work demands	•	•	•
Resource utilization			•
Participation	•	•	•
Performance management	•	•	•
Source: MSA, May 2008			

Figure 8.30 Employee satisfaction survey – Poudre Valley Health System.[31]

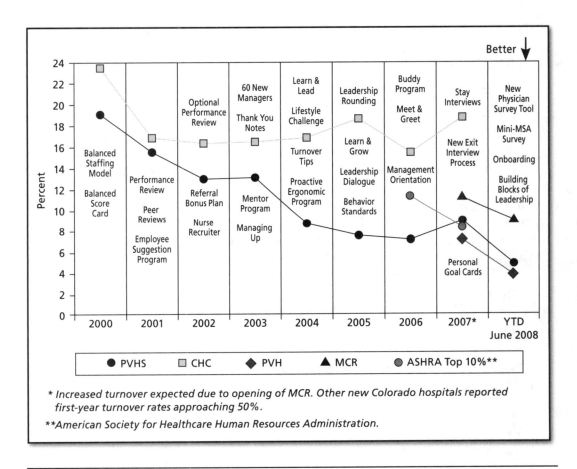

Figure 8.31 Staff voluntary turnover rate – Poudre Valley Health System.[32]

Database of Nursing Quality Indicators, the American Nurses Association named Poudre Valley Hospital the nation's top hospital for nursing quality.

Sharp HealthCare also recognizes the importance of maintaining a highly satisfied physician group. Although scores at some hospitals have declined, Sharp asserts that these data have prompted the creation of initiatives to ensure continued growth in physician partner opinions. Despite the decreases, Sharp's scores exceed Press Ganey benchmarks in most system entities with 80 percent of physicians ranking satisfaction in the top quartile (Figure 8.32).

Sharp's workforce results include results for key drivers of employee satisfaction. Positive trends are evident and all exceed best in class benchmarks as defined by HR Solutions. These results suggest to Sharp that its strategy to "engage the hearts and minds" of its staff in The Sharp Experience is successful. Survey data are evaluated at all levels of the organization, segmented on all parameters, and acted on in the Employee Opinion Survey roll-out.

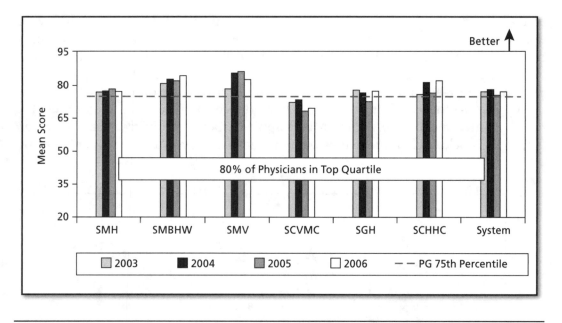

Figure 8.32 Overall physician satisfaction – Sharp HealthCare.[33]

Along with Turnover Rate and Workforce Vacancy, Sharp measures Annual Retention, segmenting results by job class. Sharp operates in an environment of significant competition for qualified staff in an undersupplied market. Sharp's Profile lists "state-mandated nurse-to-patient staffing ratios" as a key industry change and challenge for their organization. Achieving these mandates is one of their key Critical Success Factors. Figure 8.33 shows that Sharp maintains much lower vacancy rates than the benchmark in a market with the aforementioned limitations and mandates. Because the data are segmented, Sharp can demonstrate its ability to retain leadership.

Common to many Baldrige recipient applications is their achievement of success on measures developed by the Best Places to Work Institute. The institute's "trust index" is an overall measure of satisfaction that combines scores in five areas of organizational culture/climate associated with being a great place to work. Figure 8.34 shows Mercy Health System's results on the trust index for the last three years related to the "100 Best." Mercy credits its success to organizational strategy, continually enhancing feedback responsiveness, education and training, reward and recognition programs, and leadership excellence.

To demonstrate workforce development, Baldrige users frequently track hours of training provided. The American Society for Training and Development recognizes organizations that demonstrate enterprise-wide training success through its Best Awards. In 2005, North Mississippi Medical Center exceeded this benchmark and that of the Benchmarking Forum Organization, a best-practice-sharing group of Fortune 500 companies and public sector organizations. Notably, in their 2006 application, North Mississippi applied a more rigorous metric to measure training by adding a measure of effectiveness ((Figure 8.35). As a result of training, North Mississippi increased their quality of care as evidenced by the increase in percentage of resuscitations in adherence with best-practice guidelines.

Workforce-focused outcomes include evidence that the work environment is healthy, safe, and secure. North Mississippi defines a "culture of safety" as an employee's acknowledgment that patient safety is a priority of management. In

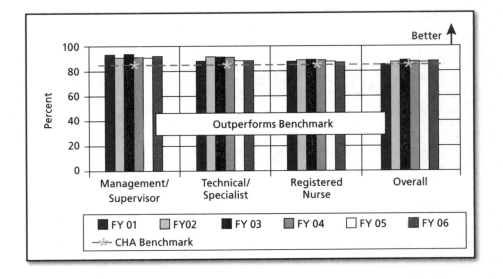

Figure 8.33 Annual retention by job class – Sharp HealthCare.[33]

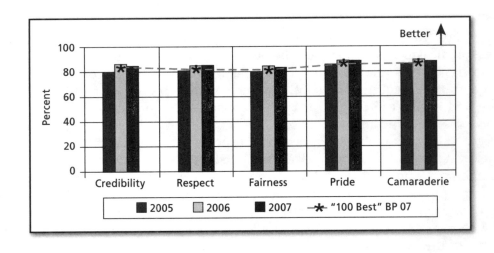

Figure 8.34 Best places to work "100 best" trust index – Mercy Health System.[35]

2004-05, North Mississippi joined the Stanford Patient Safety Consortium sponsored by the Agency for Healthcare Research and Quality by participating in an assessment of safety culture. North Mississippi met or exceeded the study group's top decile (Figure 8.36).

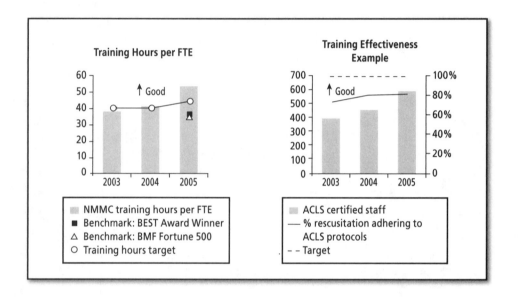

Figure 8.35   Training hours and effectiveness example – North Mississippi Medical Center.[36]

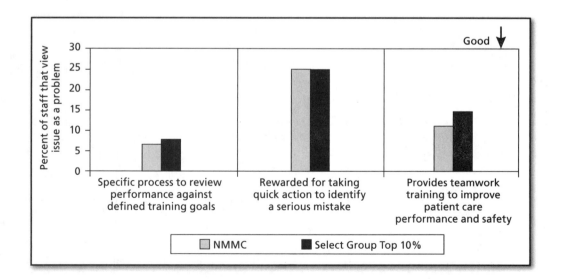

Figure 8.36   Culture of patient safety – North Mississippi Medical Center.[37]

PROCESS EFFECTIVENESS OUTCOMES

Effective processes are essential to achieve results. Process effectiveness outcomes address the performance of the organization's key work systems and processes in meeting key operational requirements. These results show effectiveness, efficiency, and innovation, as well as preparedness for events that could interrupt customary practice (that is, emergencies and disasters). Typical are results for productivity and cycle time, such as occupancy, door-to-doctor time, supply fill rate, and help desk calls. Other process effectiveness outcomes demonstrate increased use of new technology, reduction in testing and inspection, waste reduction, and the impact of various process improvement projects.

Summary of 2006-2008 Health Care Recipients' Process Effectiveness Results

---

Poudre Valley Health System (2008):

- The Abandoned Call Rate for Poudre Valley's Call Center has remained at 2 percent for four years, well below the industry average of nearly 6 percent.

- Effectively centralizing the preventive maintenance process and eliminating outside contractors has saved Poudre Valley about $300,000 annually for the last four years.

Sharp HealthCare (2007):

- Percent of gross charges denied by payers approaches 0 percent, significantly outperforming the national benchmark.

- Sharp used an innovative Web-based solution to "bring Sharp patients back to Sharp from other hospitals" and reported savings of an estimated $4.9 million since inception between the second quarter 2006 and the first quarter 2007.

Mercy Health System (2007):

- Administrative and general expenses as a percent of revenue are low, representing approximately 10 percent of revenue. Mercy is in the CMS top quartile for this measure.

North Mississippi Medical Center (2006):

- Care-Based Cost Management has led to more than $11 million in savings over the last six years. The approach has resulted in more efficient and safer patient care processes, fewer complications, and shorter lengths of stay, helping North Mississippi to earn the American Hospital Association McKesson Quest for Quality Prize in 2005.

In a targeted effort to improve timeliness of medication administration and thus prevent complications, Sharp achieved a statistically significant improvement in turnaround time for pharmacy drug delivery. A 50 percent improvement was realized by reconfiguring their physical workspace, matching staffing to peak order times, and installing a fax server.

Sharp leverages process improvement to improve financial outcomes as well as clinical results. Sharp collaborated with orthopedic surgeons and joint prosthetic suppliers to standardize the implants used and decrease the degree of profit shortfalls in orthopedics as depicted in Figure 8.37.

Like many applicants, Mercy Health System uses length of stay as a measure of work systems performance. Despite an increase in case-mix index, the increased use of protocols and targeted improvements in inpatient management have led to decreased Average Length of Stay. Mercy credits proactive efforts to reduce infections and complications as factors in continued positive trends for this measure. Mercy exceeds comparisons with state hospitals, peer groups, and a best-practice competitor (Figure 8.38).

Mercy further segments its data by hospital to analyze length of stay based on illness severity. Once again, they compare favorably to their peer groups (Figure 8.39).

Increasingly common in Baldrige applications are metrics that assess access: the patient's ability to seek and receive care with the provider of their choice, at the time they choose, regardless of the reason for their visit. Mercy uses open-access scheduling to meet patients' needs (Figure 8.40).

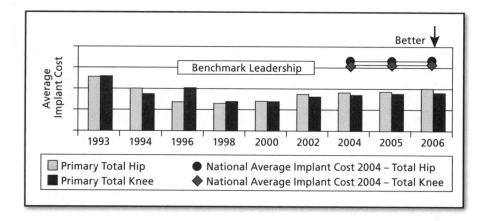

Figure 8.37   Hip and knee implant costs – ortho joint program – Sharp HealthCare.[38]

Poudre Valley Health System considers timely access to care a key process requirement. They monitor three areas of access: response times to emergency ambulance calls, length of time to see a physician in the emergency department, and outpatient clinic wait times. With respect to the clinics, Figure 8.41 shows improvement not only in door-to-doctor time, but also in door-to-departure time. Increasing the rigor of their process over time, Poudre Valley maintained their goal of wait times less than sixty minutes, despite a 21 percent increase in patient volumes. Results for the Family Medicine Center compare favorably to the average U.S. wait time. An additional increase in rigor occurred when Poudre Valley changed measures as a result of learning and instituted a goal of admission and discharge within ninety minutes.

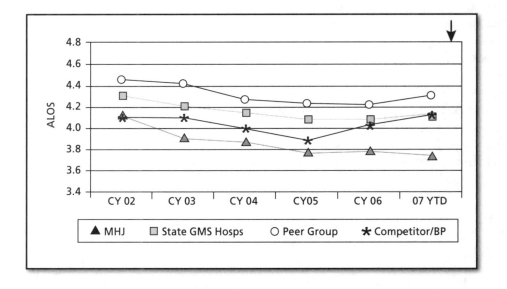

Figure 8.38   Average length of stay – Mercy Hospital, Janesville.[39]

	CY 02	CY03	CY 04	CY 05	CY 06	07 YTD
MHH	2.5	2.3	2.2	2.7	2.6	2.8
IL CAH Peer Group	3.4	3.2	3.3	3.3	3.3	3.3
MWH					3.3	2.7
WI CAH Peer Group	3.4	3.3	3.3	3.1	3.2	3.3

Figure 8.39   Critical access hospital average length of stay – Mercy Health System.[40]

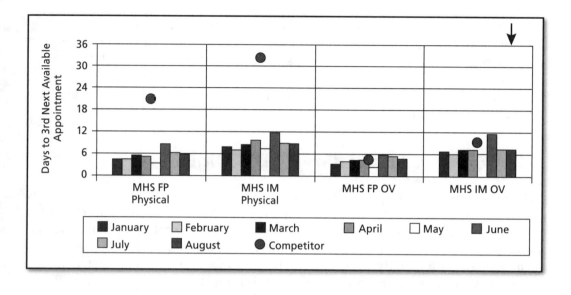

Figure 8.40   Clinic access – Mercy Health System.[41]

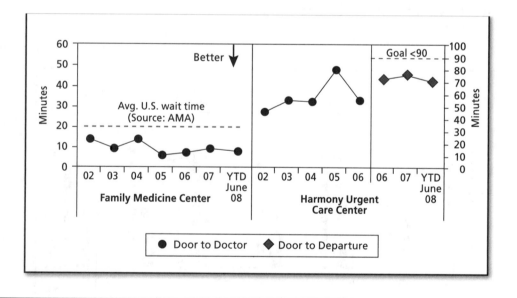

Figure 8.41   Wait time to see caregiver – Poudre Valley Health System.[42]

Sharp improved key wait times correlated to patient satisfaction. The initiation of "Expediting Discharge" Six Sigma projects at two of its largest hospitals targeted the challenges presented by capacity issues affecting satisfaction. Patient satisfaction with the discharge process improved more than 200 percent over five years (Figure 8.42). Results are segmented by entity and are benchmarked against the Press Ganey percentile.

LEADERSHIP OUTCOMES

Leaders are ultimately responsible for achieving the organizational strategy they develop and creating a successful, sustainable organization. Leadership outcomes demonstrate achievement of strategy and action plans; fiscal accountability; and organizational accreditation, assessment, and compliance. In addition, they reflect ethical behavior, stakeholder trust, and high standards of overall conduct, and they show the organization's support for and contributions to community health. Board member continuing education, community health screenings, management of ethical breaches, audit findings, waste volumes, use of volunteers, and community health status are typical results. Recent applications show results for efforts to use renewable energy sources and conserve resources. Performance comparison often requires the use of data from other industries outside of health care.

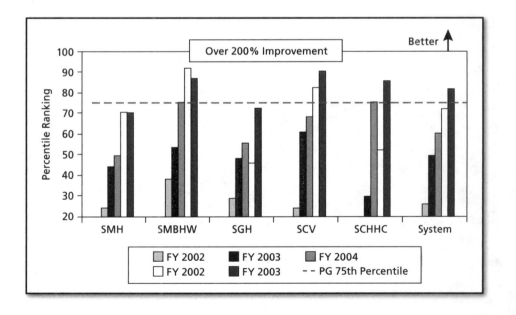

Figure 8.42 Inpatient satisfaction with discharge process – Sharp HealthCare.[43]

Summary of 2006-2008 Health Care Recipients' Leadership Results

Poudre Valley Health System (2008):

- A community case management program that pairs advanced practice nurses and social workers with high-risk, chronically ill patients decreased emergency visits annually by 50 percent and resulted in more than $850,000 savings for the past three years.

- In 2008, Poudre Valley received the Peak Performance Award, Colorado's highest award for performance excellence, marking the second time in five years for the honor.

- The American Nurses' Credentialing Center awarded Poudre Valley Hospital its Magnet Designation for Nursing Excellence in 2000 and again in 2004. The hospital was the first in the Rocky Mountain region to receive this designation.

Sharp HealthCare (2007):

- The economic value of Sharp's services to the San Diego community increased from $100 million in 2001 to more than $180 million in 2006. During the same period, the organization's financial support for San Diego's vulnerable population, health research efforts, and the broader community increased from $4 million to approximately $6.5 million.

- Between 2003 and 2006, the number of hours donated by Sharp management to community programs grew from 10,000 to almost 60,000.

Mercy Health System (2007):

- In 2007, Mercy provided more than $32 million in uncompensated care and free services to local communities.

- Mercy annually sponsors more than 3,800 health screenings, community education classes, and other activities designed to meet community needs.

- Senior Connection, a free program for those 55 and older, offers Medicare advice, referrals for home health care, and other information from trained counselors.

North Mississippi Medical Center (2006):

- In 2003, 2004, and 2005, North Mississippi was recognized by Solucient, a leading source of information for the health care industry, as one of the Top 100 Performance Improvement Leaders. North Mississippi is one of only four hospitals nationwide to be recognized for this distinction three years in a row.

- North Mississippi's charitable donations, charity care, medical cost savings, and volunteer services total about $70 million annually.

- In 2006, North Mississippi provided community services to more than 156,000 people through free health fairs, screenings, health education classes, and immunizations held throughout the rural region in locations including churches and shopping centers.

Like many health care organizations, Sharp operates in a highly competitive environment and lists capacity issues as a key strategic challenge. Nevertheless, in spite of constraints on capacity, Sharp's volume growth is 75 percent faster than that of San Diego County, its home (Figure 8.43).

Like many applicants, Sharp uses a report card to track progress on strategic initiatives, with targets and results organized in Sharp's six-pillar framework—that is quality, service, people, finance, growth, and community (Figure 8.44). Most measures remain consistent over time with the exception of the quality measures, which are adjusted as needed to inspire breakthrough improvement. For each pillar, Sharp has achieved dramatic improvements, including a 68 percent increase in net revenue from 2001 to 2007.

Mercy Health System uses an external measure of operational success to benchmark their achievement of strategy and action plans. The health care information vendor Verispan rates integrated health care networks on ten categories comprising thirty-three weighted attributes of success. Mercy uses Verispan's integration composite measure, weighted heaviest in the survey, to demonstrate sustained performance as a strong, quality-focused, integrated health care system. For the past five years Mercy has placed in the top decile of the top 100 Integrated Health Network's nationwide and has outperformed its closest competitors (Figure 8.45).

Fully integrated governance requires all levels of leadership to be included in measuring results and demonstrating high-quality outcomes. North Mississippi Medical Center takes that directive right to the top. It has been using a survey, sponsored by the Governance Institute, to assess the board's performance and planning efforts since 1992. North Mississippi has increased both the rigor and the

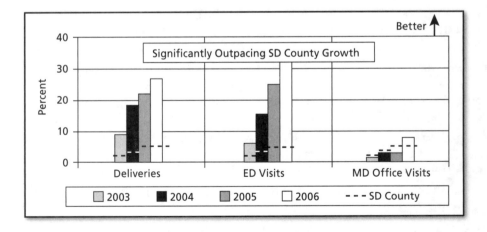

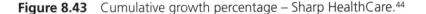

Figure 8.43 Cumulative growth percentage – Sharp HealthCare.[44]

Measure Description	Figure Reference	Improvement % / Measure of Success
Quality Pillar (FY2007 Q1 & Q2)		
Surgical Infection Prevention	7.1-23	9%
ROMACC	7.1-7	170%
Service Pillar (2002 – 2006)		
Inpatient Satisfaction	7.2-1	>150%
Medical Group Patient Satisfaction	7.2-2	>100%
Physician Satisfaction (from 2003)	7.5-2	Approaching Top Quartile Systemwide
People Pillar (2002 – 2006)		
Employee Satisfaction	7.4-2	Exceeds Best in Class
Employee Turnover (from 2001)	7.4-13	36%
Finance Pillar (2001 – 2007 Q2)		
EBITDA	7.3-4	80%
Growth Pillar (2001 – 2007 Q2)		
Net Revenue	7.3-1	68%
Community Pillar (2003 – 2006)		
Manager Hours of Community Service	7.6-13	>400%
Evidence of Strategic Success		

Figure 8.44 Summary report card performance – Sharp HealthCare.[45]

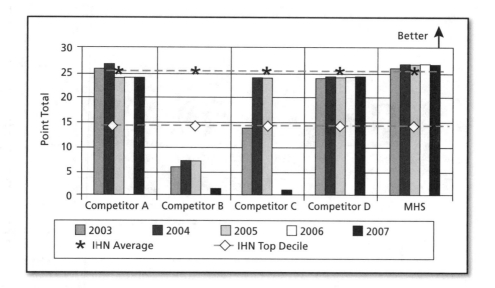

Figure 8.45 Integrated health network integration composite score – Mercy Health System.[46]

frequency of the measure to ensure its governance remains effective in achieving organizational mission and strategy. The survey changed in 2005 from assessing board members' *perceptions of governance effectiveness* to measuring how effectively the board *performs its duties and responsibilities* and how often it *follows certain board practices*, and it is now administered annually (Figure 8.46).

Leadership outcomes include results demonstrating fulfillment of societal responsibilities. North Mississippi's Live Well initiative, launched in 2002, provides community health fairs; safety, smoking cessation, nutrition, alcohol, and health education classes; blood pressure and prostate screening; and health information. North Mississippi tracks participation in these offerings, as well as Wellness Center membership growth and volunteer hours at free clinics (Figure 8.47).

Key to providing outreach is the identification of key community health needs. North Mississippi conducts a community health assessment every three years. It uses the data to track the progress of "Live Well" at addressing the health challenges of its geographic catchment area, re-assess community needs, and set priorities Figure 8.48).

The North Mississippi application drills down to a specific example of its community outreach success: data showing the impact of its smoking cessation campaign (Figure 8.49). Using robust sources of comparison, including the National Center for Chronic Disease Prevention and Mississippi State University's Social Sciences Research Center, the hospital notes that smoking rates in their service area and overall state are decreasing while tobacco use in surrounding states has increased. North Mississippi credits their focused smoking cessation campaign with increasing the numbers of adults who attempt to quit smoking.

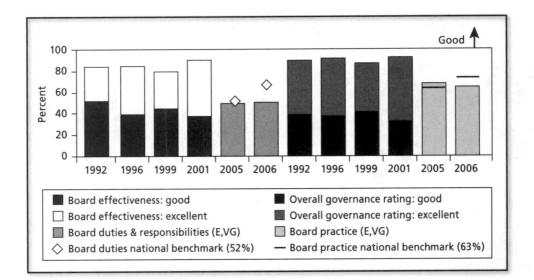

Figure 8.46   Board of directors self-assessment survey – North Mississippi Medical Center.[47]

Poudre Valley Health System provides similar impact results for community health improvement. Poudre Valley works with local community leaders and customers to identify and address specific health needs in the region, among them heart disease, prenatal care (for example, preventing low-birth weight), child safety, and injury avoidance. In 2007, total community support surpassed $110 million—or greater than 25 percent of net patient revenue (Figure 8.50). Poudre Valley compares favorably with VHA Mountain States member hospitals.

Poudre Valley's community case management program pairs advanced practice nurses and social workers with high-risk, chronically ill patients. The program has decreased emergency visits annually by 50 percent, resulting in more than $850,000 savings for each of the past three years and increased the quality of life for patients with substantial health needs (Figure 8.51).

"Live Well" Community Outreach					
	2002	2003	2004	2005	2006
Participants in health fairs, screenings, health education classes, CPR classes, immunization programs	93,917	167,831	155,981	171,376	172,814
Screening mammograms	6,690	6,132	7,286	8,540	9,453
Participants in community blood pressure screenings	5,530	11,431	7,964	5,746	5,773
Wellness Center membership	4,153	5,560	5,424	5,639	7,100
Healthcare professionals volunteer hours at the free clinic	745	832	825	813	783
Athletic trainers (students)	30,594	111,840	100,302	93,955	73,500

Figure 8.47 "Live Well" community outreach – North Mississippi Medical Center.[48]

Indicator Adults Reporting:	NMMC 2001	NMMC 2004	MS	US
Overall poor health status	25.1%	24.5%	21.2%	15.0%
Obesity	26.8%	26.4%	32.5%	22.2%
Positive blood stool test in past year	22.3%	21.0%	19.5%	N/A
Children wear bicycle helmets	19.4%	14.7%	23.7%	44.8%
Smokers – attempted to quit in past year	60.6%	68.7%	62.9%	51.8%
Binge drinking in past month	13.8%	9.2%	9.9%	16.5%

Figure 8.48 Community health assessment – North Mississippi Medical Center.[49]

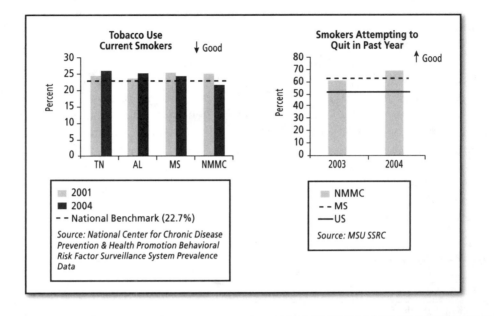

Figure 8.49 Smoking cessation campaign impact – North Mississippi Medical Center.[50]

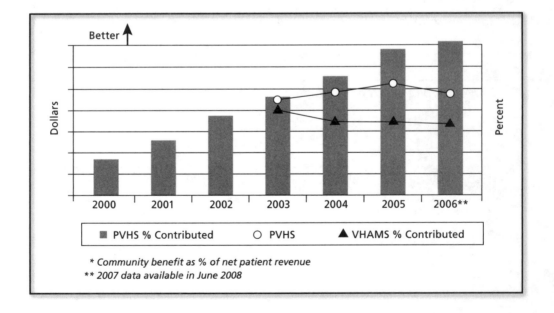

Figure 8.50 Community benefits – Poudre Valley Health System.[51]

Recognizing that community partnerships can enhance community health improvement, Poudre Valley joined area employers in a campaign to earn the designation Well City from the Wellness Councils of America. In support of the initiative, Poudre Valley created a weight-loss and fitness program called Lifestyle Challenge, an innovative approach that fosters partnership and engagement between employers and the workforce, improves employee health, and supports financial stability through reduction in health care utilization and expenses related to injury. Prior to offering the program to area businesses, Poudre Valley piloted the program with its own employees in 2004. VHA named Poudre Valley's Lifestyle Challenge the best community health program among member hospitals in 2004. Over four years, the program has shown significant results (Figure 8.52). A local employer with a national network of facilities selected the program as a best practice for implementation nation-wide. organization-wide.

Better ↑

		2003	2004	2005	2006	2007
Decrease in Visits*	Inpatient	50%	69%	62%	37.5%	43.6%
	ED	47%	53%	45%	61.5%	55.0%
Cost Savings	Inpatient	$185,584	$600,132	$831,366	$859,287	$883,005
	ED	$17,521	$10,240	$25,383	$13,145	$23,388

The patient had X% fewer visits in the 6 months following case management compared to the 6 months prior to case management.

Figure 8.51   Community case management – Poudre Valley Health System.[52]

Better ↓

		% with BMI > 25	
		at Baseline	at Completion
PVHS	2004	68%	65%
	2005	64%	63%
	2006	62%	60%
	2007	60%	51%
Employer 1	2007	71%	64%
Employer 2	2007	85%	55%

Figure 8.52   Lifestyle challenge – Poudre Valley Health System.[53]

What characterizes these health care recipients is their demonstrated ability over the course of their journeys to drive performance improvement and sustain high performance relative to competitors and the industry on a broad range of measures. For any single measure, one can likely find another health care organization with higher scores. However, these four organizations demonstrate the capability and agility to drive change and to achieve an uncommon breadth and depth of high performance for the industry—performance required to meet patient and stakeholder expectations, achieve marketplace success, and ensure long-term sustainability.

These organizations achieved significant results across a broad array of meaningful measures. They achieved these results by systematically measuring and improving the processes of leadership, management, and daily operations.

Important Questions for Health Care Leaders

- Do you have access to key health care, customer-focused, financial and market, workforce-focused, process effectiveness, and leadership outcomes necessary to assess how well your organization is performing?

- Are those measures tracked over time? If so, are you seeing beneficial trends and sustained improvement in areas of importance to your organization? Do they have clear goals?

- Are the measures evaluated against relevant comparisons and/or benchmarks? If so, do they show areas of good to excellent relative performance?

- Are results segmented by logical groupings, for example, target market segments, service lines, and job types, to make analysis more meaningful?

- Do you know your key patient, stakeholder, market, and process requirements and do you have results for most of them?

- Do you have a balanced mix of in-process and outcome measures to promote your agility in recognizing and responding to changes in your environment?

- Do your results align with your key organizational strategies and goals?

- What would you and others in your organization do differently if you had access to more of this kind of results information?

9

Conclusion

Today's unforgiving environment puts unprecedented demands on health care leaders and managers. Even organizations that historically flourished must adjust course to meet new challenges in the increasingly competitive health care marketplace. Traditional health care approaches to leadership and management are not creating needed improvement at the level or speed required. As public scrutiny grows, payers and regulators will continue to expand accountability and transparency across more dimensions of organizational performance. They will develop more ways to reward excellence and punish mediocrity because patients, payers, voters, and our government will not tolerate the status quo. These unrelenting trends put health care leaders on a quest to find effective approaches to transform their organizations, to create cultures of discipline and learning, and to build capabilities far beyond their current realities to achieve new levels of performance.

Care delivery organizations that thrive into the future will achieve not only outstanding health care outcomes but strong performance in multiple dimensions:

- Patient engagement and community perception of quality and service to build loyalty of existing patients, attract new patients, and promote growth even in mature markets

- Physician and other clinician satisfaction and perception of quality and service to maintain existing volumes and promote growth even in competitive markets where physicians have many competing practice options and places to admit or refer their patients

- Employee satisfaction and engagement to promote retention, attract new talent, and develop the skills to lead and deliver health care for the twenty-first century

- Effective and efficient work processes that can be assessed, managed, measured, and improved

- Strategic alignment at all levels

Health care organizations must change to succeed. The current challenges facing health care leaders *cannot* be met through delegating improvement to project teams, regardless of how sophisticated their methods are or how many teams get chartered. Nor is it simply a matter of delegating guidelines and care bundles of clinical best practices and ensuring these practices get fully adopted by clinicians. Superior performance across multiple dimensions can't be achieved by efforts targeted at one key process (for example, strategic planning or patient care delivery) or one key result (for example, patient satisfaction, employee turnover, or medication errors). The situation necessitates cultural transformation through a systematic approach to design and improve leadership and management processes. It calls for change at every level, from governance to culture, from financial to clinical, and from the board room to the boiler room.

LESSONS FROM BALDRIGE HEALTH CARE LEADERS

The lessons of Baldrige recipients who have taken successful performance excellence journeys and improved dramatically in multiple key areas are highly instructive for today's health care leaders. As Sister Mary Jean Ryan of SSM told us in an interview for this book, "I made the decision to improve. I knew we needed to improve and decided that Baldrige was the way to do it. If I was getting started today for the first time transforming our organization, I would go to those who have already won the Baldrige Award and ask them how they did it." Since our research team did just that, we now know that health care Baldrige recipients succeeded in transformational change through a set of common practices:

- Leaders demonstrated five critical leadership behaviors: *making a personal commitment to transformation, aligning people in support, building a culture of learning and improvement, motivating and inspiring the workforce, and building a results orientation.* These behaviors create an environment where transformation is possible (Leadership, Chapter 4).

- Throughout the organization, leaders and others sought and used the brutal truth necessary to change (Assessment, Chapter 5).

- Using that truthful evaluation, they began to understand the organization as a system of processes that create results (Sensemaking, Chapter 6).

- Over time, they created an environment characterized by the discipline of evaluation followed by action, designing, and improving the key processes essential to achieve results (Execution, Chapter 7).

Each unique in its problems and aspirations, all our study organizations found in Baldrige a roadmap forward to meet their challenges successfully. It provided them with a strategic business framework. Their assessments provoked fundamental and much needed evaluation, benchmarking, and alignment. These executives will tell you many important changes would never have happened without their Baldrige journey.

Each of the nine recipients became dramatically more capable. After their initial evaluations, they progressed beyond mere compliance with external requirements. They were able to move out of the "firefighting" mode of reactive leadership. Figure 9.1 depicts this early stage, common to many health care organizations. The arrows on the left illustrate the typical firefighting environment where leaders address problems as they come to them, moving in conflicting directions to get through immediate challenges and crises. Strategic and operational goals are unclear to the workforce, unlikely to move from theory to execution. There is no real connection between daily work of managing operations and a strategic plan for the future of the enterprise.

As the nine recipients moved into the Traction stage of their journeys and began to conduct operations through repeatable systematic processes, daily work began to align (Figure 9.2). Strategic and operational goals got defined and used to focus and

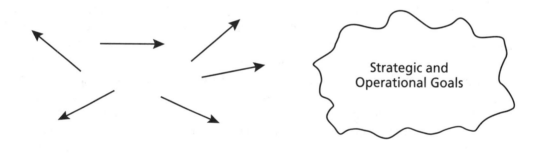

Figure 9.1 Reacting to problems: Reaction and Projects stages of the journey.[1]

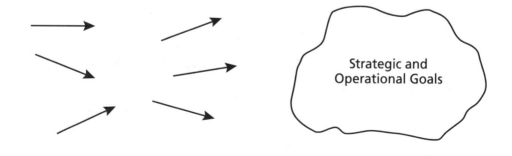

Figure 9.2 Early systematic approaches: Traction stage.

align operations with long-term objectives. Improvement projects became integrated with strategy deployment the overall organizational vision. The list of initiatives often shortened during this stage, as non-aligned work and projects were terminated. Staff and employees began to experience greater stability in the environment, with greater clarity and less stress around problems facing the organization. Evaluation and improvement grew to be routine aspects of the culture. Gaining momentum through methodical improvement of leadership and management processes, with time, brought "proof" of progress through improvements in measures of multidimensional results.

As these organizations persisted through multiple assessment cycles, their operations became characterized by repeatable processes that clearly align and address strategic goals (Figure 9.3). Effective deployment became the routine. Regular, periodic improvement of leadership and management processes manifests in staff, employee, and customer engagement with the emerging results-focused culture. Coordination of effort around key work processes by key contributing work units yielded improving performance on key measures and scorecards. By this stage, the cause-and-effect relationship between improving processes and organizational results was evident to most stakeholders. Strategy was integrally connected to routine work, and staffs understood and embraced the "line of sight" connection between their personal priorities and those of the enterprise.

To achieve the level of competency displayed in Figure 9.3 is a major accomplishment. High performance results in all domains demonstrate the return on investment for the journey. Achieving this level indicates high performance that yields market prominence, good quality, loyal customers, and engaged staffs.

Some organizations persist and even reach the highest levels of competence. This theoretical state of full integration is no doubt a rarity (see Figure 9.4). These exceptional organizations attain operations characterized by repeatable processes that are regularly evaluated and improved. Multi-disciplinary cross-unit teams

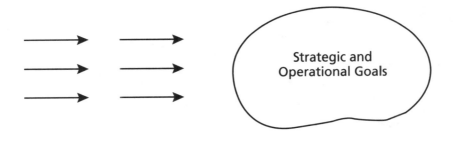

Figure 9.3 Aligned approaches: Early Integration stage.

coordinate their shared, well-defined processes. Efficiency and flawless execution of processes is sought and achieved through routine analysis and improvement. Knowledge of best and most innovative practices is shared regularly and widely. Fact-based decision making is pervasive, used to proactively address new challenges as they emerge. This state of near perfection is rarely, if ever, achieved; even Baldrige Award recipients acknowledge such limitations. Ironically, recipient CEOs deeply and realistically understand the gaps between their current culture and performance, and what it would take to achieve perfection.

CAN IT LAST?

Can high-performance cultures last? What does it take to sustain levels of performance after receiving the Baldrige Award? No conclusion of a book about the journey to excellence using Baldrige would be complete without addressing these questions. However, receiving a Baldrige Award does not guarantee superior results over the lifetime of the organization. Great companies are affected by major changes in market and industry forces like any other. Even performance giant Toyota Motors had its first operating loss in fifty years, with 2008 sales results down by 16 percent in the face of a global recession.

Several of the nine health care recipients reported significant progress after their awards. Saint Luke's Health System, the parent company of Saint Luke's Hospital, grew from three hospitals to eleven and went on to receive the Missouri State Quality Award in 2006. Tupelo, Mississippi, won a national competition for the largest Toyota plant in the U.S. around the time North Mississippi Medical Center received the Baldrige Award. Close observers noted that the commitment to performance excellence by the major health care provider in the area was a noted factor in their selection.

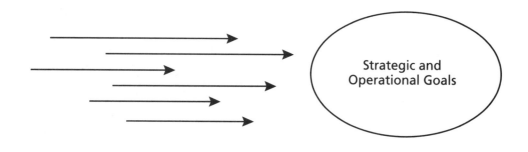

Figure 9.4 Fully integrated and mature processes: Late Integration or Sustaining stage.

Baldrige does help give leaders knowledge of their organization as a system, understanding that it promotes agility to adjust to market forces more quickly and in a more focused way than their competitors. Using Baldrige creates the possibility of sustained strength but cannot guarantee it. The Criteria drive organizations to build deep and enduring capability. Achieving scores in the highest range requires simultaneous talent, knowledge, and succession planning to sustain despite the loss of key individuals. This finding is consistent with the *Good to Great* study, where Collins and his team found that companies truly built to last have established capability deeper than individual leaders.

The task at hand is daunting and the paths forward are few. As the economy slumps and payers ratchet up pay-for-performance methodologies, those that survive and thrive will focus their attention on building the capabilities of their people and operations. They will build relationships with customers, partners, and suppliers that ensure market share and leverage demonstrated strengths.

Frequently Asked Questions

Here are questions we and leaders of recipient organizations are often asked about the national and state award processes.

WHEN SHOULD WE BEGIN?

Q: Should we begin if the whole leadership team is not on board?

We like the "ship" analogy in this question; it makes us wonder if there's a "walk the plank" analogy as well. It's great if every senior leader buys into the concept of using the Baldrige framework. But realistically, you're going to have some laggards. Building engagement starting with a few key players, as Saint Luke's did, can be effective for developing understanding and buy-in with your senior team.

Q: We have a long way to go. Now we have a financial crisis, maybe even layoffs. Should we wait?

Wait for what? Maybe things will get even worse. A crisis presents an opportunity to reexamine everything you do. The Baldrige Criteria will help you do that systematically, without the knee-jerk reactions commonly taken in times of crisis. One way to get started is to write your Organizational Profile, which will document the basic facts about your organization and may trigger discussion and learning around issues such as your strategic challenges and advantages. You also could conduct some of the high-level surveys available on the Baldrige Web site, which will help you get a broad sense of areas you need to address. Finally, consider conducting an assessment yourself. It will provide many insights and will help you demonstrate the value of the Baldrige Criteria in managing during tough times.

Q: Some of our results aren't very good. Should we wait until they've improved before applying?

Well, nobody's perfect. Baldrige is an excellence award, not a perfection award. Even Baldrige recipients get their fair share of OFIs in their feedback reports. Your application feedback will include comments on results as well as processes and will give you some insight into how to improve both.

Q: We know we can't win. Should we wait until we get better?

No. This is not about winning an award; it's about improving the performance of your organization. Doing a Baldrige assessment will help you get better faster, so get started. You may want to begin with an internal assessment. But waiting postpones developing the learning that will help your organization improve.

HOW SHOULD WE BEGIN?

Q: Can we just use the Baldrige framework without applying for the award?

Sure. Lots of organizations start in this manner. In fact, some organizations only do internal assessments without ever applying for the award. You'll develop your own set of "aha's" just by reviewing the Criteria questions. The Baldrige Web site has some useful tools for this – for free! But at some point, most organizations realize that they would benefit from more objective feedback from outside, which entails writing a state or Baldrige application. The application process brings a level of discipline and learning rarely replicated without applying.

Q: Should we start with our strongest unit or go forward as a system?

That depends on what you ultimately want to achieve. Do you want to do a demonstration project for your system to show how Baldrige can help drive improvement? Then start with your best entity. Or, do you want to build the identity and strengthen the linkages within your system as a whole? In that case, start with a system-level application.

Q: Should we start with a state-level application?

We—and the Baldrige health care recipients we interviewed—recommend this highly. The state programs mirror Baldrige, but many also offer "Baldrige light" criteria, which helps organizations just starting out develop understanding of the Criteria. Many organizations apply to both their state and the Baldrige program in the same year. This provides the opportunity for two sets of feedback, usually in different timeframes. If your state does not have a program, check with neighboring states. Sometimes their programs will allow out-of-state organizations to apply.

Q: Should we tell everyone we are "doing Baldrige"? Should we use the "B" word at all?

This is another issue for which our official answer is "it depends." Some of the health care recipients, Mercy, for example, did so from the start. Others, like Sharp, integrated Baldrige into their existing strategy and brand without specifically mentioning Baldrige. Our feeling is that at you must get beyond "doing Baldrige" and integrate the Baldrige Criteria into your own culture as the framework you're using to improve the organization. Reference to Baldrige then becomes a moot point, even though you're using it every day.

WHO SHOULD BE INVOLVED?

Q: Who needs to be on the team and how do we get them engaged? Should we involve physicians or our Board?

The answer is "yes" to both physicians and the board, but not necessarily at the very beginning. We've seen some organizations engage these two key constituencies before starting and others wait to engage them after the organization gets its first feedback report. One of the best ways to get them engaged, besides the examples we've provided in the book, is to connect them with peers in some of the Baldrige recipient organizations. You can find information about the key contact at each recipient organization on the Baldrige Web site.

Q: No one in our organization is an examiner. How do we develop internal knowledge?

Do leaders need to be experts? What resources are available? If you don't have an examiner, either at the state or Baldrige level, get one. Check the Web sites for Baldrige or your state program on how to apply to become an examiner. It's the surest way to build internal knowledge about the Baldrige process in the organization. The more senior the examiner, the better, because they're in a better position to recognize leverage points and drive change in the organization. While your CEO doesn't need to be a Baldrige expert, he or she does need to "get it." We highly recommend having senior leaders attend the annual Quest for Excellence conference in Washington, DC, where they can interact with and learn from peers in Baldrige recipient organizations. Application summaries from the Baldrige recipients, both inside and outside of health care, also are a great source of information for leaders and team members at all levels.

HOW LONG DOES IT TAKE?

Q: We've heard that Baldrige Award recipients apply for years before they receive the award.

That's true in most cases. Did Tiger Woods score below par on his first round of golf? Do you think he just plays from Thursdays through Sundays? Baldrige Award recipients "practice" Baldrige every day until they become masters, and, just like Tiger Woods, sustaining performance requires them to continue to "practice" even after winning.

Q: What can we do to speed up the pace of improvement?

We've provided some specific guidance on this at the end of the Sensemaking chapter. Also see the response to the "Do we need consultants?" question below.

HOW MUCH DOES IT COST?

Q: We've heard this is really expensive. What does it cost to apply?

This is one of the questions we hear most frequently from people who are becoming interested in the Baldrige process. There are two answers to this question, an easy one and a tougher one:

1. There are modest fees for applying for submitting national and state award applications. The fees vary according to the size of the organization and the sector it belongs to. Information on current fees for applying for the Malcolm Baldrige National Quality Award is available at http://www.baldrige.nist.gov/fees.htm. Your state program can provide its fee schedule.

2. The deeper issue related to this question is, "How much time, money, and effort will this require?" We call this the "CFO question." It's amazing that organizations rarely calculate the immense cost of mediocrity. Rulon Stacey, president and CEO at Poudre Valley Health System, said that he can document their savings due to using the Baldrige process: "If you want to guarantee quality for patients, get involved in Baldrige because quality will go up, costs will go down, and you'll be a better organization."

Q: Do we need consultants?

You don't need to use consultants. But good consultants can shorten the learning curve, saving you significant time and effort in moving forward on your journey. Consultants can provide objective assessments that can be very helpful, especially early in the process. Just remember that a consultant is there to guide you along your journey to excellence, but you must lead it.

If you have any other questions, please feel free to send us an e-mail: authors@asq.org

Notes

Chapter 1

1. Goethe, as referenced by the Committee on Quality of Health Care in America, Institute of Medicine, *Crossing the Quality Chasm: A New Health System for the 21st Century* (Washington, DC: National Academy Press, 2001), title page.

2. Centers for Medicare and Medicaid Services, *Roadmap for Implementing Value Driven Healthcare in the Traditional Medicare Fee-for-Service Program,* http://www.cms.hhs.gov/QualityInitiativesGenInfo/downloads/VBPRoadmap_OEA_1-16_508.pdf (accessed February 3, 2009).

3. James Orlikoff, *The CMS Death Penalty: Could It Happen Next Week at Your Hospital?* Reinertsen Group Web Seminar, February 2, 2009, available at http://www.reinertsengroup.com.

4. The Joint Commission, http://www.jointcommission.org/accreditation programs/09_acc_decisions.htm (accessed February 4, 2009).

5. http://www.baldrige.nist.gov. Launched in 1988 to stimulate greater quality and productivity in for-profit manufacturing and service organizations, the Baldrige Award process is now open to small business, education, and health care organizations, and all types of nonprofits, and thus effectively reaches all sectors of the U.S. economy.

6. Mike Langridge, Director, Iowa Recognition for Performance Excellence, Iowa Center for Performance Excellence, personal communication with author Kate Goonan, July 15, 2008.

7. 2002, SSM Health Care, St. Louis, MO; 2003, Baptist Hospital, Inc., Pensacola, FL, and Saint Luke's Hospital, Kansas City, MO; 2004, Robert Wood Johnson University Hospital, Hamilton, NJ; 2005, Bronson Methodist Hospital, Kalamazoo, MI; 2006, North Mississippi Medical Center, Tupelo, MS; 2007, Mercy Health System, Janesville, WI, and Sharp HealthCare, San Diego, CA; 2008, Poudre Valley Health System. For additional information about these recipients, including their application summaries, see http://www.baldrige.nist.gov/Contacts_Profiles.htm.

8. Institute of Medicine, *Crossing the Quality Chasm,* p. 6. The "six aims" correspond to the following six dimensions of care: safe, effective, patient-centered, timely, efficient, and equitable.

9. Harry S. Hertz, Director, Baldrige National Quality Program, National Institute of Standards and Technology, personal communication with author Joe Muzikowski, 2006.

10. Jim Collins, *Good to Great: Why Some Companies Make the Leap and Others Don't* (New York: Harper Collins, 2001).

11. Karl E. Weick, *Sensemaking in Organizations* (Thousand Oaks, CA: Sage, 1995). We incorporated Weick's term in our LASER model because our interpretation of the activity that occurs when organizational leaders perform an assessment or analyze feedback aligns with his definition.

Chapter 2

1. Jim Collins, author of *Good to Great*, as quoted in Baldrige National Quality Program, National Institute of Standards and Technology, *Update*, October 2008, http://www.baldrige.nist.gov/PDF_files/Update.10_08.pdf (accessed December 29, 2008).

2. The Criteria for business, education, and health care can be downloaded from the Baldrige Web site, http://www.baldrige.nist.gov.

3. Baldrige National Quality Program, National Institute for Standards and Technology, *2009-2010 Health Care Criteria for Performance Excellence* (Gaithersburg, MD: 2009), p. iv, http://www.baldrige.nist.gov/PDF_files/2009_2010_HealthCare_Criteria.pdf.

4. For details on award eligibility, visit the Baldrige Web site, http://www.baldrige.nist.gov.

5. Harry S. Hertz, presentation to the Harvard Interfaculty Program for Health Systems Improvement, January 7, 2003.

6. Booz Allen Hamilton, "Assessment of Leadership Attitudes about the Baldrige National Quality Program," commissioned by the Baldrige National Quality Program, Final Report, December 31, 2003, http://www.baldrige.nist.gov/PDF_files/Assessment_Leadership.pdf.

7. According to the Baldrige National Quality Program, "actual applications for the Baldrige Award are confidential. The 2007 award recipients have provided these summaries of their applications in the interest of knowledge sharing. All proprietary information has been removed." See http://www.baldrige.nist.gov/2007_Application_Summaries.htm.

8. Institute of Medicine, *Crossing the Quality Chasm*, p. 6.

9. William Denney, Cynthia St. John, and Liz Youngblood, "Close Health Care's Quality Chasm: Use the Baldrige Criteria to Meet Compliance Requirements and Patient Needs," *Quality Progress* (May 2009).

10. Mary Jean Ryan, *On Becoming Exceptional* (Milwaukee, WI: ASQ Press, 2007), pp. 56-57.

11. Ryan, *On Becoming Exceptional*, p. 69.

12. John Heer, personal comment at the CEO Baldrige Dialogue, Health Forum/AHA Summit, San Diego, California, July 25, 2004.

13. The process for state award programs is similar, but the dates in the cycle may vary.

14. The scoring band descriptors are shown on pp. 116-117.

15. Baldrige National Quality Program, National Institute of Standards and Technology, *Why Baldrige? A Proven Approach to Performance Improvement*, http://www.baldrige.nist.gov/Why_Baldrige.htm

16. The Alliance for Performance Excellence, "History of the Criteria." http://www.baldrigepe.org/alliance/resources.aspx.

Chapter 3

1. John P. Kotter, "Leading Change: Why Transformation Efforts Fail," *Harvard Business Review*, OnPoint (Cambridge, MA: Harvard Business School Publishing Corporation, 2005, 1995), p. 8, http://www.hbr.org.

2. Booz Allen Hamilton, "Assessment of Leadership Attitudes about the Baldrige National Quality Program."

3. Michael E. Porter and Elizabeth Olmsted Teisberg, *Redefining Health Care* (Boston: Harvard Business School Press, 2006), p.149.

4. Porter and Teisberg, *Redefining Health Care*, p.13.

5. The Centers for Medicare and Medicaid Services program to withhold payment for care associated with a publicly list of diagnoses and circumstances in which preventable harm brought on by the care delivery system itself has caused the need for health care services. These conditions are no longer reimbursable.

6. Baldrige 2007 Scoring Band Descriptions, Band Number 2; see p. 116.

7. Thomas W. Nolan, "Execution of Strategic Improvement Initiatives to Produce System-Level Results," IHI Innovation Series white paper (Cambridge, MA: Institute for Healthcare Improvement, 2007), available on http://www.ihi.org.

8. North Mississippi Medical Center, 2006 Baldrige application summary, pp. 29-30, http://www.baldrige.nist.gov/PDF_files/NMMC_Application_Summary.pdf.

9. E. David Spong, comments made at the American Hospital Association CEO Roundtable, 2005.

10. Collins, *Good to Great*, pp. 13, 71.

11. "McKinsey Global Survey Results: Creating Organizational Transformations," *McKinsey Quarterly* (July 2008), p. 5.

12. Collins, *Good to Great*, p. 69.

13. Saint Luke's Health System, 2006 Missouri Quality Award application summary, http://www.mqa.org/qualityawardrecipients.htm (accessed September 9, 2008).

Chapter 4

1. Max DePree, *Leadership Is an Art* (New York: Dell, 1989), pp. 17-18.

2. John P. Kotter, "What Leaders Really Do," HBR OnPoint, (Cambridge, MA: Harvard Business School Publishing Corporation, 2001), pp. 3-11, http://www.hbr.org.

3. John P. Kotter, *Leading Change* (Boston: Harvard Business School Press, 1996), pp. 51-66.

4. Collins, *Good to Great*, pp. 41-64.

5. The SSM Health Care Passport and a description of its use are available on the SSM Health Care Web site http://www.ssmhc.com/internet/home.

6. Collins, *Good to Great*, p. 89.

7. Al Stubblefield, *The Baptist Health Care Journey to Excellence: Creating a Culture That Wows* (Hoboken, NJ: Wiley, 2005), pp. 146-47.

8. W. Edwards Deming, *Out of the Crisis* (Cambridge, MA: Massachusetts of Institute of Technology, Center for Advanced Engineering Study, 1982), p. 87.

9. Bronson Methodist Hospital, 2005 application summary, Figure 1.1-2, p. 1, http://www.baldrige.nist.gov/PDF_files/2005_Bronson_Methodist_Hospital_Application_Summary.pdf.

10. These reflections were used in Sharp HealthCare presentations at Quest for Excellence, Washington, DC, April 2008.

11. "McKinsey Global Survey Results: Creating Organizational Transformations," p. 3.

12. Poudre Valley Health System, 2006 application summary, Figure 4.1-2, p. 16, http://www.baldrige.nist.gov/PDF_files/2008_Poudre Valley_Application_Summary_.pdf.

13. Leaders from Robert Wood Johnson University Hospital at Hamilton presented this approach at Quest for Excellence, Washington, DC, April 2005.

14. "McKinsey Global Survey Results: Creating Organizational Transformations," p. 5.

15. Kotter, "What Leaders Really Do," p. 3.

16. Baldrige National Quality Program, *2009-2010 Health Care Criteria for Performance Excellence*, p. 7.

17. Baldrige National Quality Program, *2009-2010 Health Care Criteria for Performance Excellence*, pp. 62-63.

18. Sharp HealthCare, 2007 application summary, Figure 1.1-1, p. 1, http://www.baldrige.nist.gov/PDF_files/2007_Sharp_Application_Summary.pdf.

Chapter 5

1. Collins, *Good to Great*, p. 160.

2. How the organization identifies these various segments is also addressed in the Criteria requirements for the Customer Focus category.

3. Personal communication with author Joe Muzikowski.

4. Booz Allen Hamilton, "Assessment of Leadership Attitudes About the Baldrige National Quality Program."

5. Bronson Methodist Hospital, 2005 Baldrige application summary, p. vii.

6. North Mississippi Medical Center 2006 Baldrige application summary, p. i.

7. Some self-assessment tools and background materials are available from the Baldrige National Quality Program Web site, http://www.baldrige.nist.gov, in addition to application forms for the award process.

8. The Quest for Excellence conference, held annually in April in Washington, DC, showcases current and past Baldrige recipients' processes and results. Two one-day regional Quest for Excellence conferences are held in the fall in other parts of the country.

9. Credit for this concept goes to E. David Spong, who led two Boeing divisions to receive the Baldrige Award, Aerospace Support (now Logistics Support) in 2003 and Airlift and Tanker Programs (now Global Mobility Systems) in 1998. It's safe to say that he has seen his share of feedback reports.

10. Saint Luke's Hospital of Kansas City, 2003 Baldrige application summary, p. 32, http://www.baldrige.nist.gov/PDF_files/Saint_Luke's_Application_Summary.pdf.

Chapter 6

1. Weick, *Sensemaking in Organizations*, p. 61.

2. M.S. Feldman, *Order Without Design* (Palo Alto, CA: Stanford University Press, 1989), quoted in Weick, *Sensemaking in Organizations*, p. 5.

3. The Baldrige National Quality Program develops a case study each year for use in training all examiners and judges. The feedback example in Figure 6-1 comes from 2006 case study materials, which include an application and a feedback report for Arroyo Fresco, a realistic but fictitious community health center. These materials are available at http://www.baldrige.nist.gov/Arroyo.htm.

4. Quoted in the brochure "Celebrate Excellence: Mercy Health System," which Mercy Health System developed and distributed to describe and share the organization's excellence journey. Feedback reports are confidential documents and are never publicly released by the Baldrige National Quality Program, even for award recipients, although applicants may choose to share them, as in this case.

5. Mercy Health System, 2007 Baldrige application summary, pp. i, ii, 22, 40, and 41, http://www.baldrige.nist.gov/PDF_files/2007_Mercy_Application_Summary.pdf.

6. Sharp HealthCare, 2007 Baldrige application summary, p. 26.

7. In fact, scores are of primary importance for the Baldrige Panel of Judges only during selection of organizations to receive a site visit. This decision about which organizations will receive a site visit is based solely on a detailed, blinded analysis of all the applicants' scores from the examiner teams. After a site visit, however, scoring is of secondary importance. At this point, judges are more concerned with understanding the full content of the team's report, especially the organization's areas of role-model performance and its significant gaps and vulnerabilities in order to make a recommendation about possible award recipients.

8. Beginning in 2008, the scoring band desciptors were formatted in two separate sections, one for processes and one for results, as a way to provide greater clarity for applicants on the organization's overall performance. In prior years, the scoring band descriptors addressed both processes and results in a single set of eight bands.

9. Peter M. Senge, *The Fifth Discipline* (New York: Doubleday, 1990), p. 7.

10. Senge, *The Fifth Discipline*, p. 236. Chapter 12, Team Learning, provides observations and guidance on how to effectively build team learning. Given the significant impact the Baldrige assessment process has on an organization, these insights would be useful to anyone who is leading or facilitating this process.

11. Adapted from E. David Spong and Debbie Collard, *The Making of a World-Class Organization* (Milwaukee, WI: ASQ Press), p. 64

12. Site visit teams are trained not to provide any feedback to the applicant, either positive or negative. However, applicants who receive a site visit quickly realize that the questions examiners ask are, in a way, feedback. Examiners ask questions to (1) verify the information presented in the written application, especially with regard to role model practices, and (2) clarify information that was missing or unclear in the application. They incorporate the information they gather on-site into their feedback report comments. The questions they ask on-site, therefore, often provide applicants with some "aha" moments related to their strengths and gaps.

13. Weick, *Sensemaking in Organizations*, p. 7.

Chapter 7

1. Larry Bossidy and Ram Charan, *Execution* (New York: Crown, 2002), p. 6.

2. Kotter, *Leading Change*, chap. 8.

3. Bronson Methodist Hospital, 2005 Baldrige application summary, p. 1.

4. This point is analogous with the hedgehog concept presented by Jim Collins and his team in *Good to Great*. In this and other publications, they point our that successful companies always focus on what they are good at and stop activities that are beyond their scope of core competencies. The Baldrige Criteria explicitly address the strategic importance of an organization's core competencies.

5. Collins, *Good to Great*, p. 11.

6. "McKinsey Global Survey Results: Creating Organizational Transformations."

7. Robert Wood Johnson University Hospital at Hamilton, 2004 Baldrige application summary, Figure 2.2-2, p. 16, http://www.baldrige.nist.gov/PDF_files/RWJ_Application_Summary.pdf.

8. Mercy Health System, 2007 Profile, pp. 1-2, http://www.baldrige.nist.gov/PDF_files/Mercy_Health_System_Profile.pdf. Short profiles of all Baldrige Award recipients that highlight their best practices and results can be found on the Baldrige Web site.

9. Mercy Health System, 2007 Baldrige application summary, p. 2.

10. Poudre Valley Health System, 2008 application summary, p. 7.

11. Poudre Valley Health System, 2008 Baldrige application summary, p. i.

12. Baldrige National Quality Program, *2009-2010 Baldrige Health Care Criteria for Performance Excellence*, p. 59.

13. SSM Health Care, 2002 Baldrige application summary, p.24, http://www.baldrige.nist.gov/PDF_files/SSM_Application_Summary.pdf.

14. North Mississippi Medical Center, 2006 Baldrige application summary, p. 22.

15. Sharp HealthCare, 2007 Baldrige application summary, p. 30.

16. Terry May, president and CEO, MESA Products, presentation at Quest for Excellence, Washington, DC, April, 2007.

17. Patrick Lencioni, *Death by Meeting* (San Francisco: Jossey Bass, 2004), p. 249.

18. Collins, *Good to Great*, p. 71.

19. North Mississippi Medical Center, 2007 Baldrige application summary, p. 21.

20. Poudre Valley Health System, 2008 Baldrige application summary, p. 21.

21. Sharp HealthCare 2007 Baldrige application summary, p. 30.

22. Robert Wood Johnson University Hospital at Hamilton, 2004 Baldrige application summary, p. 7.

23. Mercy Health System, 2007 Baldrige application summary, p. 12.

Chapter 8

1. Rulon Stacey, president and CEO, Poudre Valley Health System, as quoted by the Alliance for Performance Excellence, a nonprofit network of international, national, state, and local Baldrige-based award programs, http://www.baldrigepe.org/allliance/resources.aspx (accessed January 3, 2009).
2. North Mississippi Medical Center, 2006 application summary, Figure 7.1-3, p. 34.
3. North Mississippi Medical Center, 2006 application summary, Figure 7.1-1, p. 32.
4. Sharp HealthCare, 2007 application summary, Figure 7.1-15, p. 34,
5. Mercy Health System, 2007 application summary, Figure 7.1-8, p. 33.
6. Sharp HealthCare, 2007 application summary, Figure 7.1-18, p. 34.
7. Sharp HealthCare, 2007 application summary, Figure 7.1-19, p. 34.
8. Sharp HealthCare, 2007 application summary, Figure 7.1-20, p. 34.
9. Mercy Health System, 2007 application summary, Figure 7.1-21, p. 35.
10. Poudre Valley Health System, 2008 application summary, Figure 7.5-9, p. 45.
11. Poudre Valley Health System, 2008 application summary, Figure 7.2-1, p. 36.
12. Poudre Valley Health System, 2008 application summary, Figure 7.2-3, p. 37.
13. Mercy Health System, 2007 application summary, Figure 7.2-1, p. 36.
14. Mercy Health System, 2007 application summary, Figure 7.2-3, p. 36.
15. Mercy Health System, 2007 application summary, Figure 7.2-5, p. 36.
16. Mercy Health System, 2007 application summary, Figure 7.2-7, p. 37.
17. Sharp HealthCare, 2007 application summary, Figure 7.2-10, p. 36.
18. Sharp HealthCare, 2007 application summary, Figure 7.2-2, p. 35.
19. Sharp HealthCare, 2007 application summary, Figure 7.2-17, p. 37.
20. Sharp HealthCare, 2007 application summary, Figure 7.3-1, p. 38.
21. Sharp HealthCare, 2007 application summary, Figure 7.3-5, p. 39.
22. Sharp HealthCare, 2007 application summary, Figure 7.3-8, p. 39.
23. Sharp HealthCare, 2007 application summary, Figure 7.3-9, p. 39.
24. Poudre Valley Health System, 2008 application summary, Figure 7.2-9, p. 38.
25. Poudre Valley Health System, 2008 application summary, Figure 7.3-2, p. 39.
26. Mercy Health System, 2007 application summary, Figure 7.3-1, p. 38.
27. Mercy Health System, 2007 application summary, Figure 7.3-5, p. 39.
28. North Mississippi Medical Center, 2006 application summary, Figure 7.3-11, p. 41.
29. Poudre Valley Health System, 2008 application summary, Figure 7.4-1, p. 40.
30. Poudre Valley Health System, 2008 application summary, Figure 7.4-2, p. 40.
31. Poudre Valley Health System, 2008 application summary, Figure 7.4-3, p. 40.
32. Poudre Valley Health System, 2008 application summary, Figure 7.4-11, p. 42.
33. Sharp HealthCare, 2007 application summary, Figure 7.5-2, p. 43.
34. Sharp HealthCare, 2007 application summary, Figure 7.4-12, p. 42.
35. Mercy Health System, 2007 application summary, Figure 7.4.15, p. 42.
36. North Mississippi Medical Center, 2006 application summary, Figure 7.4-6, p. 43.
37. North Mississippi Medical Center, 2006 application summary, Figure 7.4-10, p. 44.
38. Sharp HealthCare, 2007 application summary, Figure 7.5-8, p. 44.
39. Mercy Health System, 2007 application summary, Figure 7.5-1, p. 43.
40. Mercy Health System, 2007 application summary, Figure 7.5-2, p. 43.
41. Mercy Health System, 2007 application summary, Figure 7.5-3, p. 44.
42. Poudre Valley Health System, 2008 application summary, Figure 7.5-8, p. 45.

43. Sharp HealthCare, 2007 application summary, Figure 7.5-23, p. 47.
44. Sharp HealthCare, 2007 application summary, Figure 7.6-2, p. 48.
45. Sharp HealthCare, 2007 application summary, Figure 7.6-1, p. 48.
46. Mercy Health System, 2007 application summary, Figure 7.6-2, p. 47.
47. North Mississippi Medical Center, 2006 application summary, Figure 7.6-5, p. 48.
48. North Mississippi Medical Center, 2006 application summary, Figure 7.6-14, p. 50.
49. North Mississippi Medical Center, 2006 application summary, Figure 7.6-15, p. 50.
50. North Mississippi Medical Center, 2006 application summary, Figure 7.6-16, p. 50.
51. Poudre Valley Health System, 2008 application summary, Figure 7.6-8, p. 49.
52. Poudre Valley Health System, 2008 application summary, Figure 7.6-9, p. 49.
53. Poudre Valley Health System, 2008 application summary, Figure 7.6-11, p. 50.

Chapter 9

1. Figures 9.1 – 9.4 show the journey and stages of our study organizations in relation to the steps toward mature processes described by the Baldrige National Quality Program, *2009-2010 Health Care Criteria for Performance Excellence*, p. 68.

About the Authors

Kathleen Jennison Goonan, MD, is the executive director of the MGH Center for Performance Excellence, a Baldrige-based consulting group within the Massachusetts General Hospital/Partners Institute for Health Policy in Boston. Prior to founding the center with David Blumenthal, MD, in 2002, Kate spent twenty years as a health care executive, including senior vice president, Institute for Healthcare Improvement; vice president of quality, UMass Memorial Health Care; and senior vice president, Blue Cross Blue Shield of Massachusetts. She has served on the Panel of Judges, Malcolm Baldrige National Quality Award (2000-02), and as a judge for the AHA McKesson Quality Award and the JCAHO Codman Award. She is a member of ASQ.

Joseph Muzikowski is a senior consultant at the MGH Center for Performance Excellence. Joe formerly was vice president, business processes and strategic supply, for Solvay America, based in Houston. He has been a member of the Board of Examiners, Malcolm Baldrige National Quality Award, for sixteen years (1994-2009) and served as the chair of the Panel of Judges (2001-02). He also serves as a judge for the Veterans Administration Carey Award program. Joe is an ISO 9000 lead auditor and a Six Sigma master black belt.

Patricia K. Stoltz is a senior consultant at the MGH Center for Performance Excellence. She was formerly a leader in quality improvement at Henry Ford Health System in Detroit. She has been a member of the Board of Examiners, Malcolm Baldrige National Quality Award, for ten years (1999-2004, 2006-09). During the mid-1990s she helped draft and pilot the first Baldrige Criteria for Performance Excellence for the health care sector. She also serves on the Panel of Judges for the Michigan Quality Leadership Award.

Index

Page numbers in *italics* refer to tables or illustrations.